AMIE BRIAN

Amie is a London-Irish editor, author and playwright. Since graduating from Pembroke College, Cambridge, she has worked across the theatre and publishing industries as an editor, producer and writer. She now works as an Editorial Assistant at Aurora Metro & Supernova Books, and as an Assistant Producer at Andy Jordan Productions. As a playwright, her play *Of Silent Words*, which she co-wrote with Diya Sengupta, was shortlisted for the Paines Plough Women's Prize for Playwriting and her historical fiction play *Negotiating With The Dead* won the Pembroke Player's Prize for Playwriting. She is currently completing an MA in Creative Writing at Royal Holloway University.

CHERYL ROBSON

Australian-born, Cheryl worked at the BBC in London for several years then developed and produced new writing for theatre before working as an editor and publishing over 200 writers, winning numerous awards. As a playwright, she won the Croydon Warehouse International Playwriting Competition, was longlisted for the Bruntwood Prize and has had several stage plays produced. Her co-translation of *David's Story* by Stig Dalager was shortlisted for the Marsh Award for Children's Literature in Translation and her co-edited book *Silent Women: Pioneers of Cinema* (Supernova Books) was voted best book on silent film in 2017. As a director, her film *Rock 'n' Roll Island* won four awards at US film festivals and was nominated at Raindance London. It was broadcast on BBC 4 in 2020 and was named Sunday Times' Critics Choice. Cheryl is best known for her successful campaign to erect a statue of Virginia Woolf on Richmond Riverside.

First published in the UK in 2026 by Aurora Metro Publications Ltd.
80 Hill Rise, Richmond, TW10 6UB
www.aurorametro.com   info@aurorametro.com

FB/AuroraMetroBooks X @aurorametro Instagram @aurora_metro

Production by Amie Brian

With many thanks to Tiffany Woodsmith, Liliana Oliveira and Thea Telfer

Printed in the UK by 4edge printers on sustainably resourced paper.

ISBN: (print) 978-1-912430-96-3
ISBN: (ebook) 978-1-910798-15-7

SPHINX PLAYS

SIX FEMINIST CLASSICS

Introduced by Sue Parrish

AURORA METRO BOOKS

Philippa Buxton in *A Berlin Kabaret* by Peter Cox, Sue Parrish and Joseph Atkins
Photo © Pau Ros 2013

CONTENTS

THE ROARING GIRL'S HAMLET

CLAIRE LUCKHAM

A PROLOGUE

MOLL enters. She is dressed as a man and looks stunning. She starts the prologue alone on stage, possibly in a spotlight.

MOLL Welcome!

We are clear bounding with joy at seeing so many here tonight.
Welcome!
– and jittery.
See my hand shake? Jangled with nerves.
Jumpy and shaking with fear – but, never the less, overjoyed
I am. Mad Moll is, since that is I...
She who lives off her wits, and has no humour to marry,
Who lives among the cheaters, lifters, nips and foists, the puggards,
And arbers of this – And am not one – she, who sleeps both sides
Of the bed, and am man enough for any woman...
And like a man am supposed to know no fear –
I am not afraid of a brawl 'tis true, but this...
I quake, shake... and verily, want to puke...
On two counts I am fearful: –
One, the first, is that I may harm those I love –
These women

The rest of the cast appear in two groups. One dressed traditionally, as women. The other group are dressed as men.

And these others
That I have implored to join us –
These plain ordinary women... whose lives are made tough enough
By childbirth, drudgery and the pleasing of men –
Ay, they please themselves too, but the price they pay for

A small pleasure is a lifetime of service –
These mothers, daughters, whores –
These wives, these nuns, these workhorses here
Joined with us to defy the law.
Remember we break the law to appear here in costume and in public
On a stage.
Second –
I am fearful second... Moll has to say it,
I who care that... *(MOLL clicks her fingers)* ...for public opinion,
Fear yours... what you might think... will think...
I fear your expectation...
That you do think that you do know what it is,
That you will see tonight...
...that you will know what you want to see...
And... I...
You expect to see the play 'Hamlet' performed by women...
That is, by women who will pretend they are men...
Who will ape the way men do the play...
Ay, I know we set ourselves up like skittles to be
Knocked down by your opinion, in choosing this,
This most best loved, best known...
The play that men shelter in their hearts away from woman –
This sacred play.
I beg you judge us not by all the 'Hamlets' that have gone before.
Allow us our women's voice.
Yea, I say this, I, Moll, that dresses in man's attire –
So am I part male, part female –
So are we all. So Hamlet is.

One thing more – a practical thing –
We have our look-outs positioned
All around.
Should the watch be spied, and danger approach,

Three owl hoots will signal to our stage manager.
She will stop our playing by blowing on her whistle.
Thus –

THE STAGE MANAGER demonstrates.

Then you must all leave here fast, like lightning,
Taking care not to trample on your fellows –
And God help her that is left behind!
This is a precaution only... we hope!
I pray you, gentle audience enjoy the play.

Music!

The play starts with a funeral procession.

INTRODUCTION

From the rough and tumble of the early tours to our acclaimed trailblazing Glass Ceiling events at the National Theatre, it has been a blast!!!

By the time I arrived at the Women's Theatre Group in 1990, shortly before it was relaunched as Sphinx, I had already been a founding member of both the Conference of Women Theatre Directors and Administrators in 1980, and The Women's Playhouse Trust in 1982-3. These were the two key feminist organisations which enlightened, empowered and galvanised women in theatre. At the heart of my mission for Sphinx was the advancement of women playwrights and female protagonists, inspired by the work of the Women's Playhouse Trust.

By 1990, the backlash to feminist politics was in full swing, and it was clear to me that we must make the case for women's artistic advancement in the mainstream. This was not necessarily a popular strategy, even among women, who were committed socially to the grass roots and opposed to 'elitism' in established theatres. The 1983/4 Status of Women in UK Theatre Survey gave us solid data, and confirmed that opportunities for women to tell their own stories were meagre and often limited to social issues.

Discussing these concerns with my first Arts Council Officer, a woman, she uttered the immortal words, "Oh but Sue, women can't be artists, women are mothers." I was dumbfounded and furious that after nearly twenty years of feminist fringe theatre groups toiling up and down the motorways, artistic equality remained a distant country. But it laid out the battlefield!

Throughout the life of Sphinx, I have remained steadfast in our aim to advance women playwrights. It has been my guiding principle and the beating heart of the company. It has taken many different forms and levels, and taken us on many adventures as well as maintained a constant dialogue with the profession, our policy makers and with the Arts Council. We have led campaigns for funding equality, and produced many industry reports. We have produced eighteen touring plays, many of which toured the UK and internationally several times, and produced eighteen major conference events to bring together and share the creative experiences of leading women artists. I well remember trying to explain to Germaine Greer the disapproval of the Glass Ceiling audience of her book *Slip-Shod Sibyls*, and returning Taslima Nasrin to Heathrow airport under the mysterious direction of Special Branch.

When, in 2012, the Arts Council rejected our UK-wide women's playwriting project, a project which would later become the blueprint for Sphinx 30, they instead funded our two Women Centre Stage Festivals at the National Theatre and Hampstead Theatre. This gave groundbreaking opportunities for a programme of developing work from new writers. The project, significantly, also provided new performance platforms for experimental companies, including both Graeae and Kali Theatre. We had created a fizz and a buzz which brought new audiences to both theatres. I was warmly and tearfully thanked by a leading actress in the audience for 'speaking for us'. Eight of the plays from this programme were published by Nick Hern Books.

Beyond the established touring grid, we took Diane Esguerra's characters Freud and Dora into schools, drama schools and universities (in *Sweet Dreams*); our aerial version of Pam Gems' *The Little Mermaid* into a tent, and workshops into Holloway Prison. We reached out to new audiences and

The Little Mermaid by Pam Gems
Photo © Robert Day 2004

engaged with young minds, receiving back a consuming sense of being on a roller coaster of discovery and creativity.

It is my good fortune and tremendous gift to have met and worked with many remarkable women over these thirty tumultuous years and especially the writers of these six landmark plays. Each of these plays chart explorations into unseen and unknown territories, none of them domestic.

I was fortunate to have witnessed the sophisticated and spectacular production of *New Anatomies* at the ICA in 1981 by Nancy Diuguid. In her preface to *New Anatomies*, Timberlake Wertenbaker recognizes her protagonist, Isabelle Eberhardt, 'as a woman in love with adventure, on a quest'. She was an independent woman seeking freedom in the world. She sets the stage for this stunning collection of complex female protagonists.

Claire Luckham's Prologue to the all-female *Hamlet* of 1992 – enacted by the anarchic, raucous Moll Cutpurse – launched our new mission. It was inspired by Mary Frith, the 'Roaring Girl' immortalised by Middleton and Dekker as Moll Cutpurse in 1610/11, a pickpocket who lived in male clothing. An insurgent woman.

Every Bit of It portrays the fascinating and emotional meeting on a train between two very different women who discover a mutual love for the great Blues singer, Bessie Smith. Accompanied by pianist Kate Williams, it was cast with a rising Scottish singer, Suzanne Bonnar, and Elizabeth Quinn, a leading deaf actress, fresh from her West End triumph in *Children of a Lesser God*. Together, they broke hearts in Jackie Kay's poetic drama about loss, bereavement and violence, and redemption through music. It also crossed theatrical boundaries by integrating text, poetry and song. The finale brought the house down with a sensational fall of cherry blossom.

In *Playhouse Creatures,* the first English actresses, a glittering troupe led by the magical Frances Cuka, forged their place in history in April De Angelis' pungent and vibrant modern classic. Followed by *Goliath*, a narrative creation by Bryony Lavery based on Beatrix Campbell's book about the urban riots of 1991, for a solo performer. Nichola McAuliffe played nineteen characters in a celebrated bravura performance and was nominated for the TMA Best Actress Award in 1997.[1]

I well remember taking Janet Suzman, who directed *The Snow Palace,* to meet Pam Gems. We met to discuss how to shape a play originally destined for the RSC with a multiple cast, for a Sphinx cast of six, and firmly rejected Pam's plea for a cat! *The Snow Palace* told the story of a Polish writer, Stanislawa Przybyszewska, who wrote the play *The Danton Case*, and died of hypothermia in her unheated hut in her thirties. Kathryn

1. Known since 2011 as the UK Theatre Awards.

Pogson was universally acclaimed as Stanislawa and *The Snow Palace* was nominated for the Barclay's Award for Best Touring Production 1998. The mesmerising first ten minutes of crows cawing in the cold of a Polish winter will remain with me as a profound evocation of a woman's loneliness. The eminent Polish film director Andrzej Wajda attended the first performance of *The Snow Palace* in Poland. Wadja made the classic 1983 film of the novel *Danton*, which Pam Gems had based her Royal Shakespeare Company production, *The Danton Affair*, on. When we were introduced, Wadja gave me a hug to pass on to Pam Gems, who had not come to Poland. I duly delivered the hug on our return.

Sweet Dreams by Diane Esguerra explored a close encounter with Sigmund Freud and his famed, or notorious, Dora case. It was written at a time when sexual abuse was seldom acknowledged, with little comprehension of the horror and harm brought by crashing the sexual boundaries between adult and child. A young woman is subjected to a predatory older man, and Freud alone believed her account and her trauma. The play was enhanced by the spirited performances of Sophie Walker, Gabrielle Jourdan and Ann Marcuson, playing Dora, and the intellectual and empathetic Freud of Jonathan Oliver. A deeply prescient piece!

I have worked with all these playwrights on many occasions over the years and in our collaborations, we always sought to express a distilled modern feminism, without recourse to grievance or victimhood. In re-connecting with these wonderful plays, I have been struck by their freshness and significance, and by the landmark contribution they have made to the contemporary theatre landscape. I hope that they will be studied and produced again and again and again.

My goal to take a major fringe company from touring in a van to creating mainstage theatre has been exhilarating to say the least, and I would like to express my heartfelt thanks to every one of our collaborators – actors, musicians, designers, all of you! – for playing your part in this journey, and placing women centre stage.

Sue Parrish

Sue Parrish addresses the first 'Vamps, Vixens and Feminists Conference' at the Olivier Theatre, the National Theatre. Photo © Pau Ros 2009

Sue Parrish graduated from UCL with a BA Hons in English Literature. She is an Associate of the Guildhall School of Music and Drama and has been Sphinx Theatre Company's Artistic Director and Producer since 1990. Sue has extensive experience producing and directing Fringe, Repertory and Musical Theatre. For three years, Sue created Shakespeare productions with leading orchestras and conductors for the City of London Festival in the Guildhall Great Hall.

For Sphinx as a Producer, her credits include: *Goliath* by Bryony Lavery, *The Snow Palace* by Pam Gems, *Vita and Virginia* by Eileen Atkins, *A Wedding Story* by Bryony Lavery and *Blame* by Beatrix Campbell and Judith Jones. Sue has also directed classical works by Congreve, Vanbrugh, Shakespeare and Japanese Noh theatre by Seami and Mishima. As a Director, her credits include: *Playhouse Creatures* by April De Angelis, *Every Bit of It* by Jackie Kay, *Sweet Dreams* by Diane Esguerra and the award-winning *A Berlin Kabaret*.

Sue produced the Glass Ceiling feminist conferences at the National Theatre for ten years from 1991 and Women Centre Stage Festivals at the National Theatre (2015), Hampstead Theatre (2019) and Trafalgar Theatre (2020). She was a founding member of the Conference of Women Theatre Directors and Administrators, in 1979, and of The Women's Playhouse Trust in 1982, and has remained involved in developing the feminist dialogue in theatre.

PREFACE TO NEW ANATOMIES

New Anatomies was originally going to be a one-act of a play about three women who dressed as men. The other two were George Sand and Ono Kamachi, a Japanese poet and courtesan. Eventually, the fascinating Isabelle Eberhardt, a historical character whose diaries I discovered by chance, took up a whole play to herself. She was a woman in love with adventure, on a quest, and this was a theme that obsessed me.

This question of cross-dressing is rich and also complicated and, of course, I was fascinated by it. I was intrigued by the mental liberation in the simple physical act of cross-dressing. I think it's to do with being able to shed the external gaze. Women are always looked at, even today. And women themselves can often play into that or feel obligated to play into it. For a woman, to dress as a man is a way to bypass all of that and no longer to feel so much an object. To turn into a subject. Hence the person can suddenly become active, free to explore, to stride out, to breathe. They no longer have to think of themselves as female and hence this and that (all those expectations that come from being female). It's an act of general disobedience, rebellion, a refusal to obey imposed norms and a discarding of the particular burden of being female. It's also safer. For Isabelle Eberhardt, it was all of those things: the desire to explore and the need for safety when traveling.

There were many discussions during the rehearsals for the first production of *New Anatomies*. Not all the actresses wanted to play men, particularly Arab men. Algeria, however, had a very different history, a history that was much in evidence when I was growing up on the French side of the Basque Country and Algerian men and women were fighting together for Independence (I must have watched *The Battle of Algiers* at least five times).

What was great about the whole experience of *New Anatomies* was working with women in theatre. Having something called the 'Women's Theatre Group' was a declaration, among other things, that it was necessary for women to write plays and to write more roles and more complex roles for women. It was also interesting, in that context, to write small roles for men, roles that were not dominant. I had a good time writing Bou Saadi and Saleh, the two young Algerians Isabelle encounters. I still remember that scene in particular, the way it looked.

I think there are quite a few plays written by men that have one good role for a woman. But there are not many plays written by men that have a lot of different and interesting roles for women in one play. That was the challenge of the Women's Theatre Group.

Timberlake Wertenbaker

Hazel Maycock and Adele Salem in *New Anatomies* by Timberlake Wertenbaker
Photo © Leslie McIntyre 1981

NEW ANATOMIES

TIMBERLAKE WERTENBAKER

New Anatomies was commissioned for, and produced by, the Women's Theatre Group. It was first performed at the Institute of Contemporary Arts (ICA), London, in 1981.

Director	Nancy Diuguid
Designer	Iona McLeish
Stage Manager/Musician	Jo Richler
Composer/Musician	Liz Kean
Cast	Sandy Mayberley, Hazel Maycock, Susan McGoun, Penny O'Connor, Adele Salem

Characters

The play is designed for a cast of five women and a musician. Except for the actress playing Isabelle, each actress plays a Western woman, an Arab man and a Western man. Changes should take place in such a way as to be visible to the audience and all five actresses can be on stage at all times. The roles are distributed as follows:

ISABELLE EBERHARDT/SI MAHMOUD

SÉVERINE, ANTOINE, BOU SAADI

NATALIE, EUGÉNIE, MURDERER, JUDGE

JENNY, SALEH, LYDIA, COLONEL LYAUTEY

VERDA MILES, ANNA, SI LACHMI, YASMINA, CAPTAIN SOUBIEL

PASHA *(non-speaking)*. The role of Pasha in Act II, Scene One is silent, and should be taken by the musician.

Notes

Songs are not necessary but they can be used in the play. They need to be popular music-hall songs from the turn of the century and from the repertoire of male impersonators. The only place a song is needed is at the top of Act 2.

The action of the play takes place at the turn of the century in Europe and Algeria.

ACT ONE, SCENE ONE

AIN-SEFRA, a dusty village in Algeria. ISABELLE EBERHARDT looks around, none too steady. She is dressed in a tattered Arab cloak, has no teeth and almost no hair. She is 27.

ISABELLE Lost the way (*She steadies herself*). Detour. Closed. Pause *(as if an order to herself)*. Go inside, (*She sings, softly, Arabic modulations, but flat.)* 'If a man be old and a fool, his folly...' *(She burps.)* That's what it is. (*She takes out a cigarette and looks for a match through the folds of her cloak*). Match *(She forgets about it, sings)*. 'If a man be old and a fool, his folly is past all cure. But a young man...' What it is is this *(looking around)* I need a fuck. *(Pause.)* Definitely. Yes.

SÉVERINE enters. She is a slightly older woman, dressed uncomfortably for the heat, in a long skirt and jacket.

ISABELLE Trailed... *(to SÉVERINE)* Trailing behind me.

SÉVERINE Come inside.

ISABELLE Inside? Trailed: the story, I know. Stealing it.

SÉVERINE You have a fever.

ISABELLE remembers her cigarette.

ISABELLE Matches. Stolen. *(louder)* You stole my matches

SÉVERINE finds the matches, tries to light ISABELLE's cigarette.

ISABELLE *(apologetic)* Desert wind: makes the hand shake.

SÉVERINE lights two cigarettes and sticks one in ISABELLE's mouth.

ISABELLE Pay for my story with a match. European coinage!

SÉVERINE You need rest.

ISABELLE No, later. *(She burps)*. Found out what it was. What was it? Ah, yes. It was: I need a fuck. I need a fuck. Where am I going to find a fuck? Bunch of degenerates in this town. Sleeping WHEN I NEED A FUCK. It's the European influence. Keeps them down.

SÉVERINE Come inside, Isabelle.

ISABELLE 'Please go inside mademoiselle, and stay there.' Out of the wind. Saw a couple of guards earlier. That'll do. One for you, one for me. I'll give you the younger one, rules of hospitality. No? Sevvy the scribe prefers a belly dancer, eh, dark smooth limbs and curved hips. Or the voluptuous tale. Your face looks like a big hungry European cock. No offence: not your fault you look European. Must find those guards.

(staring) Coolness of the night as it filters through the sand. The smell of sand, Séverine, do you know it? It's like the inside of water. Smell...

She leans down and falls flat.

SÉVERINE Isabelle, please...

They struggle to get her up.

ISABELLE You going to write I couldn't walk straight enough to find a fuck? They'll want to know everything. I'm famous now, not just anybody, no, I'll be in History. *(near retch)* They hate me, but I forgive them. You tell them... that when the body drags through the gutter, it is cleaved from the soul. Tell them the soul paced the desert. They take baths, but lice crawl through the cracks of their hypocritical brains. Bunch of farmers. Wallowing in the mud of their ploughed fields. Turnips, cabbages, carrots, all in a line, all fenced in. *(cries)* Why do they hate me so? I didn't want anything from them.

Pause.

Si Mahmoud forgives all. Si Mahmoud paced the desert. Heart unmixed with guile, free. Why aren't you writing all this down, chronicler? Duty to get it right, no editing. *(She burps).* Edit that.

SÉVERINE Please, Si Mahmoud. Let's go in.

ISABELLE Listen. The dawn's coming. You can tell by the sound, a curve in the silence and then the sand in the desert moves... Write down: a third of a centimetre, they'll want to know that in Europe.

(Pause. SÉVERINE, resigned, sits with ISABELLE.)

When I was growing up in the Tsar's villa in St Petersburg...

SÉVERINE Geneva.

ISABELLE What?

SÉVERINE You said Geneva earlier.

ISABELLE Did I? Yes, ducks... must have been Geneva.

SÉVERINE *(delicately)* Your brothers...

ISABELLE Didn't have any.

SÉVERINE You said...

ISABELLE I was the only boy in the family.

SÉVERINE Your brother Antoine...

ISABELLE Beloved. *(Makes a gesture for fucking)* Didn't. Would have. Nasty little piece got her claws in him first. No, did.

SÉVERINE Si Mahmoud, the truth.

ISABELLE There is no god but Allah, Allah is the only God and Muhammed is his prophet.

SÉVERINE What brought you to the desert?

(ISABELLE makes a trace on the ground.) It's in Arabic.

ISABELLE *(reads)* The Mektoub – it was written. Here. That means, no choice. Mektoub.

SÉVERINE Your mother?

ISABELLE No choice for her either. The Mektoub.

SÉVERINE You told me she was a delicate woman. What gave her the courage to run off?

ISABELLE Even the violet resists domestication.

SÉVERINE But in the 1870s...

ISABELLE Séverine, it is a courtesy in this country not to interrupt or ask questions of the storyteller. You must sit quietly and listen, moving only to light my cigarettes. When I pause, you may praise Allah for having given my tongue such vivid modulations. I shall begin, as is our custom, with a mention of women.

SCENE TWO

GENEVA. A house in disorder. ANNA, a woman in her late thirties, with remnants of style and charm.

ANNA And then the children... They won't stay.

ISABELLE and ANTOINE appear. ISABELLE is 13, dressed in a man's shirt and a skirt much too big for her. ANTOINE is 16, frail and feminine.

ISABELLE Antoine. Don't let him frighten you.

ANTOINE *(near tears)* Drunken tyrant.

ISABELLE Let's dream.

ANTOINE He threatened to hit me. Brute. I have to go away, now.

ANNA *(paying no attention to any of this)* First Nicholas, not a word... He must have come to a bad... Too many anarchists in the house. It's a bad influence on children.

ISABELLE Oh yes, let's go away. We're in Siberia. The snow is up to our knees, so hard to move. Suddenly, look, shining in the dark, a pair of yellow eyes.

ANTOINE I have no choice. I'll have to run away and join the army.

ISABELLE I'll come with you, we can take Mama.

ANTOINE The army's only for boys

ISABELLE We can't leave Mama.

ANTOINE I wish I was a girl. He doesn't treat you that way.

ISABELLE I'm strong.

ANTOINE He'll kill me

ANNA If only Trofimovitch had allowed some fairy tales, even Pushkin... not all these Bakunin pamphlets at bedtime.

ISABELLE It's snowing again. Darkness. Another pair of yellow eyes, glistening. Another. We're surrounded. Are they wolves?

ANTOINE *(joining in reluctantly)* No, those are the eyes of our enemies.

ISABELLE You're shivering.

ANNA And now Natalie...

ANTOINE I'm cold. It's too cold up there. I want to go further south.

ISABELLE The Crimea. Lemon groves.

ANTOINE 'Knowst thou the land, beloved, where the lemons bloom...' No, I want to go further south. Far away. The Sahara.

ANNA And Natalie's so good with...

ISABELLE Our camels are tired.

ANTOINE That's the sort of thing Natalie would say.

ISABELLE *(offended)* The transition from Siberia was too sudden. I haven't acclamitated.

ANTOINE Acclimatized.

ANNA It's all so difficult.

Flute music.

ISABELLE This stillness.

ANTOINE Dune after dune, shape mirroring shape, no life... weariness.

ISABELLE How rapidly the sun seems to plunge behind the dunes. This stillness.

ANTOINE Let us rest, my beloved.

ISABELLE I'll build our tent. There's a storm coming, I can see the clouds.

ANTOINE There aren't any clouds over the desert.

ISABELLE That's what Natalie would say.

ANTOINE You don't understand, the corners of a dream must be nailed to the ground as firmly as our tent: no rain in the desert.

ISABELLE A wind then. Listen, the wind's galloping over the dunes.

ANTOINE It's a sandstorm.

ISABELLE Quick. Where are you? I can't see you.

ANTOINE Here, come here, my beloved.

They throw themselves into each other's arms, roll on the floor.

ANTOINE Beloved.

Their embrace lingers.

ANNA Natalie mustn't... she's too good with (*She notices the two children.*) Antoine, I'm not sure you should... with your sister... like that.

ISABELLE We're playing, Mama, we're dreaming.

ANNA Are you too old? I don't know. The poets... But Natalie...

ANTOINE Wants us to behave –

ISABELLE Like Swiss clocks. Tick tock.

ANTOINE Tick tock.

ANNA You mustn't... She is sometimes a little... but she's the only one, she's so good with dust. I don't seem to manage very well. There's so much of it and it's complicated finding it. I wasn't brought up to... But this new world of Trofimovitch, where it's wrong to have servants, well yes, but what about the dust? I suppose when the revolution comes, they'll find a way, deal with it.

ISABELLE We don't mind.

ANNA Natalie... wants to leave us.

ANTOINE Even Natalie can't take the beast any more.

ANNA Isabelle, she's always been very fond... Tell her she absolutely mustn't...

ISABELLE She's free.

ANNA But Trofimovitch.

NATALIE enters. She is a tightly pulled together young woman. An awkward silence and a sense that this is not unusual when she comes into a room.

ANNA Natalie, I was saying... to abandon your home...

NATALIE How can you call this pigsty a home?

ANNA Darling, a young lady's vocabulary shouldn't include... Your family...

NATALIE Family. (*She looks around at them.*) In a family you have first a mother who looks after her children, protects them, teaches them.

ANNA Didn't I? You knew several poems of Byron as a child.

NATALIE A mother who teaches her children how to behave and looks after the house, cooks meals, doesn't let her children eat out of a slop bucket –

ANNA Trofimovitch says meals are a bourgeois form of... But don't we have...?

NATALIE When I cook them. And secondly, in a family a brother is a brother, a boy then a man, not this snivelling, delicate half girl. You've allowed him to be terrorized by that drunken beast.

ANNA Natalie, his mind, philosophy...

NATALIE Philosophy? Don't make me laugh. Yes, and finally in a family you have a proper father, not that raving peasant, who's driven us to this misery and filth, who's now trying to get into my bed at night.

ANNA He's not always very steady at night, he must have thought... He didn't notice it wasn't his.

NATALIE *(exploding)* And you defend him. My mother defends the man who's ruining all of us, you defend the man who's trying to seduce your own daughter. You won't leave that filthy lecherous drunk, you prefer to ruin us.

ANNA Leave him... go... where?

ISABELLE Natalie, love forgives.

NATALIE Love, that spittle of stinking brandy. Love?

ISABELLE *(gently)* 'Love has its reasons...

ANTOINE ...which reason cannot fathom.'

NATALIE The two of you with your books!

ANNA *(feebly)* Isabelle is right... She doesn't mind...

NATALIE At her age you love anybody, even beggars, even a snivelling brother. *(to ISABELLE)* I'll come back and get you later, then you can come live with me in a real home, with a real family, with my husband.

ISABELLE A husband, Natalie. That's different. Is he dark? Is he foreign? Does he visit you only at night and wrap you in a blinding veil of torrid passion? A secret husband, how wonderful, like Eros and Psyche. Does he let you look at him?

NATALIE What are you talking about? I'm marrying Stéphane.

ANTOINE Stéphane, the shopkeeping weed. He's driven you to that?

NATALIE You're one to talk, you fine figure of manhood.

ISABELLE He does look like a dandelion, you said so yourself.

NATALIE He'll soon be my husband and I'll have him talked about with respect. We'll be very happy.

ISABELLE How? If he knows you don't love him.

NATALIE Love, look where that got us. Oh, I tell him I love him, men like to hear that. Sometimes I tell him I adore him.

ANNA To lie... I'm not sure...

NATALIE I can't have you at the wedding. I explained he was too ill. Stéphane's family's a little upset that we're from Russia and not properly Swiss. But they'll see, I'll make a wonderful home for him. *(Pause.)* I must get my things. Don't tell him, it won't do any good,

She leaves.

ANNA I don't understand. What have I done? But you, my babies, you'll never leave, no, you couldn't now. What did you say, Isabelle? Torrid passion, yes, I think, with Trofimovitch, it was... He was so strong, so convinced, impossible to think clearly... And then, how wrong it was to have servants, husband, hypocrisy of the sacrament, he said, and how my life made millions suffer. Would you have preferred a big house? You see, there are so many rules when you... The doctor says a frail heart... There's no choice when your heart is...

She drifts off.

ISABELLE At last the silence descends on the darkening dunes. How still is our solitude, my beloved, how still the desert.

ANTOINE Let's stop here.

ISABELLE Yes, let's grow old together and watch the hours stretch on the ground.

ANTOINE *(moving away)* Beloved, forgive me, but I must.

ISABELLE I can't see you. You sound so far away.

ANTOINE I don't have the strength any more, forgive me...

ISABELLE Where have you gone? Oh, please. Abandoned, alas, nothing to do.

ANTOINE *(from off)* But wait.

ISABELLE Wait... and all around me, death. *(Screams)* Dead.

SCENE THREE

GENEVA, a few years later. NATALIE and ISABELLE.

NATALIE Dead?

ISABELLE Dead. Both of them. Mama first, almost immediately after she received Antoine's letter. It broke her heart, those years of silence, not knowing, her frail heart. And then the letter from the Legion! Antoine a Legionnaire; he'll never survive.

NATALIE It might be just the thing for him. Turn him into a man.

ISABELLE He didn't even tell me, the coward, the traitor. He must have planned it for months in secret. And then a cool letter describing life in the barracks and, now, marriage. I'll have to find him before it's too late.

NATALIE And him? Drank himself to death?

ISABELLE Poor Trofimovitch. He'd begun to put his ear to the ground listening for the sound of the revolution. He said he'd hear it when it came, he still had the ear of a Russian peasant. And he despaired of the silence. When Mama died, he... turned and twisted, crumpled himself into a knot and kept his ear to the floor, but this time I think he was listening for her. 'Three be the ways of love: a knitting of heart to heart' – that's Antoine and me – 'a pleasing of lips and eyes, and a third love whose name is death.' That's Trofimovitch and Mama. It's from an Arabic poem. Trofimovitch taught it to me. There's a similar one in Greek.

NATALIE Mama should have taught you to sweep instead. If I'd learnt properly when I was young my mother-in-law wouldn't have found so much to complain about. But Stéphane has been very patient. I'm lucky. *(Taking in the disorder).* We can start on this house. Stéphane thinks we'll get a lot of money for it, sell it to some English aristocrats. They like these gloomy old places.

ISABELLE The house belongs to Antoine. He'll want to come back here and live with me.

NATALIE He'll want his own little home now.

ISABELLE 'And the screen of separation was placed between us.'

NATALIE The house belongs to all of us. Your share of the money can help towards the expense of having you live with us, and you'll have some left over for your marriage. I wish I'd been able to bring some to my husband although he never reproached me.

ISABELLE What's marriage like?

NATALIE We're doing very well with the shop now and soon we'll build our own house, a big one.

ISABELLE I mean at night.

NATALIE You get used to it.

ISABELLE Brutal pain and brutal pleasure, and after, languor. 'And the breeze languished in the evening hours as if it had pity for me.'

NATALIE You've been reading too much. You mustn't talk like that to men. When they come into the shop you must be seen working very hard, dusting things very carefully. That always inspires young men. We've thought a lot about Stéphane's cousin. He has a flower shop and he won't mind the fact that you look so strong. You could help him in the garden. You'd like that.

ISABELLE Does he grow cactus plants?

NATALIE They're the wrong plants for this climate.

ISABELLE It's the wrong climate for the plants. I'm going to Algeria.

NATALIE The thought of marriage frightened me too, but I'll help you make a good choice. You'll need a roof over your head.

ISABELLE No rain in the desert. No need for a roof.

NATALIE We're in Geneva and I'm here to protect you until you're safely married.

ISABELLE Geneva of the barred horizons. I'm getting out, I need a gallop on the dunes.

NATALIE You'll forget all that when you're married. You'll forget all those dreams.

ISABELLE *(looking at NATALIE for the first time)* Poor Natalie, left the dreams to look for order, but order was not happiness.

NATALIE You always made fun of me, you and Antoine, but I always cared for you and I'm determined to help you. When you understand what life is like without the books, you'll understand me, you'll see.

ISABELLE Geneva to Marseilles by train, Marseilles to Algiers by boat and then a camel for the desert.

NATALIE That's enough now. It's your duty.

ISABELLE Words of a Swiss preacher, song of the rain on the cultivated fields.

NATALIE You have to obey me. You have no choice.

ISABELLE Trofimovitch told me obedience comes not from direct fear, but fear of the rules. I have no fear; he always said I was the bravest.

NATALIE He had no right to treat you as if you were an exception. (*Pause.*) You're still so young, we won't force you. We'll give you a year, even more. (*Silence.*) If we sell this house, we can take a little trip to Algeria. I want to see what they have over there. They say Arabs are very stupid and give you valuable jewels and clothes for trinkets. Will you agree to that?

ISABELLE The desert.

NATALIE Stéphane's arranging the papers for the house and then he'll get us all passports. You couldn't get one by yourself.

ISABELLE Antoine, we'll gallop over the desert.

NATALIE I'll be so pleased to sell this house. All buried at last.

ISABELLE Antoine!

SCENE FOUR

Algiers. ANTOINE in a crumpled civil service suit sits smoking, tired, grey. JENNY, young and very pregnant, is bustling. ISABELLE is staring out and YASMINA, a servant, is polishing something, extremely slowly.

JENNY *(to ANTOINE)* Why doesn't your sister ever help? She hasn't lifted a finger since she's been here. She talks too much to the servant. I have enough trouble making that woman work. They're so lazy, these people. She's said more to that girl than to me. Call her over, Antoine. She never listens when I talk to her.

ANTOINE *(weakly)* Isabelle.

ISABELLE turns.

JENNY Please remember that Fatma is a native and a servant. They don't respect you if you treat them...

ISABELLE Her name isn't Fatma.

JENNY Their names are unpronounceable. We call them all Fatma.

ISABELLE Her name is beautiful: Yasmina. Poor girl, they tried to marry her to a cousin she hated. It was death or the degradation of becoming a servant. I'll write about her.

JENNY I wouldn't believe anything she says. Help me polish some glasses. I can't trust Fatma with them.

ISABELLE Throw over a cigarette, will you, Antoine?

JENNY Women shouldn't smoke. It makes them look vulgar, doesn't it, Antoine?

ISABELLE Matches.

JENNY And you work very hard for your cigarettes. They don't grow on trees. Some people have to pay for everything and soon we'll have another mouth to feed.

ANTOINE Isabelle will help us when she sells some articles.

JENNY She won't sell any by just sitting around smoking.

ISABELLE Inspiration doesn't come from frying potatoes.

ANTOINE laughs.

JENNY You always take her side. You don't care what happens to me. She hasn't even offered to knit something for the baby.

ISABELLE *(bored)* Yasmina will help me find something.

JENNY I'm not going to put some horrible native cloth around my beautiful new baby.

ISABELLE *(to ANTOINE)* I'll get Natalie to send you a collection of poems when she goes back. Do you remember that beautiful one by Lermontov, that Mama used to recite, about the young soul crying out its entrapment in the womb? The dumb joy of the mother but for 'a long time it languished in the world, filled with a wonderful longing and earth's tedious songs...' how does it go?

ANTOINE *(awkward)* I don't remember.

ISABELLE 'Could not drown out the last sounds of Paradise...'

JENNY You're jealous, that's all, because you can't find a husband. Natalie told me how you frightened Stéphane's cousin away.

ISABELLE He looked like an orchid.

ANTOINE You're worse than Arabs, you two, fighting about nothing.

ISABELLE Is that what they teach you in the barracks?

JENNY He's not in the barracks any more. He has a very good job.

ISABELLE Sitting on your bum, staring at numbers.

JENNY And he'll be promoted soon.

ISABELLE To longer numbers.

JENNY If you don't ruin his chances. You've been heard talking to the natives in their own language. There's no reason not to talk to them in French.

ISABELLE *(to ANTOINE)* You hate it, don't you, this life?

JENNY People are becoming suspicious. This is a small community.

ISABELLE Tick tock, a Swiss clock, the needle that crushes the dreams to sleep.

JENNY You think food just appears on the table. It has to be paid for.

ISABELLE And only ten miles from the desert. You might as well have stayed in Switzerland for all you've seen of it.

ANTOINE I did see it. It's not how we dreamt of it. It's dangerous, uncomfortable, and most of it isn't even sand.

ISABELLE Freedom.

JENNY Life is much cheaper here than in Switzerland. We'll go back when we have enough money to buy a decent house.

ISABELLE 'Oh the bitter grief of never again exchanging one single thought.' Remember how we knew all of Loti by heart and we dreamt of moving, always moving.

ANTOINE Life isn't what we dreamt.

ISABELLE It could be... the rolling movement of camels, movement, Antoine.

JENNY Rolling stone gathers no moss. I don't want my baby to be poor.

ISABELLE Remember when we followed the Berber caravan and we had the sandstorm, 'oh, my beloved'...

ANTOINE I saw the Berbers. One wrong move and they slit your throat. They don't like Europeans.

ISABELLE Not Europeans with guns, but we could talk to them. Freedom.

JENNY You keep talking as if Antoine was a slave. He has a good job. We'll be able to take holidays, have a house. That's freedom: money.

ANTOINE I see how things are now.

ISABELLE What dictionary are you using? The Swiss clockmaker's or the poet's?

An Arabic flute, offstage.

ISABELLE Or his? Listen. I hear him every evening, but I've never seen him come or go. He's just there, suddenly, calling.

JENNY It's probably a beggar and he'll come asking for money. Chase him away, Antoine. They carry diseases these people. It's bad for the baby. (*They ignore her. She shouts.*) Go away, you savage, go away, go away! (*Silence. Embarrassed.*) I'm so tired and nervous. This isn't a friendly country. It's not easy to have a baby. It doesn't happen all by itself.

NATALIE enters, arms full of materials and clothes.

NATALIE It's wonderful how stupid these people are. They give you things for nothing.

ISABELLE The word is generosity, gifts of hospitality.

NATALIE Look at this one, it's worth a fortune, that embroidery, that detail. They're terribly clever for savages. Look at this woman's cloak.

ISABELLE It's not for a woman.

NATALIE We'll be the first shop in Switzerland to sell these oriental things. They're all the rage in Paris. You could even model some of them, Isabelle. Here's a woman's dancing costume.

JENNY Give it to me.

NATALIE I can't wait to get back. We'll make a fortune.

ISABELLE I'm not coming back with you.

NATALIE Nonsense.

NATALIE continues to lay out the clothes. JENNY wraps her face in a veil.

JENNY I'm in your harem. You're the sheikh. Oh, come to me.

ANTOINE You look grotesque.

JENNY You're so cruel. I'll hide behind my veil.

ISABELLE That's not a woman's veil. Women in the desert don't wear veils, only the Tuareg men do. (*She starts dressing JENNY.*) It should be wrapped around the head and worn with this. This is called a jellaba. It can be worn in any kind of weather. The hood will protect you against the elements, or against the enemy. It's very useful for warriors.

JENNY I don't want to be dressed as a man.

ISABELLE Why not? The baby might end up looking like an Arab? He'll run away from you into the desert.

NATALIE You look lovely. Don't tease her, Isabelle. When you're pregnant you have these caprices. I couldn't wear red or walk into the house without making three turns in the garden.

ANTOINE It's like the Arabs. They'll never do anything without going through fifty useless gestures.

ISABELLE The word is courtesy.

ISABELLE takes a jellaba and puts it on, slowly, formally. Freeze while she is doing this. Once in it, she feels as at home in it as JENNY obviously feels awkward.

NATALIE And they gave me this in secret.

She takes out a captain's uniform.

ANTOINE Someone they killed probably. They have no respect for human life. You see how dangerous they are.

ISABELLE 'Always behave as if you were going to die immediately.' Remember when we were Stoics and we tried to live in that barrel for a month?

NATALIE *(going over to JENNY and putting a 'feminine' scarf over her head)* I'm afraid reading is a hereditary disease in our family. I would keep books well away from your children when they're young, otherwise it's very hard to wean them from all that nonsense when they're older. If only we could get her married, she'd forget all those books, but it's the quotes that drive men away. I'm glad Antoine, at least, is saved.

As NATALIE is saying this ISABELLE is putting the captain's jacket on YASMINA. The two girls giggle, YASMINA doing a military stance. JENNY suddenly notices them.

JENNY Don't do that, it's... blasphemy.

ISABELLE Why, do you think clothes make the monk?

ANTOINE Isabelle looks like all our recruits. No one would know you were a girl. Is this male or female?

He puts on a jellaba, joining in the game.

JENNY If anyone sees us, we'll be ruined.

ISABELLE *(to ANTOINE)* Let's go to those dark dens in the Arab quarter and have a smoke.

ANTOINE If they recognize us *(throat-slitting gesture).*

ISABELLE We'll say we're from Tunis. That'll explain my accent.

JENNY You can't go out. What about me?

ISABELLE Come, Antoine, for at least one evening, let's go back to our dreams.

NATALIE I want you to come with me to the market.

ISABELLE I told you I won't help you cheat those people any more.

NATALIE I'm only trying to save some money.

ISABELLE One evening, Antoine.

They begin to go.

JENNY Ooooh – ooooh my stomach. I think I'm going to faint. Don't leave me, Antoine.

ISABELLE You have Natalie and the 'captain'.

JENNY Oooh. *(She doubles over.)* Put your hands on my forehead, Antoine. It's the only thing that'll help.

ISABELLE Why don't you just tell him you want him to stay instead of acting ill, hypocrite?

NATALIE Don't upset a pregnant woman, Isabelle.

ISABELLE Antoine...

ANTOINE goes over to JENNY and puts his hands on her forehead. ISABELLE turns to leave.

NATALIE What are you doing?

ISABELLE I'm going outside.

NATALIE A woman can't go out by herself at this time of night.

ISABELLE But in these... I'm not a woman.

SCENE FIVE

THE KASBAH. ISABELLE, alone.

ISABELLE If, down an obscure alleyway, a voice shouts at me: hey you, shopkeeper – I'll not turn around. If the voice pursues me: foreigner, European – I'll not turn around. If the voice says: you, woman, yes, woman – I'll not turn around, no, I'll not even turn my head. Even when it whispers, Isabelle, Isabelle Eberhardt – even then I won't turn around. But if it hails me: you, you there, who need vast spaces and ask for nothing but to move, you, alone, free, seeking peace and a home in the desert, who wish only to obey the strange ciphers of your fate – yes, then I will turn around, then I'll answer: I am here: Si Mahmoud.

SCENE SIX

THE DESERT.

ISABELLE, SALEH and BOU SAADI are sitting passing around a pipe full of kif. They are very stoned, from lack of food and the hashish. Long silences, then rapid bursts of speech. The poetry must not be 'recited'. For the Arabs, it is their natural form of speech.

SALEH 'The warrior was brave. Alas the beautiful young man fell. He shone like silver. Now he is in Paradise, far from all troubles.'

ISABELLE Was he fighting the Tidjanis, Saleh?

SALEH No, Si Mahmoud, that is a song against the French.

Silence.

ISABELLE Tell me more about the wise men.

SALEH Usually they're sheikhs who have been handed their knowledge by their fathers and then give it to a son. They live in the monasteries. We'll stay in one tomorrow.

BOU SAADI But sometimes they wander and look just like beggars.

SALEH There used to be very many, but the French are getting rid of them.

BOU SAADI You must be careful what you say against the French, Saleh, it was God's will they become our rulers, it was written.

SALEH Have we not read it badly?

Silence.

BOU SAADI One of the most famous marabouts used to live not far from here. Lalla Zineb. Many people visit her tomb.

ISABELLE A woman?

BOU SAADI Not an ordinary woman.

ISABELLE But a woman?

SALEH What difference does it make, Si Mahmoud, if she was wise? They say she predicted the victory of the French and then died of grief. *(Silence.)* If it is wisdom you seek, Si Mahmoud, you should spend some time in the monasteries. We could take you to the one where the leader of our sect lives.

ISABELLE And you, my friends, what have you found in the desert?

SALEH I had a cousin who had a beautiful white mare. She was fast, exquisite. He'd had her since he was a boy. She was his treasure and his love. One night, she disappeared. He searched for months and found her at last in the camp of a few Tidjanis. He waited until the night to get her back, but someone must have seen him because he stumbled on her body on his way to the camp. Her throat had been slit, his beautiful white mare. Some time later he managed to kill the man who had stolen her. It's only fair, a mare is more valuable than a wife to us. But the Tidjanis told the French about it. They're very friendly with the French. He was judged in the city and then sent away to forced labour in a place called Corsica. Very few men come back from Corsica and then only to die. That's the law of the French.

BOU SAADI We were born crossing the desert, but now we have to ask permission to go to certain places.

ISABELLE Was it better always to fight the Tidjanis?

SALEH It was our custom. *(Silence.)*

'She said to me:

Why are your tears so white?

I answered:

Beloved, I have cried so long my tears are as white as my hair.'

ISABELLE One day we'll understand, Saleh.

SALEH Ah, Si Mahmoud, perhaps you will, you're learned.

BOU SAADI We'll leave a few hours before dawn. I hope you're not feeling too weak, Si Mahmoud.

ISABELLE No, my friends, but why didn't you tell me to bring food? I've eaten all of yours.

BOU SAADI We're used to this life.

SALEH 'She said to me:
Why are your tears black?
I answered:
I have no more tears, those are my pupils...'

CAPTAIN SOUBIEL enters.

CAPTAIN SOUBIEL You there, who are you and where are you going?

BOU SAADI and SALEH jump up, acting increasingly stupid as the CAPTAIN stares at them. BOU SAADI in particular almost caricatures 'oriental servility'.

BOU SAADI We're traders on our way to El-Oued, Allah willing.

CAPTAIN Don't give me any of this Allah business. The three of you are traders?

BOU SAADI This is a young Tunisian student on his way to the monasteries down south.

CAPTAIN Monasteries, we've just had a report on those monasteries. Fortresses, that's what they are, hotbeds of resistance. All those sheikhs with their wives and slaves pretending to teach religion when they're shouting propaganda against the French. Don't talk to me about monasteries. *(He stares at ISABELLE)*. A Tunisian student, we've had a report about that too. You're not very dark.

BOU SAADI Men from the city are lighter than us. Much sun in the Sahara.

CAPTAIN Can't he speak for himself? What's your name?

ISABELLE Si Mahmoud.

CAPTAIN Si Mahmoud. You two, go make some tea.

BOU SAADI We have no tea.

CAPTAIN Well, then, go have a piss and don't come back until I call you. Stay where I can see you and you, stay here. *(He has a good stare and then becomes extremely courteous)*. Remarkable, I must say, remarkable. I wouldn't have known. I'm honoured. You've become a legend in the Legion: it's one thing to go out looking for some Arab scum criminal, but a mysterious young lady...

ISABELLE My name is Si Mahmoud.

CAPTAIN You can of course rely on the honour of the French Army to keep your secret. Ha, ha, you Russian girls are extraordinary. One of them blew up the Tsar or his cousin the other day and now we have this young thing living it out with the Arabs. They say Dostoevsky does this to you, gives you a taste for cockroaches. But, mademoiselle, if you wished to see the country, you should have come to us. We would be only too pleased to escort you and you would find our company much more entertaining than that of those sandfleas.

ISABELLE You shouldn't speak of the Arabs in that manner, Captain. They resent it.

CAPTAIN You must tell me how to run the country, mademoiselle. It'll pass the time as we travel. Dunes get monotonous.

ISABELLE I am travelling with my friends, Captain.

CAPTAIN What? Are there more of you? Do we have a whole boarding school of romantic young girls?

ISABELLE My friends Saleh and Bou Saadi.

CAPTAIN She calls these dregs of humanity friends. Ah, youth, the female heart. I admire your spirit, mademoiselle, but it is the duty of the French Army to rescue damsels in distress.

ISABELLE My friends will look after me.

CAPTAIN Mademoiselle, I'm here to protect you. These people smile at you at one day and cut your throat the next. You see, they have no logic, no French education. And if they ever found out... You're not at all bad looking you know.

ISABELLE I choose to travel with them.

CAPTAIN You're quite a brave little character. I like that. I think we'll get on very well. You remind me of a delightfully unbroken young filly.

ISABELLE Whereas you, Captain, remind me of a heavy cascade of camel piss. Mind you, nothing wrong with camel piss, I just don't choose to have it on top of me. Or, to put it another way, I'd rather kiss the open mouth of a Maccabean corpse dead of the Asiatic cholera than 'travel' with you, Captain.

Freeze.

CAPTAIN May I see your papers?

ISABELLE What papers?

CAPTAIN You must have government permission to travel through French territory.

ISABELLE This is the desert. It's free.

CAPTAIN This is French territory, under the rule of law and civilization and we require even sluts to have the correct papers. I'm waiting. I see you have no papers. You there!

(BOU SAADI and SALEH come back.)

Do you know what this friend of yours Si Mahmoud is?

ISABELLE Captain, the honour of the French Army.

CAPTAIN We save the honour of our own kind. You'll kick yourselves when you find out. This little Tunisian friend of yours, ha, ha...

ISABELLE Captain, please.

CAPTAIN This Si Mahmoud is a woman.

(Silence. BOU SAADI laughs stupidly. SALEH doesn't react at all.)

Look under her clothes if you don't believe me.

SALEH *(slowly)* Si Mahmoud has a very good knowledge of medicine. He's helped people with their eyes and cured children.

CAPTAIN Probably told them to wash. It's a woman I tell you. You must be stupider than I thought not to have noticed or at least asked a few questions.

SALEH It is a courtesy in our country not to be curious about the stranger. We accept whatever name Si Mahmoud wishes to give us.

ISABELLE You knew.

SALEH We heard. We chose not to believe it. *(to the CAPTAIN)* Si Mahmoud knows the Koran better than we do. He's in search of wisdom. We wish to help him.

CAPTAIN Wisdom? That's the story she's spreading. I think it's more like information to pass on to people who don't belong here, like the English. They're always using women for this sort of thing. They can't forgive us for having produced Joan of Arc. You have ten days to bring this agitator back to the city. You know what happens if you don't.

ISABELLE I'll appeal.

CAPTAIN Yes, in Paris. It's never wise to refuse the protection of the French Army. A good journey, mademoiselle.

He leaves.

ISABELLE I'm doing no harm...

BOU SAADI It's not a good idea to irritate Europeans. It's best to pretend you're stupid and keep laughing. I'm very good at it. Saleh is learning very slowly.

ISABELLE I want nothing to do with these people. Why won't they let me alone? Ah, my friends, it's written I must leave you, but I'll come back, I'll come back.

ACT TWO, SCENE ONE

A SALON IN PARIS.

VERDA MILES, SÉVERINE, LYDIA, EUGÉNIE, ISABELLE, and PASHA, a servant.

SONG.

VERDA MILES as a young man in Paris.

LYDIA Isn't she extraordinary? Do you know I am almost in love with that man about town. And it was so kind of her to come and sing for my little salon.

EUGÉNIE Ah, but your salon, such a setting for an artist.

SÉVERINE Don't be a hypocrite, Lydia. She knows everyone is at your little salon. And I've been invited tonight because you want me to write a story on her.

LYDIA What she is doing is so important – for us.

SÉVERINE Lots of women have gone on stage dressed as men. It shows off their figures.

LYDIA When Verda Miles is on stage, she *is* a man.

EUGÉNIE And 'man is the measure of all things'.

LYDIA Do interview her, Séverine.

SÉVERINE You can't interview English people, they don't know how to talk about themselves.

PASHA comes in with a tray of champagne.

SÉVERINE I say, is that real?

LYDIA No, it's just Jean. But the clothes are real. I had them copied from the *Arabian Nights.*

SÉVERINE The Countess Holst has one, a genuine one, but he's not as convincing.

LYDIA And she had to sleep with the Turkish Ambassador to get him.

EUGÉNIE When I was in Cairo I thought of bringing one back with me, but it's cruel to take them out of their natural environment.

LYDIA Why don't I engage Verda Miles in conversation? You can simply listen.

SÉVERINE You'll make it too philosophical and I'll miss the story – if there is one.

LYDIA My dear, you can't talk philosophy with English women, they think it's something naughty their husbands did as boys. No, I'll start with dogs.

EUGÉNIE *(seeing ISABELLE)* Lydia, what do I see? Ah, there, there is a true one, I can tell. A young oriental prince, look at the simplicity, the dignity. Oh, do present him to us.

SÉVERINE It's even an Arab who looks a little like Rimbaud, the Countess will be green when I tell her. How very clever of you.

LYDIA Yes, that's quite a find, but that's not a real Arab either. Much more interesting, you have there a young woman who travels with the savage tribes in the Sahara. Her name's Isabelle Eberhardt. Russian, I think, she won't talk much about herself.

SÉVERINE Eberhardt's a Jewish name.

LYDIA Yes, well, they're all nomads, aren't they? She had some troubles with officials in North Africa and she's come to Paris to ask the French Government to help her. She's very naïve.

SÉVERINE She must be to think the Government will help anyone. Does she have enough money to bribe them?

LYDIA She seems to have left everything behind – somewhere.

EUGÉNIE The nomadic spirit, it's so noble, so carefree.

LYDIA She knows almost no one here, but look at her, she could become quite the rage. You might help her. I believe she writes.

SÉVERINE Oh dear. Descriptions of the sunset in sub-Wordsworthian rhymes. So many interesting people would still be remembered if they hadn't left behind their memoirs.

LYDIA has been waving ISABELLE over.

LYDIA Pasha, more champagne please.

SÉVERINE *(courteous, intrigued)* Would you like some champagne, mademoiselle?

ISABELLE Is that what it is? It's good, I've had six glasses already.

EUGÉNIE *(with an exaggerated Arab salutation, or an attempt at one)* I am so delighted. I too have been There.

ISABELLE ?

EUGÉNIE Why didn't we discover it before? All those trips to Athens and Rome staring at ruins when we had the real thing all the time in the Orient.

ISABELLE chokes on her drink, coughs and spits.

ISABELLE Oh, forgot, used to the sand. Sorry, Lydia.

EUGÉNIE The Homeric gesture, is that not so? *(to the others)* You can't imagine what it's like to see lying in the sun, or mending shoes, men of such consular types, all clad in white like the senators of Rome. Each one with the mien of a Cato or a Brutus.

LYDIA There's Verda, excellent.

Champagne. ISABELLE drinks another glass.

VERDA No, I never drink. *(to ISABELLE)* What a charming costume you have.

EUGÉNIE The flowing simplicity of the African garb, so free, so... Athenian.

VERDA I'd like to copy it. You see. I have an idea for a new song, it would be an oriental melody, exotic, and with that costume...

ISABELLE It's not a costume, it's my clothes.

VERDA Of course, that's what I meant. Do you know any oriental songs?

EUGÉNIE Those oriental melodies – so biblical.

ISABELLE *(very flat)* Darling, I love you, darling, I adore you, exactly like to – maaa – to sauce. When I saw you there there on the balcony, I thought... *(She hiccups.)* That's all I know.

LYDIA They have the most beautiful breed of hounds in Egypt. They're called Ibizan hounds...

ISABELLE I ate some cat in Tunisia. They said it was rabbit, but I could tell it was cat, I found a claw. It tasted all right.

EUGÉNIE I found them so admirable in the simplicity of their needs. A population of Socrates.

LYDIA What made you decide to sing men's songs, Miss Miles?

VERDA I started singing on the stage when I was three and at the age of six I had run through most of the female repertoire. By the time I was seven I thought I would have to retire. But then, one night, I noticed by chance – if there is such a thing as chance – my father's hat and cape hanging over the back of a chair. You see my father was also in the music-hall, as was my mother. As I was saying, I saw the hat and cape and put them on. I went to the mirror and when I saw myself I suddenly had hundreds of exciting roles before me. I've been a male impersonator ever since. It is, how shall I say, much more interesting, much more challenging to play men. There is more variety... more...

LYDIA More scope. How well I understand you. I myself occasionally scribble. Oh, not professionally, like Séverine, not writings I would necessarily show. Although, of course, if Séverine did ask to see them, I might, just as a friend... Do you know that in order to write seriously I must dress as a man? I finally understood why: when I am dressed as a woman, like this, I find I am most concerned with the silky sound of my skirt rustling on the floor, or I spend hours watching the lace fall over my wrist, white against white. But when I dress as a man, I simply begin to think, I get ideas. I'm sure that's why Séverine is such a brilliant journalist, she always dresses as a man.

SÉVERINE My dear Lydia, you know perfectly well I wear male clothes so I can take my girlfriends to coffee bars without having men pester us.

VERDA *(nervous)* Of course I never have that sort of problem because I am always with my husband. And I love to wear women's clothes. My husband says I am the most womanly woman he has ever known.

SÉVERINE Lydia was quite falling in love with your man about town.

VERDA It's puzzling how many letters I get from women, young girls even. Sometimes they are so passionate they make me blush. One girl quite pursued me. She sent flowers to my dressing room and every time I performed I would see her, up close, staring at me. It was most disturbing. And her letters! At last, I had to invite her to my dressing room. I let my hair all the way down and wore the most feminine gown I could find. And then I gave her a good talking to. She never came back.

SÉVERINE Have men never written you love letters ?

VERDA Yes, but that's different. That's normal.

SÉVERINE Normality, the golden cage. And we poor banished species trail around, looking through the bars, wishing we were in there. But we're destined for the curiosity shops, labelled as the weird mistakes of nature, the moment of God's hesitation between Adam and Eve, anatomical convolutions, our souls inside out and alone, always alone, outside those bars. Do you love normality, Miss Miles?

EUGÉNIE I was never considered normal. At school, my dancing master said my feet were perfect examples of the evils of anarchy. My deportment had revolutionary tendencies and the sound of my voice, I was told, was more raucous than the Communist Manifesto. No amount of hours spent practising in front of empty chairs taught me how to engage a young man in conversation and at last my poor parents said in despair, let her travel. I have not been unhappy, but I would have liked to be useful, or at least a philologist.

LYDIA I think normality is a fashion. Here we are, five women and four of us are dressed as men. And I'm only wearing skirts because there are some German diplomats here and they're very sticky about these things. I believe the century we're entering will see a revolution greater even than the French Revolution. They defrocked the priests, we'll defrock the women.

VERDA We'll lose all our strength.

SÉVERINE Tell us about the desert, Miss Eberhardt.

ISABELLE Sand.

LYDIA Can't you help her, Séverine?

SÉVERINE Do you remember the Marquis de Mores?

LYDIA Spanish? Stood around looking passionate? With an American wife? He hasn't been seen in ages.

SÉVERINE He was killed down there. His wife – you know what Americans are like – has taken it very personally. She wants the French Government to find out what happened. It seems they're showing a most unusual lack of curiosity. *(to ISABELLE)* We might persuade her to send you down there to collect some information. I'd like to go myself. I smell a story which might be quite embarrassing to some people. We could travel together. I'd enjoy that.

ISABELLE Do you really like women?

SÉVERINE *(seductive)* Have you lived in the Orient and remained a prude?

ISABELLE Me? Ha!

SÉVERINE There are thousands of women in this city who would do anything to be made love to by me. But I like women with character.

ISABELLE I'm not a woman. I'm Si Mahmoud. I like men. They like me. As a boy, I mean. And I have a firm rule: no Europeans up my arse.

Freeze.

VERDA I really must go. My husband...

ISABELLE Did I say something wrong?

EUGÉNIE The nomadic turn of phrase: so childlike.

SÉVERINE I don't like vulgarity. I'm afraid I can't help you.

ISABELLE You look just like Captain Soubiel now. He wanted to 'protect me'. And there was something to protect then. *(She drinks, hopeless.)* I spent nine months working on the docks of Marseilles to pay for this trip. Loading ships.

SÉVERINE Too bad it was a waste.

ISABELLE Yeah, it was written. Too free with my tongue. Too free.

She drinks another glass and passes out.

LYDIA I'll have to teach her some manners. I'm sorry.

SÉVERINE That spirit isn't for corsets. Look at her. She's younger than I am and she probably has malaria, who knows what else. Nine months loading ships – that's the work of ex-convicts. What a story.

LYDIA She's ruined everything tonight.

SÉVERINE I'm not sure... No, I'll help her.

The melancholic sound of an Arab love song...

SCENE TWO

SI LACHMI, SALEH, BOU SAADI and ISABELLE.

ISABELLE *(slightly out of it)* Oh, these happy, these drunken hours of return.

BOU SAADI *(to SI LACHMI)* It was written Si Mahmoud would come back to us.

SALEH He can now become one of us, a Qadria.

ISABELLE I wanted to possess this country. It has possessed me.

SI LACHMI There are at least a hundred different Sufi orders, but the Qadria is one of the oldest.

ISABELLE I've been in such a hurry to live.

SI LACHMI We are also the most numerous.

SALEH There are more of us than Tidjanis.

SI LACHMI You will have twenty thousand brothers.

ISABELLE The senses have tormented me.

BOU SAADI The Qadrias are bound by links of affection.

SALEH And solidarity, limitless devotion.

ISABELLE A certain languor in these sands.

SI LACHMI You'll be safe in our territories.

ISABELLE Take off at last the grimacing, degraded mask.

SI LACHMI All our monasteries are open to you.

ISABELLE This is my property: the extended horizon.

SI LACHMI Keep this chaplet, it'll protect you.

ISABELLE The luxurious décor of the dunes: mine.

SI LACHMI There is no dogma. We believe only in the equality of all men and gentleness of heart. You must also show absolute obedience to your sheikh. Our founder, Abd-el-Qader was most loved for his friendship with the oppressed. He loathed hypocrisy, all lies. You must be generous and show pity to all.

ISABELLE And wisdom?

SI LACHMI That comes later, Si Mahmoud. You're still young. Free yourself first from the vulgarity of the world.

ISABELLE Doesn't the word Sufi come from the Greek *sophos*, wise?

SI LACHMI It comes from a Berber word that means to excel. But that isn't important. Try to be a brave and good man, that's all we ask. *(Pause.)* So you have been visiting France?

SALEH Si Mahmoud has been asked to find the murderers of a European called the Marquis de Mores.

ISABELLE Oh yes, I'd forgotten. He was an explorer.

SI LACHMI The *French* have asked you to look for his murderers?

ISABELLE Not exactly the French. His wife.

SI LACHMI Indeed.

ISABELLE She gave me a lot of money. I should make an effort. Why would anyone want to murder an explorer?

SI LACHMI He himself was not French?

ISABELLE I don't think so. Why?

SI LACHMI I am fascinated by the European tribal wars. They are more bitter than ours, but are conducted with much more subtlety. I am learning much from them.

SALEH We kill people we don't like openly, in battle.

ISABELLE You think it was the French themselves who wanted to get rid of him?

SI LACHMI God alone knows the hearts of men. Do the French know with what purpose you've come back?

ISABELLE I don't hide anything. I'm not a hypocrite.

SI LACHMI We don't forbid prudence, Si Mahmoud.

SALEH You're our brother now. We'll help you.

ISABELLE If Allah's willing, I'll find the murderers, if not – then I suppose it's not written they should be found. Does poverty allow the possession of a horse?

SI LACHMI We don't deny pleasure. Each follows his own capacities.

During this last exchange, the MURDERER comes in, unseen. He strikes with a sabre. ISABELLE turns just in time to avert it and only her arm is struck. The MURDERER is caught by SALEH and BOU SAADI.

SI LACHMI What's your name, you dog?

BOU SAADI That's a Muslim brother. Do you know what you've done?

SI LACHMI What's your name?

SALEH Who ordered you to do this?

MURDERER Allah.

SI LACHMI God told you to kill a brother?

MURDERER That's a woman.

SI LACHMI It's no business of yours who this person is if we accept him as our brother. You question a sheikh?

MURDERER Allah ordered me to kill that person who offends our law.

SI LACHMI What law, fool? My sisters dressed as young men when they travelled. Who are you to judge? Who told you to do this?

MURDERER Allah.

SALEH Or the Tidjanis, or the French?

SI LACHMI hands the sabre to ISABELLE.

SI LACHMI You may kill him.

ISABELLE seizes the sabre, then stops herself.

ISABELLE Why? *(gentle)* Have I offended you without knowing?

MURDERER You have done nothing to me, but if I have another chance, I'll kill you.

ISABELLE Strange... I don't hate you. No, I forgive you. But I did you no harm.

MURDERER You're offending our customs.

ISABELLE But that's why I left *them. (She throws the sabre down.)* No, you're an instrument, but why? A riddle... Brothers, if it was written that I must die... But so young, without understanding... no. I can't die in this silence. Don't let me die here. Don't let me disappear, without a trace. Who wants to do this to me?

SCENE THREE

THE COURTROOM IN CONSTANTINE.

ISABELLE and the MUDERER. As the MURDERER speaks, he changes into the JUDGE.

MURDERER/JUDGE "An angel appeared to tell me the Marabout of the Qadrias, Si Lachmi, would be proceeding to El-Oued accompanied by Miss Eberhardt who called herself Si Mahmoud and wore masculine dress, thus making trouble in our religion." This, Miss Eberhardt, is what the accused has to say in his defence. Have you anything to add?

ISABELLE There is no law in the Muslim religion that says a woman may not dress as a man.

JUDGE There should be. It's un-Christian. Why do you wear it?

ISABELLE It's practical for riding.

JUDGE Women have traditionally ridden in dresses.

ISABELLE Side-saddle! Imagine me joining a battle riding side-saddle. I'm greatly admired for my riding.

JUDGE A battle, Miss Eberhardt? Have you joined many battles?

ISABELLE *(modestly)* Just a small raid.

JUDGE Tell us about it.

ISABELLE The sun was rising. It seemed covered in blood. There were about a hundred of us. And then we began the charge. Shouts, sand and dust, the gallop down –

JUDGE May I ask whom you were charging, Miss Eberhardt?

ISABELLE I don't know. We were close together to give the charge more force, we could hardly see and the wind –

JUDGE Could this charge have been against the French, Miss Eberhardt?

ISABELLE No. No.

JUDGE Didn't you just say you did not know whom you were attacking?

ISABELLE It was the Tidjanis. It must have been the Tidjanis. They are our traditional enemies.

JUDGE Our?

ISABELLE The Qadria. I am a Qadria. That is why I am sure my attacker is a Tidjani.

JUDGE Don't the Qadria also fight against the French? Unlike the Tidjanis. *(Pause.)* You have been heard to complain against the French, Miss Eberhardt.

ISABELLE France could have helped this country so much, with medicine, with technical knowledge. But for some reason it has made the people here worse off than they already were. And soon the French will be so hated –

She stops herself.

JUDGE Do go on, Miss Eberhardt. *(Pause.)* The Arabs will rise against us, isn't that what you were about to say? And with your help and encouragement, Miss Eberhardt?

ISABELLE I am no more than a humble brother.

JUDGE A brother?

ISABELLE I am a member of the Qadria. Please find out if my attacker is a Tidjani or paid by the Tidjanis. If the Tidjanis are allowed to get away with this, I'll no longer be safe –

JUDGE You would be safe in Europe, Miss Eberhardt.

ISABELLE What would I do in Europe?

JUDGE What are you doing here, Miss Eberhardt?

ISABELLE I belong here.

JUDGE You are a European.

ISABELLE No, I am not –

JUDGE Were you lying when you told us you were born in Switzerland?

ISABELLE No.

JUDGE You are a European, Miss Eberhardt. You are also a young woman.

ISABELLE No I am not.

JUDGE You are not a young woman? Twenty-six is not old, Miss Eberhardt.

ISABELLE I belong in the desert.

JUDGE You belong at home, Miss Eberhardt, in Europe. We consider ourselves responsible for your safety.

ISABELLE Then find out who tried to murder me!

JUDGE We know it was a poor Muslim you drove to madness with your behaviour. And in order to protect you from further attacks –

ISABELLE If he is punished – not too severely, please – I will be safe.

JUDGE We must ask you to cease your wanderings.

ISABELLE I have to travel.

JUDGE We do not consider that safe, Miss Eberhardt.

ISABELLE My friends and brothers will protect me. I wish to go further south.

JUDGE I'm afraid we must ask you to refrain from visiting places where your presence might cause an unpleasant incident, Miss Eberhardt.

ISABELLE I'll be safe in the desert.

JUDGE The desert is a troubled place.

ISABELLE I'll spend some months in one of the monasteries.

JUDGE We particularly do not want you in the monasteries.

ISABELLE Where do you suggest I go?

JUDGE I have told you, Miss Eberhardt. Back to Europe.

ISABELLE Ah. No. No.

JUDGE We cannot force you. But no more gallivantings in that offensive masquerade.

Pause.

ISABELLE It's you. *(Pause.)* It's not the Tidjanis. It's you. You're afraid of me.

JUDGE Your activities are obscure, Miss Eberhardt to say the least, but the French government is not afraid of women.

ISABELLE You've been trying to get rid of me all along. How much did you pay him?

JUDGE I would think twice before you make accusations against France, Miss Eberhardt.

ISABELLE It's not even what I am doing, is it? It's what I am. You hate what I am. But what harm am I doing? What?

JUDGE May I point out, Miss Eberhardt, that a man was recently sent to prison in England for a much lesser offence than yours.

ISABELLE What? He took a walk on the beach?

JUDGE This Mr Wilde had a perversion of inclination. You, Miss Eberhardt, have perverted nature.

ISABELLE Nature defined by you, confined by you, farmed by you to make you fat.

JUDGE We will of course imprison your assailant.

ISABELLE My friends, my brothers, where are you? Help me.

JUDGE But you're to stay out of the desert.

ISABELLE No. Please. No.

JUDGE For good.

ISABELLE Fenced out. Again. Always.

SÉVERINE Fenced in, Isabelle. All of us.

SCENE FOUR

ISABELLE and SÉVERINE.

ISABELLE Blocked. Detour. Blocked again. Need some absinthe. Buy me an absinthe, girl scribe.

SÉVERINE I thought Muslims didn't drink.

ISABELLE Shouldn't. Do. Have you seen how supple Arabic writing is? Not like that French print. Need some absinthe. Si Mahmoud is dying of thirst. Hang on my every word. Steal my story and won't give me a drink. European!

SÉVERINE I'm trying to keep you sober for Colonel Lyautey It would help if you made sense.

ISABELLE Make better sense with absinthe. Understand the world then: nice blur. 'Alas my soul for youth that's gone.'

SÉVERINE You're twenty-seven!

ISABELLE Lived fast. Too many detours and had to run.

SÉVERINE Here comes the Colonel. Try to behave yourself.

ISABELLE The French: camel piss. I forgive them.

SÉVERINE He's an exception. The Arabs like him.

ISABELLE Europe has taught them ignorance.

SÉVERINE Isabelle – it's your last chance.

COLONEL LYAUTEY enters.

SÉVERINE Colonel. I've heard so much about you.

LYAUTEY And I about you, Séverine. Your pen strikes more terror in the heart of the French Government than the rattle of the Arab sabre.

ISABELLE His speech jingles like his medals.

SÉVERINE Colonel, you wished to meet Isabelle Eberhardt.

LYAUTEY *(bows)* Si Mahmoud.

ISABELLE My sister married a dandelion. I was courted by his brother, a radish, no, his cousin, an orchid, and here's a multicoloured bouquet of medals bowing before me. The grace of Allah follow your footsteps, master. *(Bows down to the ground)* A drop of absinthe for the poet's soul, Colonel, to remember Paradise.

SÉVERINE Colonel, you must excuse her – she's been so badly treated.

LYAUTEY I've wanted to meet you for some time, Si Mahmoud.

ISABELLE Yeah, I'm famous. All bad. They hate me. Why?

LYAUTEY Bloodthirsty mercenaries defend the boundaries of convention, Si Mahmoud, and your escape was too flamboyant. You remind me of the young Arab warrior who wears bright colours so he'll be seen first by the enemy.

ISABELLE Ah, you're the firing squad. Here. *(Points to her heart, spreads her arms)* Scribe, take down the martyr's last words: Si Mahmoud, heart without guile, dies, crossed by European civilization...

SÉVERINE Colonel, I'm sorry.

LYAUTEY It's all right. I like refractory spirits.

ISABELLE Why do compliments in French always sound translated? I hate flowers, that's why I like the desert. Barred by the hedges now. Are you very brave, Colonel, to have picked so many medals?

LYAUTEY Yes, Si Mahmoud, and so, I'm told, are you.

ISABELLE With me bravery is a languor of the instincts. Are you languid, Colonel?

SÉVERINE Isabelle, stop playing.

ISABELLE Why? Travelling show: examine here the monstrous folds of uncorseted nature, the pervert seed that would not flourish on

European manure. Complete with witty and scientific commentary by our own Sevvy the Scribe, straight from Paris...

SÉVERINE It's hopeless, we had better go.

LYAUTEY Wait. Si Mahmoud, I don't like hedges either. I come from Provence: it's dry there and barren. And you can still hear in the walls the echoes of chivalry and nobility, what you have here, what we're destroying.

ISABELLE I believed in French civilization once. Is it the climate that makes it rot?

LYAUTEY The wrong ones came. You used to travel with the Qadrias.

SÉVERINE Isabelle can go places where no other European would be safe.

LYAUTEY Do you want to travel again?

ISABELLE When I came out of hospital after my wound, the dunes had shrivelled. I wondered if they'd been empty all the time.

SÉVERINE You were ill. You know you want to travel.

ISABELLE 'Anywhere, anywhere as long as it's out of this world.' Let the little cloud of oriental perfume that was my soul vanish. No trace.

LYAUTEY They say, Si Mahmoud, you're a young man in search of knowledge.

ISABELLE Was.

SÉVERINE She's accepted by all the marabouts. It's only the French who prevent her from returning.

LYAUTEY My predecessors have a lot to answer for. *(to ISABELLE)* The Zianya sect is known for its pious and disinterested leaders. The Qadria have great respect for the Zianya.

ISABELLE How do you know all this?

LYAUTEY You forget, I love this country.

ISABELLE 'The tongue is a man's one half.'

LYAUTEY 'The other the heart within.' And who can judge the heart? Have you heard of the Zianya leader, Sidi Brahim?

ISABELLE Even our marabouts look up to him.

LYAUTEY Would you like to visit his school?

ISABELLE Can't. It's in Morocco.

LYAUTEY I can get you in.

ISABELLE Is it written that Si Mahmoud shall speak to Sidi Brahim, that wisdom might be gained at last?

LYAUTEY What will you need?

ISABELLE A good horse.

LYAUTEY When can you leave?

ISABELLE Tomorrow.

SÉVERINE Morocco. She'll never come back, Colonel.

LYAUTEY You can only stay five months this first time, Si Mahmoud. Please tell Sidi Brahim the French will help him if he wishes to extricate himself from his enemies.

SÉVERINE I see. The conquest of Morocco.

LYAUTEY Not this time, I hope. But Si Mahmoud will tell you that country is devastated by marauding tribes.

ISABELLE Too much bloodshed, yes.

LYAUTEY We would help, no more.

SÉVERINE Shall we call it then the digestion of Morocco?

LYAUTEY I'll expect you in Ain-Sefra in five months, Si Mahmoud, and then we'll have long chats about this country. How did my predecessors not appreciate you?

ISABELLE From the point of view of bread and Swiss cheese, the love of the desert is an unhealthy appetite.

LYAUTEY What idiots not to have understood you. Poor Si Mahmoud.

ISABELLE Poor Si Mahmoud.

SÉVERINE She loves pity, Colonel.

ISABELLE We Slavs are like that. We love the knout and then we love being pitied for having suffered the knout. And you, chronicler, must make no judgements. We souls of the desert *(hiccups)* love the knout.

LYAUTEY Five months then. Your word of honour. I'll find a way of thanking you, Séverine.

SÉVERINE It may be too late, Colonel, you should have found her before.

LYAUTEY They should have found me before. It may be too late for me too. Territories exploding, violence sowed and reaped, so unnecessary. Only you, Séverine, it's not too late for you.

ISABELLE It's never too late for the chroniclers.

SÉVERINE But that's not what you meant, Colonel, is it?

LYAUTEY No.

SCENE FIVE

Ain-Sefra. Same as the first scene, a few hours later.

ISABELLE and SÉVERINE.

ISABELLE Very strict at the monastery. Walk towards the gate and a shadow bars your path. But Sidi Brahim let me pace. He understood Si Mahmoud had been locked in too often. His son lived in another quarter. There were many young men of great beauty in those rooms, and we don't hate love. But I couldn't join. They would know I was not completely a man, and also, much of that was gone. Slowly, slowly, the torment of the senses opens to the modulation of the dunes. Only a ripple here and there betrays the passage of the storm. Sidi Brahim wanted me to go further south and describe the country to the Colonel.

SÉVERINE Why didn't you?

ISABELLE Promised I'd come here.

SÉVERINE You had more than a month left.

ISABELLE If a man be old and a fool... suddenly, suddenly Si Mahmoud felt a shiver of fear. Suddenly my destiny: forgot the script. So I thought I'll come back, word of honour, and Si Mahmoud is important now, not broken.

SÉVERINE Shouldn't you get some rest? You must be coherent if you're seeing the Colonel later.

ISABELLE Always coherent. It's the letters that get scrambled.

SÉVERINE I must go in. I feel faint.

ISABELLE Hard work chronicling. Keep you up all night unravelling the Mektoub. Rest. Will you write my story? Practical guide for girls with unhealthy desires. With diagrams for the Europeans, the Cartesians. They couldn't fence in my tongue. Poor Sevvy, sweet scribe of uncartesian appetites, rebuild your dream.

SÉVERINE Will you find your way?

ISABELLE Stay outside, head against stone and the soul more pure. If a man be old... but a young man may yet cast off his foolishness. I'm not wise, I'm not wise.

She feels something, sticks out her hand.

Rain? It doesn't rain in the desert. Mirage. No, rain, that's nice. Sleep in the rain. What's that noise?

SÉVERINE Thunder probably. There have been storms in the mountains. Don't wander off.

ISABELLE Make my report to the Colonel, then wander off. Tell them Si Mahmoud... *(But Séverine has left.)* The rain. Get clean that way, wash the traces and the letters. Fresh sand, new letters.

She lies down.

SCENE SIX

Ain-Sefra. SÉVERINE, COLONEL LYAUTEY and the JUDGE

SÉVERINE Drowned!

LYAUTEY We came too late.

SÉVERINE Drowned in Ain-Sefra.

JUDGE In the middle of the desert? That's no place to drown.

SÉVERINE A flash flood. The whole native quarter washed away.

LYAUTEY My men rushed down. We couldn't find her.

JUDGE It's said she didn't even try to save herself

SÉVERINE Our rebel warrior, Colonel.

JUDGE Close the file. This person must be officially forgotten.

LYAUTEY We found some journals. Would you like to see them, Séverine?

SÉVERINE With pleasure.

They walk off, arm in arm.

Lights fade to blackout.

The end.

PREFACE TO EVERY BIT OF IT

It's kind of funny looking back on work I wrote years ago. It's another way of telling the time. Even before writing *Every Bit of It*, I'd had a passion for the brilliant bravura Blues singer Bessie Smith. (My dad bought me *Any Woman's Blues* when I was twelve. It was my first album.) Not only did I love the raunchy, raw, unplugged sound of her voice, but I loved the narratives of the blues. Nothing seemed out of bounds in blues songs; murder, betrayal, floods, money... I didn't exactly understand the double entendres in a song like *Kitchen Man*, but I kind of intuited them.

I started to wonder how a deaf person would feel music – that maybe writing about the blues from the point of view of a character that doesn't hear them would free me to take risks. The character that Elizabeth Quinn played, a deaf woman who loves the blues without having 'heard' them, emerged. When I first met Elizabeth – who I knew had been in the stage version of *Children of a Lesser God* – she said to me, 'You're Scottish, aren't you?' I was fascinated. How could she tell I was Scottish by reading my lips? She said it was to do with how I rolled my 'r's'. From Elizabeth I learnt about sign language and started to think about all the ways that people are mistreated or excluded from mainstream society.

But when I look back on *Every Bit of It,* I'm most grateful for Sue Parrish introducing me to Suzanne Bonnar. I hadn't heard of Suzanne. Sue sent me the documentary about her life – *Fly Me to Dunoon*. It was like watching my own life back at me. It was unusual to get to meet other Black Scottish sisters then. Before Suzanne, I had only met one other, Maud Sulter. It was a joy to have Elizabeth and Suzanne to write for.

And at the end of it all to have not just a play, but a beloved friendship: that has been one of my life's greatest joys. Suzanne, to me, was like a modern-day Bessie. Her voice blew me away. It took me back to the past and hurled me toward the present. Watching her sing and play Bessie, was to witness her inhabit a force and a spirit.

Writing is a curious thing. You make things up and somehow some part of them becomes real. The line between what happens and what could happen is very thin. The poems that I wrote for *Every Bit of It,* influenced by the twelve-bar beat of the blues, formed part of my second poetry collection *Other Lovers*. Later, I went on to write a whole book about Bessie Smith. Bessie has been with me since I was a girl singing *Nobody Knows You When You are Down and Out* into a hairbrush microphone in my back bedroom. If you can find a way to hang on to your passions, to change with them, the imaginative road leads all the way to a real one. I'll never forget seeing various performances of *Every Bit of It* in Edinburgh, in Oxford, how much a play that seemed to be about such a singular topic, resonated with people in unexpected ways. Looking back at this play that I wrote over half my life ago, I realise that Faulkner was right. The past is never past. This play is probably as accurate a picture of me then as any photograph. Maybe even more so. Telling the story of your life through the things you have imagined and created is somehow more truthful.

Jackie Kay

Suzanne Bonnar and Elizabeth Quinn in *Every Bit of It* by Jackie Kay
Photo © Sheila Burnett 1992

EVERY BIT OF IT

JACKIE KAY

Every Bit of It was first produced by Sphinx Theatre Company at Warwick Arts Centre in 1992.

Director	Sue Parrish
Designer	Annabel Lee
Music	Claire Van Kampen
Lighting	Di Stedman
Choreographer	Deirdra Lovell
Piano	Kate Williams
Cast	Suzanne Bonnar and Elizabeth Quinn

Characters

GEORGIA – A 42-year-old white academic who is on her way to her brother's funeral. She is writing a biography about Bessie Smith, although she never reveals this. She had a son eighteen years ago who she gave up for adoption. She has a hard wit, feels very confident about her intelligence, but not much else. She is deaf, and became deaf when she was around five years old. She comes from a well-off American family.

CATHY – A 33-year-old Black Scottish woman who is escaping from her violent husband. She is emotional, funny and defensive. She knows all of Bessie Smith's songs by heart. Her self-image has been badly affected because of her husband's violence. She was brought up by her mother in a working class part of Glasgow. She has just killed her husband, although you never find out how she did it.

ACT ONE, SCENE ONE

GEORGIA is sitting on the train on her own, looking out the window.

GEORGIA Strange things are happening to me.

I walk down my street and I see Bessie.
Strange things are happening to me.
I look out a window and I see Bessie.

But tonight I won't be in.
Tonight I will close the curtain.
She will not get in.

Under the cotton sheets,
under the dim lamplight,
I refuse to dream.

GEORGIA gets out her books and reads. CATHY asks if the seat is taken and GEORGIA indicates for her to help herself. GEORGIA returns to her work.

CATHY Are you going far? *(GEORGIA continues reading her book.)* I'm going far. Far as I can go. I'm getting out of it for a bit. It's driving me crazy. I wasn't even that bothered about where to go. Do you know what I mean? (*CATHY waits for GEORGIA to reply. GEORGIA doesn't.)* Suit yourself then. Stuck up cow.

CATHY puts her Walkman on and sings I AINT GOT NOBODY unaccompanied.

There's a saying all around
And I begin to think it's true
It's hard to love some man
When he don't care for you.

I ain't got nobody, nobody
Nobody cares for me.

GEORGIA looks up and smiles at her.

CATHY Where are you going?

GEORGIA Right to the end of the line.

CATHY Same here.

SPEAKER We'd like to apologise to passengers for the lateness of this train leaving this stop. This is due to the early arrival of this train at this stop.

CATHY (*laughs*) That's typical. Maybe neither of us will get very far.

GEORGIA What is?

CATHY What's the matter with you? Are you deaf or something?

GEORGIA Yes. I am deaf. I've been deaf since I was as kid.

CATHY I was just joking. I wasn't serious. Right. So what do you do, lipread?

GEORGIA When I'm not reading books, I'm reading lips. You're Scottish aren't you?

CATHY How can you tell that?

GEORGIA In the shapes your mouth is making.

CATHY Really?

GEORGIA Yes. It's all in the Rs. An English 'really' looks like this:

GEORGIA does it, CATHY laughs.

CATHY They make me remember things. Trains. The way the land whizzes back like a flashback.

Things I haven't thought in years.

Maybe it's the people on them. See that woman looks just like this primary teacher of mine called Mrs Blackie. She was the one that said she had a darky living next door. So guess what my name is the next day. Then she'd always pick me to read 'Little Boy Sambo'. Or say Cathy'll know how to do this if we had to dance the Black bottom.

It was a laugh. Most of my mates liked me. Actually, thinking back, I was quite popular. Strange, eh?

To think of that, actually being popular.

SPEAKER We would like to offer complimentary drinks for the lateness of this train. This is due to a failed engine.

CATHY They're offering us drinks now. Free. Do you want one?

GEORGIA No thank you.

CATHY walks down the train to get the drinks.

Bessie and I are in her Pullman heading for Tennessee

Bessie and I are in her Pullman heading for Tennessee.
We got so much heartbreak, we can't divide it easily.
I take one piece, she takes another, we both drive
and our sadness drives further,
It's way up ahead, ahead of Bessie and me.

And even in the springtime, it's hanging from the paw paw tree.
The road is long and flat; the fields repeat the cotton.
A Black man's head, snapped like a branch, is all we can see.
We drive without moving. We try and carry on, but
There's this big sadness hanging from the paw paw tree.
It's way up ahead, ahead of Bessie and me.

CATHY returns with the drinks, gives GEORGIA one anyway.

SCENE TWO

GEORGIA My brother's dead. I'm on my way to his funeral. He was only 48. It was sudden. He wasn't even sick.

CATHY See when I'm sick nobody notices, except my mother who still says you're looking awful peelie wally.

GEORGIA Peelie wally?

CATHY Pale.

GEORGIA Everything feels oddly familiar on this train. As if I've been on it before.There's lots of men that look exactly like him. I keep stopping myself from saying, you're supposed to be dead. What's that word for that, you know when something's happened before.

CATHY I feel a bit like I've emerged. Do you know what I mean?

Like I haven't seen anybody for years? Even looking out this window is nice. I've been collecting timetables.

I'm a right one for not being able to throw anything away.

At least I was like that until yesterday.

MFI, B&Q, I loved those shops. I'd collect paint charts and things.

You should see the colours in my basement. What can you do with
half tins of electric blue.

GEORGIA Or buttercup yellow, hollyhock pink, seaweed green?

CATHY Exactly.

My favourite painted colour was always white. Plain white. Fresh and clean. That's the most important thing being clean. Some people think having a bath three times a day is over the top. But I think it's absolutely necessary. Don't you. Otherwise you start to smell, sort of mid afternoon. Sometimes you can never get rid of it. Same with the walls.

You've got to whitewash them regularly to keep up. Spanking. Brilliant white.

GEORGIA Paint me a picture of yourself.

CATHY I lived with my man Jack who... let's say, wasn't very nice.

GEORGIA That's him. What about you.

CATHY I'm 33. I was married at 18. My marriage was... *(gets frustrated)* Och. This is stupid. I don't want to do this. You do it.

GEORGIA I live on my own. I'm doing research for a book I'm writing.

CATHY Have you got any children?

GEORGIA *(hesitates)* No. No I haven't.

CATHY can't think what else to say. Looks out the window.

GEORGIA *(to herself)* I'm trying to think of what else I could have done. At the time there seemed nothing else to do but what I did. I used to brush it off by saying to myself he was better off, I was doing the best thing for him, the unselfish thing. The hardest thing. Now, I'm not so sure. Maybe it was selfish. Maybe it was the worst thing.

CATHY I haven't got any myself.

GEORGIA Strange things are happening to me.

I look out the window and I see Bessie.

CATHY She's got a voice bigger than the ocean. Could knock you down.

A voice that sings of being kicked around. Loaded with pain.

I got a picture of her from a book. I cut it out carefully and put it in my purse. I was away the trip.

I talked about her all the time. I like her. I like her so much.

I'd do things for her. I wish she wasn't dead.

I even named my goldfish after her.

GEORGIA I know exactly who you mean.

CATHY No you don't. You think you're awfully clever don't you?

GEORGIA I'm almost as clever as I think I am. I know more about her than you do.

CATHY You weren't even listening.

GEORGIA Name me one thing you'd like to know. One thing.

CATHY How did she die?

GEORGIA In a car crash. Name another.

CATHY How much money did she make?

GEORGIA When?

CATHY I don't know when.

GEORGIA In the '20s, two thousand dollars per week. In the '30s, a lot less.

CATHY This could be anybody.

GEORGIA They are your questions.

CATHY I'm not playing. It still could be anybody.

GEORGIA You were talking about Bessie Smith.

CATHY You weren't joking.

GEORGIA A lot of people say they know about things and they don't really. But I'm quite particular in that I do know an awful lot. I memorize things. You could put me on *Mastermind*.

CATHY Have you not got a bit of a tip for yourself?

GEORGIA I don't see any point in pretending to be thick.

Bessie was born in Chattanooga, Tennessee.
Her father, William Smith, was a Baptist minister.
Her mother went by the name of Laura.
Laura died when Bessie was only nine.
Bessie was raised by her sister Viola.
Her brother Clarence got her an audition
For the Moses Stokes Travelling Show.
My brother liked Bessie Smith.

CATHY Is this the one whose funeral you're going to?

GEORGIA Yes.

CATHY Were you close?

GEORGIA Not really. Not recently. We used to be. (*GEORGIA pauses, then tells CATHY this almost against her will.*) There was this hotel called Dad's hotel near where we lived. When our dad was acting up we went out and stood outside this hotel. All the Black people went there. Dressed up to the nines. Danny would stand, his hand against the wall. I'd stand with my hand against the wall. He'd sing Nat King Cole's 'Unforgettable' and I'd watch his mouth moving, singing to me, holding the wall. And his fingers snapping, his foot tapping to give me the rhythm. His hand conducting high or low to give me the pitch. And then he'd sing 'Nobody Knows You When You're Down and Out'. We'd swing and dance against the wall, watching Black people come and go. How did that song go? It was slow, wasn't it, really slow!

I haven't ever told anyone that.

CATHY My father liked Bessie. The only times I remember meeting him, he would sing that song to send me to sleep. Only it kept me awake, thinking. He'd say, this is Bessie's song. I thought Bessie was his sister for years, no kidding.

GEORGIA You thought Bessie was your aunt?

CATHY Actually I wondered what had happened to her to get her in such a bad way. I mean I wondered why are people nice when you're loaded with money, and don't want to know when you're not? Whenever I felt rotten, I thought Aunt Bessie's got it worse. And that cheered me up. I didn't even know what she looked like, but I pictured her a cross between Shirley Bassey and Yvonne Goolagong.

GEORGIA It was a sad song, I remember.

CATHY sings 'Nobody Knows You When You're Down And Out.'

Once I lived a life of a millionaire
spending my money, I didn't care
I carried my friend out for a good time
Buying bootleg liquor, champagne and wine.

When I began to fall so low
I didn't have a friend and no place to go
So if I ever get my hands on a dollar again
I'm gonna hold on to it till them eagles grin.
Nobody knows you
when you're down and out

In my pocket not one penny
And my friends, I haven't any.
But if I ever get on my feet again
Then I'll meet my long-lost friend
It's mighty strange without a doubt
Nobody knows you when you're down and out.
I mean when you're down and out.

GEORGIA Have you ever seen a dead person?

CATHY Quite recently actually.

GEORGIA Really who?

CATHY Jack. My husband. But there's worse things than death.

GEORGIA Yes – surprise birthday parties. Golden weddings. Alopecia. Babies' nappies.

CATHY You're a scream.

GEORGIA is surprised.

GEORGIA I wonder what happens to them afterwards. I'm interested in that. What's it feels like. We can't ask the question. What's it like. Is it like being walled in? Is it like floating?

CATHY Don't ask me.

The train goes through a tunnel. It's dark. They can't talk. Lights up.

GEORGIA I've got a dress with me. Do you want to see it? I haven't worn it for years. But he gave it to me. I thought I'd wear it for the funeral. He'd like that. Do you think he can see us from where he is?

CATHY Frankly, no. I like wearing a dress now and again. Haven't worn one for ages. It caused too much trouble.

That's it now though. First thing I do when I get there is go shopping. A nice shimmering sort of a dress, that's what I'd like.

GEORGIA Shimmering?

CATHY Shimmering and elegant. My time's my own now.

CATHY says the announcement alongside the SPEAKER to interpret for GEORGIA.

CATHY & SPEAKER We would like to apologise for the continued delay to your service. This is due to an unexpected fall of blossom from the cherry trees. A blossom we are not familiar with. If passengers would like to make their way to the buffet car now, we are offering a free cup of cherries. (*GEORGIA looks at her watch, worried.*) What about those cherries?

GEORGIA No thank you. They won't be good. It's the wrong time of year. *(CATHY makes her way down the train.)*

They followed the tobacco crops in the spring,
the cotton crops in the fall, all along the flat plains.
It had to be the right time, the right town,
where for the blues, people had enough money to spend.

Call it a blues trail. A trail that led to a big tent.
Town after town, people packed in like rice in a bowl.
On she would come, the Empress, the Voodoo Queen.
Blast the blues into them so people remembered who they'd been.

Took them to the sad place. The place they were scared to go.
Took them to the mean place where they knew they'd been low.
Somebody was waiting and it might have felt like home.
Somebody knew them; somebody could see right into their soul.

And she took them there in feathers and plumes.
She took them there in extraordinary costumes:
a wig of horsehair and a lampshade fringe.
Her blues were shocking bits of news,

travelling on the underground railroad,
or the Jim Crow car. Quicker than the engine.
Where to meet. Which house was safe. Which friend.
Carrying the blues from Chattanooga to Chicago.

The tobacco crops in the spring, the cotton in the fall.

CATHY returns with cherries in a cup.

CATHY Go on. Take some. They're all right. So they are.

GEORGIA takes a fistful and they share them in silence.

I saved the money up and hid it in a cup in the cupboard. I knew one day I was going to catch a train out of town. I had to be quite clever to hide the money from Jack's beaver eyes. He always imagined I was having affairs, spending the money on these young men. I'd be so lucky.

Want a laugh? There's this bloke who wants to have an affair, a married man, you understand, so he calls up a dating agency and the woman they match him with is, guess who?

GEORGIA His wife?

CATHY No. His mother.

GEORGIA I never bothered with marriage. Men are just a nuisance.

CATHY I bet you never wanted for anything. I mean your parents were well off weren't they?

GEORGIA Well, off their heads, yes. My father was a fish pathologist. He was more interested in fish diseases than in our mumps, chicken pox or measles.

CATHY I don't blame him. What about your mother?

GEORGIA She leaned on the bottle a bit heavily. I think she was jealous of the fish.

CATHY You can tell I'm not from money, can't you? Stone cold sane. Marriage is peculiar really. See my mum and dad, they stayed married less than two years. That's sensible. I remember my dad sat at the kitchen table and ate all his dinner and I didn't eat my dinner. I don't even know what happened. All I really remember is thinking, my dad left because I didn't eat my dinner.

GEORGIA Did you want for something?

CATHY A BMW.

GEORGIA Bessie's house before she went on the road

with her brother and the Moses Stokes

Show had more rats than children

and Bessie's sister Viola had a heavy load

scrambling for scraps of food to show

her love; a young mother for her children.

This poverty that had a secret code.

Never discuss it, weep about it, or make a show

of it – pretend not to be children.

CATHY There's worse things than poverty too.

GEORGIA I don't know about that. Do you know how many people are living below the poverty line?

CATHY I've probably got a better idea than you. I know what it's like wondering about your next meal. Do you?

GEORGIA Well, how can you say that then? Worse things than poverty?

CATHY Staying somewhere. Staying in the same place you need to get out of. Staying there and being scared in that place. Somebody doing things to you. Horrible things. Not repeatable. No words for them. None. No shapes for them. None. Saying to yourself, go, now, get out. And not being able to move your own body. Washing yourself. Washing the house. Cleaning the sheets. You're clever but you're not that clever. I bet you don't know what it means.

Feeling sick at yourself. Disgusted. Have you felt like that. Sick. Ashamed. Guilty all the fucking time. Your eyes shifty when you're out for your messages.

GEORGIA I don't understand why you're telling me this.

CATHY You think you know everything. That's what I'm saying. You don't. Even the words you use aren't right. How many poor people have come up to you and said 'I'm living below the poverty line?' You might know some kinds of things, but you don't know everything. What good does writing your book do for poor people?

You're middle class aren't you, comfortable.

What is this book? What's it about?

GEORGIA The origins of the Ku Klux Klan.

CATHY You're joking.

GEORGIA Yes. I am. I don't talk about my books before they're published.

CATHY Why not?

GEORGIA All of us academics, we're very tight.

CATHY Tight arsed.

GEORGIA If you like. We're very isolated, very much in our own worlds. Sometimes you don't see anybody for days.

CATHY What I'd give to see nobody for days.

GEORGIA Sometimes it is quite... well, we're just completely on our own.

CATHY Poor things. Shame. You ain't got nobody. What a shower. Look. I might not know she had a sister Viola but I can sing her songs. All of them. I've got them in here, that's where they belong.

CATHY sings 'I Aint Got Nobody'.

I'll sing good songs all the time

Won't some bounder be a pal of mine?

I ain't got nobody, nobody

Ain't nobody cares for me.

GEORGIA Don't you hate the past? Don't you hate remembering things? I read. I write. I make things up. I research. I notate. I put things down in writing. Wherever I go, there it is. The past. I can't get away from it. There it is, a heavy weight across my chest.

CATHY It wasn't the past. It was the present. Don't you know that?

SPEAKER & CATHY We'd like to apologise for the continued delay to your service. This is due to something else on the line. At this point we're not exactly sure what. Would the passenger over from France come to the guard van now, that's if they've lost anything.

GEORGIA At this rate I'm going to miss his funeral.

CATHY Ah well.

GEORGIA How will I say goodbye if I don't get there on time?

CATHY Write him a letter. Send it airmail.

GEORGIA *(crossly)* What's the matter with this train? Deja-vu. That's it. Deja-vu.

CATHY Who cares? Who cares what anybody thinks now? The thing is to stand up for yourself.

GEORGIA She was beaten up a lot too you know.

CATHY Who said anything about anybody being beaten?

GEORGIA Wasn't that what you were trying to tell me?

CATHY Naw. It's not true. It's not possible. Bessie was a big woman, wasn't she?

GEORGIA So are you.

CATHY What is this?

GEORGIA Twice now. Twice in my life I've been on a train and I've missed it, and it's been so important.

CATHY Only twice? You're lucky.

GEORGIA No I wasn't lucky at all. Clever people aren't lucky. Only thick people.

CATHY Don't talk daft.

GEORGIA No. Clever people don't take risks so they rarely get lucky. They play safe. They're selfish. They think of their career and number one. They don't like the unexpected. They don't like chance.

CATHY Nonsense.

GEORGIA Do you take chances?

CATHY If I say yes, I'm stupid, right?

GEORGIA Do you take risks?

CATHY Yes. Quite big ones as a matter of fact.

GEORGIA What's the biggest one you ever took?

CATHY You don't want to know, believe me.

SCENE THREE

GEORGIA Hell. I can't even take my own advice,
that's what she thought often, when her left eye
(always the left) was swollen and a blue river
ran underneath the brown; or when
whole parts of her body could not
be walked on, or swam in, or touched even.
When her body had no-go areas; something-only areas.
Danger a fence right round her skin, wooden
as her own voice the morning after
all that violence. It was in the way they looked at her.
It was not in her mind. She did not grow such looks
in her own backyard. The hard stare; the furtive one where
the eyes were a fast car swerving as she walked near.
Nothing could persuade her not to be funny.
She could not stop being funny. *Making* people
laugh till they cried, hurt themselves, howl.
She *was a* shouter. She could barrelhouse.
But on the morning after all that violence
she could not raise the roof of her voice.

She could not embellish or endow or growl.
Laugh, yes. Grunt. Giggle. Once she caught herself
in the trembling mirror. *A minstrel.*
She tried to be completely still.
As if she was committing a murder.
A clown. An Aunt Jemima. She had a smile
that could cross a river. And she had a laugh
that could build a raft. And that was all she had.

CATHY I would say white. My dad is white. This is a tan. My dad is a white American GI. This is a tan. I got it when I went to Majorca. It's never gone away. I told the girl from the farmhouse on the hill. It was the sun. I get dark fast.

So the girl from the farmhouse on the hill asked her mother if this was true or not. And her mother told her it wasn't.

The next day she said, you really are that colour. Aren't you?

GEORGIA Memories coming up like dead things in a river. Rising. Nothing else to do but remember. I keep going to pull something out of my bag and pulling out something else. Have you seen this. Of course you haven't. This is a photo of Danny, my brother. (*She pulls it out the bag.)*

Half the things I don't even remember putting there.

Isn't he good-looking?

CATHY He's all right.

GEORGIA What do you mean all right?

CATHY Black men are better looking.

GEORGIA Mike Tyson. Sammy Davis Junior. Idi Amin?–

CATHY All right. Some Black men. My dad was good looking. The Black one. Not the one my mum went out with later who brought me up.

I used to feel so guilty about that. Having a different daddy to my real daddy.

GEORGIA I don't see it like that. Surely you adjusted? Surely children adjust. Accept and love what they have. Don't they?

CATHY sings 'Mistreating Daddy'.

CATHY Daddy, Mama's got the blues
The kind of blues that's hard to lose

Cos you mistreated me
And drove me from your door.
Daddy, you ain't heard the news –
There's another Papa in your shoes.
You ain't even got a chance with me no more,
So be on your P's and Q's.

Mistreating Daddy, mistreating Mama all the time.
Yes, because she wouldn't let you.
Mistreating Daddy, Mama's crossed the danger line.
Yes, you cross it I'll get you.

I got a feel for people talking about
I will grab my Dad and turn him wrong side out.
Mistreating Daddy, I've got a good Papa now.

GEORGIA Did you know Bessie had a son? Bessie adopted a son who she called Jack after her husband Jack, the one who beat her. After Bessie adopted Jack, she started to change. She mellowed. Didn't drink so much gin. Stayed at home more. Was on the road less. Wasn't so promiscuous. She surprised herself. Having Jack Junior brought out the best in her.

CATHY There was one single moment when I decided that was it. The moment was so fast it was quicker than a split second, or a hurricane. One moment when I said, "yes, enough, I'm leaving". After that, planning it was easy. Do you know what it was? All these years of being frightened.

And suddenly it came like that – anger like a volcano that's been dormant and safe for years suddenly erupting. Hot. Bubbling. Dangerous. Fucking euphoric.

GEORGIA I don't want to remember I'm sick of being on this train. I'm tired.

CATHY There's nothing else to do. Everyone else is doing the same. We'll never get there if you don't. This is what's holding us up. You're on the line.

GEORGIA Stop joking. Your jokes aren't even witty.

It's over. It's all over and I'm grown up. That's what gets me. I am forty-two and I am still thinking about him. He'll be eighteen now. He might try and find me. He might be on this train.

CATHY Do you want to know what the last straw was? He started digging in the back garden. He said this is for you. Wait until it's finished. It'll be comfortable. He was off his head.

GEORGIA And why do I remember the Blues?

I am five or six or seven in the back garden;

the window is wide open.

Her voice is real slow motion

through the heavy summer air.

Jelly roll. Kitchen man. Sausage roll. Frying pan.

CATHY I said the neighbours would know. People see more than you think.

He says: 'Yes and they're not bothered. You don't belong here anyway.

And if they did and I got caught, so what? You'd be dead.

And that's the main thing. We're talking about objectives here.' Do you know what I did?

GEORGIA Why do I remember her voice now

and not the sound of my mother's?

My mother's voice. What was it like?

A flat stone for skimming a rock.

Long grass. Asphalt. Wind. Hail. Cotton. Silk. Salt. Treacle.

I think it was a peach.

I heard it down to the ribbed stone.

CATHY I waited until he was sleeping. Why catch such an early train. I must say I enjoyed every bit of it. I got out a current timetable from the box of timetables. I fed Bessie. You can't pack a goldfish, can you? Anyway Bessie would have driven him mental, staring, just staring, the way fish do.

GEORGIA Words are stones in a wall. Words are a glass bowl. Words are thin wires, cut, ripped, slashed.

CATHY He won't get any peace. No way. Slow death. No peace. Aye. It's going to drive him mental. And you know what? I don't feel guilty. I think it serves him right. So it does. What a way to go.

GEORGIA I am coming down the stairs in my parent's house.

I am five or six or seven.
There is fat thick wallpaper
I always caress, bumping flower into flower.
She is singing. Did they ever play anyone else?
My father's feet tap a shiny beat on the floor.
Christ. My father says. That some voice she's got.
I pick up the record cover. My fingers are all over her face.
Her black face. Her magnificent Black face.
Why do we remember some things, and not others?

CATHY At first I tried to explain. I said, you know what you've done, don't you? But the bastard never remembered anything. Ah, I thought, Fuck it. And left it at that.

GEORGIA Bessie loved her son Jack more than anything. All of her generosity and good sense, she poured into him. She would have been a great mother, don't you think. Imagine being sung to sleep.

But, you know what happened, don't you? Her husband, her husband, stole him, didn't he? Went off with their son Jack and never came back. And Bessie never recovered. Can you imagine that? Isn't that awful?

CATHY It's not very nice, no. How long did you have your son for? Go on tell me.

GEORGIA Who are you? Who are you to ask such questions? Leave me alone. Pushing yourself into my life. You've got a bloody cheek. Who do you think you are?

CATHY Look, all I'm trying to do is help.

GEORGIA Keep your help.

CATHY sings 'St Louis Gal'.

CATHY Worried in the night-time
Worried in the day
Cos another woman
Took my boy away

Down in St Louis
There I lost my pride and joy
St Louis woman

Stole the heart of my big boy
I'm crying:

St Louis gal
Just look what you done done
I said what you done done
St Louis gal
You gonna have some fun
I mean – a lot of fun

St Louis gal
I'm gonna hammer you
I mean manhandle you
You'll find yourself in a jam
As sure as anything what am

Down in Missouri
They'll come a time
Your life
Won't be worth a dime
You stole my pal
St Louis gal.

SPEAKER & CATHY We are dreadfully sorry for this continued delay to your journey. We should be able to set off again soon. We have had signal failures, very large oak leaves, and a failed engine to cope with. The buffet is still open. Free Cokes for children under eight only. Could adult passengers ensure that under-eights are present when requesting the Free Coke.

ACT TWO, SCENE ONE

CATHY and GEORGIA are still on the train. Though it has now lost all semblance of a real train.

GEORGIA Do you see that? That rock next to the sycamore tree? That's where I went to be alone, after the violence of children grabbing me and poking me and looking down my ears shouting,

"You're deaf. She's deaf. You're deaf. She's stupid."

Annie Marie Brown born 19 May 1945. Died suddenly 19 May 1951. Beloved daughter of. Will be missed. Revenge was sweet.

You smell. You think we're saying something nice, don't you.

CATHY *(fast and loud)* Margaret Jones born 10 November Tennessee. Died suddenly in hospital. T.B. At the tender age of seven.

GEORGIA There are some stones that open in the night like flowers. Down in the red graveyard where Bessie haunts her lovers. There are stones that shake and weep in the heart of night. Down in the red graveyard where Bessie haunts her lovers.

CATHY I stopped remembering childhood insults. Anything that was ever said, Jack said worse. Things you couldn't believe or imagine. Words that would start to play inside your head until you started to say them to yourself, call yourself the names.

"It's your fault. You deserve it. You made this happen. What was it you did?"

GEORGIA Bessie was beaten up by her men. Badly. Sex and violence. A cycle of it. A pattern repeating itself. Maybe she enjoyed it. She beat them up too though. She had a temper like a bomb on a timer.

CATHY How can you say that? Nobody can enjoy it. That's what Jack said, but it wasn't true. *(becoming Jack)* You love it don't you? You want it. Where do you want it. Show me where and I'll do it for you.

GEORGIA No. Jack. Stop it.

CATHY "You've been with someone else again. Haven't you. I can smell it on your pussy. Answer me. Bitch. Answer me. Bitch. You paint me a picture. Go on. *Now*."

GEORGIA Annie-Marie was my best friend. Once she stood by when these kids were beating me up. She just did nothing. I couldn't believe it. Just the night before we'd been playing doctors and nurses and it'd been so intimate. I remember her so clearly. I can see her. I'm standing in the school playground with Annie-Marie. Next to me, Annie-

Marie is the cleverest girl in the school. Apart from each other we have no friends. Clever children are despised and feared. We are signing a story, a year long, about the end of the world. A teacher catches us and makes us stand in the dark, in her cupboard – the stink of chalk. Signing is bad for us. We cannot talk in the dark.

CATHY What happened to her?

GEORGIA I don't know. Anyone who betrayed me ended up in my imaginary graveyard with a fitting headstone.

CATHY You're a hard woman, Georgia.

GEORGIA It was because I loved her. After her my best friends were in books. I read about blues singers. I imagined I had Heathcliff for a lover. Or I was Madam Bovary. Or I was Hedda Gabler. Or I was Lady Macbeth. Or Anna Karenina. Or when I wanted to be plain I was Jane Eyre. Books were more real to me than the real world.

CATHY I never do much reading.

GEORGIA Bessie knew how to stick up for herself and friends. There was this time when the Ku Klux Klan came and tried to pull the blues tent down

See that day, Lord knows, did you hear what happened then.
A shadow like a dagger always chases the sun.
And in the thick heavy air came the Ku Klux Klan
To the tent where the Empress was about to sing her song.

They were going to pull the Blues Tent down.
Going to move the Empress out of the town.
Take her twelve bar beat and squash it into the ground.
She tried to get her Prop Boys together, and they got scared.

She tried to get the Prop Boys together, and they got scared.
She said Boys, Boys, get those men out of here,
But they ran away and left the Queen on her own.
She went up to the men who had masks over their head.

With her hand on her hips she cursed and she hollered,
'I'll get the whole damn lot of you out of here now

If I have to. You are as good as dead.
You just pick up the sheets and run. Go on.'

That's what she done. Her voice was cast-iron.
You should have seen them. You should have seen them.
Those masks made of sheets from somebody's bed.
Those masks flying over their heads. Flapping.

They was flapping like some strange bird migrating.
Some bird that smelt danger in the air, a blue song.
And flew. Fast. Out of the small mid-western town.
To the sound of Black hands clapping.
And the Empress saying, 'And as for you' to the ones who did nothing.

CATHY sings 'Young Woman's Blues'.

Woke up this morning when chickens was crowing for day
And on the right side of my piller my man had gone away
By his piller he left a note
Reading I'm sorry Jane, you've got my goat
No time to marry
No time to settle down

I'm a young woman and ain't done running round
I'm a young woman and ain't done running round
Some people call me a hobo, some call me a bum
Nobody knows my name, nobody knows what I've done

I'm as good as any woman in your town
I ain't no high yeller, I'm a beginner brown
I ain't gonna marry, ain't gonna settle down
I'm gonna drink good moonshine and run these browns down.
See that long lonesome road.
Lord you know it's gonna end,
And I'm a good woman
And I can get plenty men.

SCENE TWO

CATHY This train's going right past my house.

See that house over there. The one on the right. The washing's still out. That's mine. I should have packed that skirt. No. I didn't have time.

GEORGIA Who is that in the garden? Looks like police.

CATHY So it does. So it does. The last time they were round they told me it was a waste of time trying to prosecute. He'd broken my jaw. Knocked out these two teeth. Chipped my rib. A friend of his was round. He made me make his pal a cup of tea. I made his pal the cup of tea. He drank the tea. And when his pal had gone he started in that quiet awful way. Why were you rude to Dylan? Dylan only wanted a cup of tea. Cup of tea too much to ask?

GEORGIA I made him a cup of tea.

CATHY Do you think you're too good for my pals?

GEORGIA I made the tea. What's the matter?

CATHY You know what the matter is.

GEORGIA Look Jack, I made him tea the way he likes it with two and a quarter level spoons of white sugar.

CATHY You're taking the piss. You're taking the fucking piss. Bitch.

GEORGIA No Jack. Don't Jack. Please Jack. I'll say sorry to Dylan.

SPEAKER & CATHY Something quite serious has happened Ladies and Gentlemen. We have had to return to our starting point. We will begin our journey again as soon as we can clear the lines. We apologise for any inconvenience this may be causing.

GEORGIA When will we ever get there? This is driving me crazy. I'm just going to get out.

GEORGIA gets up to get out.

CATHY You can't get out. They're not letting anyone out.

GEORGIA *(angry)* This has happened to me before. I've been on a train and I've not managed to get where I was going.

CATHY The other time was something to do with the boy wasn't it?

GEORGIA What do you think he looks like now? I asked them to send a photograph to me and they never even did that. They probably changed his name to something ridiculous. Do you think he's missed me like I've missed him?

Eighteen years, I've been trying not to think of him.

On his birthday, I'd make sure I had lots of work to do.

I can't think how I did it. It wasn't just him I pushed out of my mind. It was myself. I haven't been myself. All this time and I haven't been myself. I can't remember what that is.

Do you know that? I've been a different person all these years.

I've never felt like this about it before. It's this train. It's strange isn't it? I don't feel myself. I don't know what to do.

I didn't even tell my brother. I wished I'd told him now. We'd have been closer then. I bet he knew there was something I couldn't bring myself to tell him.

CATHY Same with me and my dad. Years I pushed him away. Pretended he wasn't my father. I was ashamed. When people asked I'd just lie and say my stepdad was my real dad. Go on have a good greet.

It's good for you. I know what you mean. Do I know what you mean?

I've not been myself either.

It got so bad that I was waking up in the morning wondering who I was. So I've just got to find out. That's it. I'm just finding out. What things I like. What things I want to say. Talking to you. Not stopping myself. Not being frightened that I'm going to say the wrong thing. The wrong thing. I mean there's no such thing as the wrong thing is there?

GEORGIA What happened to your father? Where did he go?

CATHY Where do you go? They went North. North to Chicago. Men like my father. To be able to order a drink without lowering their heads. Just to be able to do that. It's fucking scandalous. I was with my dad. I was told he was my dad. A big Black man with black hands. I turned his hands over and saw the rivers, the lines. I remember thinking are my hands like these?

GEORGIA My brother held my hand. The blues man was singing about going to Chicago and not taking his woman. The song is wind at the top of the mountain, my brother said. It's a black-eyed Susan. It's the sea crashing on rocks.

It's a car with on open roof whizzing through a corn field. Cutting it open. It's a tight euphoric fist. It's *a grown man weeping*.

People flocked to hear the Empress for miles around.

Women recognised the blues, their lives.
Only the blues women spoke the unspeakable;
Drugs, violence, sadism, alcohol.

SCENE THREE

GEORGIA Do you want to see the dress I was going to wear to his funeral?

CATHY Get it out then.

GEORGIA gets out a dress like Bessie's covered in rhinestones and beads. It is huge, much too big for her.

CATHY Is that not a bit irreverent?

GEORGIA It was his dress.

CATHY What do you mean his dress?

GEORGIA My brother's. We used to do shows, Danny and me. We clapped each other. He enjoyed dressing up. I mimed to the songs with a hairbrush microphone. It was a scream.

At the top of the staircase is the trunk of things that belonged to my mother. Our mother. She walked into the attic room and my brother was wearing this dress and my mother went berserk. She didn't see it like dressing up. She said he was too old. And he was eighteen, I suppose that's quite old. Then he left for the Navy.

The song he liked the best was that one 'Do Your Duty'. He'd do this dance step to it.

CATHY Go on show me.

GEORGIA No.

CATHY Go on.

GEORGIA I'm too old now.

CATHY Go on.

CATHY sings 'Do Your Duty' as GEORGIA dances. GEORGIA teaches CATHY the dance step.

GEORGIA I don't know what his wife thought. I thought he stopped it after his marriage, but apparently not. I think marriage is made to make secret desires stronger.

CATHY His wife probably thought it was disgusting. And can you blame her?

GEORGIA Bessie wouldn't have bothered.

CATHY She would so.

GEORGIA Bessie was bisexual. She fancied her husband's niece and had an affair with her. Ruby Walker. Ruby was in love with Bessie and jealous of her uncle Jack. She wanted Bessie all to herself. Bessie loved sex with men and women.

CATHY So? Nothing you say about Bessie surprises me now. Each to their own. That's what I say. You want both? Have both. I don't want any.

GEORGIA You might when you get out of this train.

CATHY Oh. We're actually moving. Feel that. Going somewhere.

GEORGIA She was always on the move. Place to place. Moving. Tent to tent. And all those people coming for miles around.

CATHY It served him right. I don't feel the least bit guilty. You haven't asked me how I did it.

GEORGIA He did it. He did it to himself. That's what's so awful.

SCENE FOUR

SPEAKER & CATHY Would the passenger who just bought the phonecard please bring it back if there are any remaining units. We need to make an urgent phonecall and our line is not working. I repeat the passenger with the card please return to the buffet car now.

CATHY Look it's her. She looks pissed off, doesn't she? No wonder. What a swizz. *Next* thing, it'll be the clothes off our backs. Have you noticed something about this train?

GEORGIA I've noticed quite a bit about this train.

CATHY Have you noticed how the people on it are all staring at us? Do you not think that's odd?

GEORGIA We're good-looking. What else could they do?

CATHY *(chuffed)* Do you think so? What else have we in common?

GEORGIA Both of us have been at parties wearing the wrong dress.

Both of us have been in crowded rooms under duress.

Both of us have cracked up under stress.

CATHY When somebody turns and does a body swerve.

When somebody looks at us as if to talk is a nerve.

When it's both of us somebody doesn't want to serve.

GEORGIA Pity cannot laugh at itself which is a shame.
Pity goes Aw. Its eyelids go heavy. Who is to blame?
What was it about Bessie? What was its other name?

CATHY Both of us were mad about the Empress.
Both of us have cracked up under stress.
Both of us have on occasion worn the wrong dress

GEORGIA Bessie didn't like those parties for dicty Blacks.
Those parties when everyone had upturned noses.
Black folks talking hoity toity.
Every nigger saying Bessie's too rough.
Struts her stuff. Bessie saying gimme
a pig foot party, gimme a whole bottle of gin.
Don't gimme no Van Vechten's tiny wife rolling her eyes.
Gimme a pint of gin. I'm going to knock it down.
Knock it down before I sing anything.
She look at me like that one more time
and I'm gonna knock her down. That's it.
That's done it.

She punches.

Now who did she think she was?
Then Bessie sings 'Workhouse Blues'.
She's in this posh apartment with stars in jewels.
A woman sings an aria. Another drinks Martini.
What is that stuff? Cole Porter is here.
So's Adele and Fred Astaire.
Bessie was a shouter. None of this whispering jive.
Frank Walker told Clarence Williams go and get her.
Well that's what Frank Walker says, who knows?
Clarence was a honky tonk piano player.
When Black Swan tried to record her
she shouted in the middle of her blues,
Hold on I gotta spit.

Black Swan was so disgusted they cancelled

the recording. I bet they were sorry.

SPEAKER & CATHY We're sorry to announce to passengers that the cause of the hold up has been discovered. We have found an unidentified body on the line. The workmen have managed to bring the body onto the train.

We strongly suspect that someone on this trains knows the deceased person. We are asking passengers to come up carriage by carriage for questioning.

GEORGIA I hope it's not anyone we know.

CATHY It is someone we know.

SCENE FIVE

GEORGIA What do you mean it is someone we know? You're frightening me.

CATHY Don't be frightened.

GEORGIA Tell me.

CATHY It's nothing really. I'm joking.

GEORGIA I really can't tell with you what's a joke and what's not.

CATHY What I'm saying is you never know the minute. You've got to grab it. You can't keep waiting. That boy of yours, he could be sitting on this train and you wouldn't know it. He wouldn't know you are his mother either, would he? He's probably turned out well. Dressed quite trendy, I'd think. It's not him. You're the one. You've to forgive yourself first.

GEORGIA To pardon an offence, to remit a debt, to give up resentment, to abandon one's claim, to make excuse for... to–

CATHY Stop that nonsense. Just forgive yourself that's all.

GEORGIA To forget that's what I need.

CATHY No. If you forget you can never forgive. You've got to remember to forgive properly. All that forgive and forget's a load of shite. I've forgiven myself because I remember.

GEORGIA Two weeks I had him for. Two weeks of this small, so small, mouth lapping at my breast. Two weeks holding these tiny fists, my anchors. Looking into the old, wise eyes he had. Wise dark eyes. A mass of black curly hair.

I already knew him. When he was born I realised I'd known him all that time. The time I'd been telling myself this was just an embryo; I was just a carrier. And he took so long to be born. As if he didn't want to come out. I'll never forget that feeling, a huge force thundering through me, taking me over, possessing me.

Just two weeks and then I handed him over. All that weird time-in-between-time, sleep-in-between-sleep, the smell of my own breastmilk. All that time and suddenly I was alone without my baby. Utterly alone. *(tries to pull herself together)* But I don't regret it. No. What could I have offered him? How would I have fed him? I prayed for him. For good parents. For him to understand.

Do you think he will?

She tries to pull herself together.

The first day without him was a day in November. I could tell you the exact date but I don't want to sound obsessive.

It was raining. I remember exactly how it looked in the street outside the hospital. And my tears pouring down my face. Thinking to myself you can't cry now, you're a mother.

And then thinking the opposite, you can't cry now, you're not a mother.

And then thinking to yourself, you're nobody. Nobody.

When I watch your mouth, I remember her voice. I remember being
five and hearing her voice. This big voice, bigger than a church,
than the wind, than a warning. This voice that took me, owned me,
never left me. Do it. Sing 'Every Bit of It' for me. Please, Cathy.

(*CATHY sings 'Every Bit of It'. GEORGIA clearly knows all the words.)*

Listen to my speech this morning
Mama gonna get you told
Pay attention to my warning
Cos you been acting twice too bold
Everything you give me
Must suit me to a tee.

I want every bit of it
Or none at all,
Cos I don't like it secondhand

I want all you kisses
Or none at all
Give me lots of candy, honey
Love is grand
Mama likes loving
Both night and day,
I don't like choosing
That's what I say
I want every bit of it
Or none at all
Cos I don't like it secondhand.
No, I don't like it secondhand.

CATHY This is the blues. You live it. You are down there up to your neck in it. Blues. All you can think is why did I let myself down, How did this happen to me? What went wrong with my life? Your voice is hoarse at itself. You can't swallow. You practically wet yourself saying things like, 'Sorry, sorry, sorry' for something you haven't even done. How come you think? How did this get to be my life? You crawl on the floor like a baby and howl. It is the end of the world. Your eyes are bruises. Your skin is bruises. Inside your head is bruises. You are a bad person. Dirty. Someone is punishing you, telling you how bad you are. You could explode in a fireworks of bruises. You could throw yourself off a train. Or you could throw him off a train.

You could wait till he's asleep. You could give him chloroform. You could either stab him or cut his wrists with his own razor. Or bury him in the hole he made for you. Or set him alight.

The world is all of a sudden full of possiblity. You could do that, and then get on a train.

SPEAKER & CATHY We are making one stop only. Passengers in carriages G and F stop who have not seen the body are welcome to disembark at this stop.

GEORGIA Let's get out. Where are we? I suppose it doesn't matter?

CATHY No. It doesn't, does it? Not a whit.

GEORGIA Do you want to wait for the body?

CATHY No I'm not all that bothered.

GEORGIA Are you at your wit's end? I'm not.

CATHY Me neither.

CATHY and GEORGIA leave the train.

SPEAKER All other passengers have seen the body. We are in the unusual position. Ladies and Gentlemen, of most of you feeling you know the body. As you know, we deal with, snow – all kinds of snow – leaves – all kinds of leaves – and blossom – all kinds of blossom. Bodies are not our line. The Body Squad will meet this train. Those of you who wish to get out, do so now. The buffet car is still open selling slightly off sandwiches for those passengers that are really hungry.

We apologise for this and for all delays to your journey.

Thank you for travelling with us.

SCENE SIX

CATHY and GEORGIA enter a blues tent. CATHY is dressed up as Bessie Smith. GEORGIA is dressed up as Clara Smith. They are both giggling and excited. They are in complete control. CATHY makes a movement like a magic wand and the speaker comes on. It is the same voice from the train, only much more lively.

LOUDSPEAKER The Smith Girls are in town. Come and hear them. The curtain raiser is Rastus and Jones. Then the prima donna Margaret Scott, then the dancers, Three Baby Vamps. And Bessie Smith, the Empress of the Blues. She's singing with Clara Smith. And you know how she usually doesn't like anybody else singing blues but her. This is sure going to be a special show.

GEORGIA Might as well get on with the show cos you know these people have paid 25 cents to get in to see us.

GEORGIA sits down in the audience. CATHY sings 'Gimme A Pigfoot'.

CATHY 25 Cents! Ha No, no!

I wouldn't pay 25 cents to go in nowhere

'Cos listen y'here

Up in Harlem every Saturday night

When the highbrowns get together

It's just too tight

They all congregates at an all night strut

And what they do is tut, tut, tut.
Old Hannah Brown from cross town
Gets full of corn and starts breakin em down
Just a the break of day
You can hear old Hannah say:

Gimme a pigfoot and a bottle of beer
Send me, gate
I don't care
I jus like I wanna clown
Give the piano player a drink
Because she's bringing me down
She's got rhythm – yeh
When she stomps her feet
She send me – right off to sleep.
Check all your razors and your guns
We're gonna be razzlin when the wagon comes.
I wanna pigfoot and a bottle of beer
Send me cos I don't care,
Slay me cos I don't care.

Slay me cos I'm in my sin
Slay me cos I'm full of gin.

CATHY I ain't never heard of such shit. That's just about the most stupid idea I ever heard. This is my show. You don't like it? Kiss my Black ass and give me my drops.

GEORGIA You don't like our show? Nothing stopping you. Get the hell out.

GEORGIA and CATHY giggle like children.

CATHY They still there, Clara?

GEORGIA Yes Bessie, they still there.

CATHY Well then, let's sing them the 'Bye Bye Blues'.

GEORGIA and CATHY sing 'Bye Bye Blues'.

GEORGIA & CATHY Now I feel blue, I'm going to do something that may look wrong.
When my man comes, he'll be surprised to find that I am gone.
I done found out, we can't agree no matter how I try.
I wrote a note, will get his goat when he reads this last goodbye.

I've got those bye bye blues.
I mean them long gone blues
I'm going to where you off my mind.
I've got those low down blues,
I mean those graveyard blues
That keeps me worried all the time.

So I'm making a change I think will do me good
Because everybody told me in my neighbourhood.
As long as I stay I'm gonna be confused.
I'm sorry sweet Papa, I've got those bye bye blues.
I mean I've got those bye bye blues.

Lights fade down.

The end.

PREFACE TO PLAYHOUSE CREATURES

When Sphinx Theatre Company asked me to write a play about the first English actresses, I realised I had never even considered those women before. I knew there were boy actors in Shakespeare's day and I knew at some point women were 'allowed' to act but I had never pinpointed that moment in history nor had it ever been taught to me, despite being an English graduate. The power of silence!

I had heard of Nell Gwyn of course, but only as an orange seller and the feisty mistress of Charles II. I didn't know that she was the most acclaimed comic actress of her day. All this awaited me as I descended into the cellar of the Aldgate Women's library to be shown the books on the first women actresses, which were all written pre-1960 (this was the early 1990s) apart from Elizabeth Howe's brilliant *The First English Actresses*. There were very few contemporary accounts of the lives of actresses but, thankfully, Pepys' diary holds some salacious accounts. He was obsessed with the theatre and used to go backstage to watch the actresses change (for a fee, they weren't stupid). This fact alone blew my mind. What blew his mind was their 'confidence'. Mrs Marshall and Nell Gwyn exchanging blue banter while still dressed in breeches, which they did whilst playing men's roles. All the better for the audience to admire their legs. My admiration grew for them, as for the first time women got to taste the incident, glamour and pay of a theatrical life.

Directed by Sue Parrish, the Artistic Director of Sphinx, I had the joy of watching these women come to life in the studio theatre of the Lyric, Hammersmith, where the play opened in 1993 – the consensus of the performers being 'nothing has really changed'! I was a young writer at the time and I had no inkling that the play would survive beyond its original outing. In fact, it has gone on to be produced many times over the next thirty plus years in the UK and other countries. It was my 'break-through' play and I like to think that, whilst the actresses depicted helped themselves to a new life in the theatre, they extended that hand to me. What wonderful spirits.

No one knows who the very first actress was. At a good guess it was Mary Betterton, wife of actor-manager Thomas Betterton, but that was the only fact I had about her. I truly felt I was raising ghosts. Doll is the only fully made-up character. I had been asked to write for four but one day she came into my head and made the page. She is, in a way, our portal to the past.

April De Angelis

Playhouse Creatures by April De Angelis
Photo © Hugo Glendinning 1993

PLAYHOUSE CREATURES

APRIL DE ANGELIS

Playhouse Creatures was commissioned by Sphinx Theatre Company, and made its world premiere at the Theatre Royal Haymarket in 1993. It has since been expanded and revived at the Old Vic in 1997, the Dundee Rep in 2007, the Chichester Festival Theatre in 2012 and the Orange Tree Theatre in 2025.

Director	Sue Parrish
Designer	Annabel Lee
Music	Claire Van Kampen
Lighting	Di Stedman
Movement	Linda Dobell
Cast	Fleur Bennet, Frances Cuka, Geraldine Fitzgerald, Nicola Grier, Jean Marlow.

CHARACTERS *(In order of appearance)*

DOLL COMMON
NELL GWYN
MRS FARLEY
MRS BETTERTON
MRS MARSHALL

PROLOGUE

DOLL COMMON enters. She is sixty or so. She seems vagrant, timeless. She warms her hands at a small fire.

DOLL It is a fact that I was born. That is a fact. The how was in that old eternal way, but the when I shall not divulge. No. I'll keep that hugged close to my chest like a sick cat. *(Pause.)* Once this was a playhouse, and before that, a bear pit. On a hot day, I swear you could still smell the bears. They used to rag me; 'that ain't the bears, Doll, that's the gentlemen!' But it was bears because upon occasion as I swept I came upon their hair. Tufts of it bunched up in the corners which I saved. As a small child, my father was the bear keeper. I remember the bears moaning at night, and licking the wounds at their throats where the irons cut in and sighing, for while bears love to dance they hate to do it for a whip. Indeed, under those conditions, I believed they preferred fighting to the dancing, even as blood was spilt and death faced. Sometimes I still hear their cries very faint and in the wind.

She stops and listens.

ACT ONE, SCENE ONE

NELL *(off)* Doll? Doll?

NELL GWYN enters.

NELL Is that you, Doll? I'm cold. I swear I've never been so cold.

(DOLL laughs.)

It ain't funny, Doll. Let's have a bit of your fire.

She muscles in.

DOLL You ain't changed.

NELL I fancy something. I fancy hot chocolate. Warm and frothy in a silver cup.

DOLL There ain't none here, your ladyship.

NELL I'll ring a bell.

DOLL There ain't no bell.

NELL No bell? How do you change the scenes then?

DOLL You're slow, ain't you?

NELL looks about her.

NELL This is an odd place.

Pause. It's dark. Dark and it stinks. DOLL begins to recite as a taunt, a reminder.

DOLL 'Our play we perform for you this night

For no greater cause than your delight.'

NELL This is a dream. One where I forget me lines.

DOLL 'We ask alone but one small favour

That you critics have some sweet flavour

'cos heaven be praised 'tis not so wise an age

But that your own follies may supply the stage.'

She does a little dance. NELL gives a cry.

NELL Here, Doll. We're not... are we?

(DOLL laughs.)

No, Doll, no!

DOLL *(mimicking)* Oh no, Doll, no.

NELL Stop it, Doll, stop it! We need a priest! A priest!

DOLL What do we want one of them for?

NELL Cos we're...

DOLL Go on...

NELL Aren't I at rest, then?

DOLL rings a small bell she has about her.

NELL You had a bell you bleedin' liar!

DOLL A priest! A priest!

DOLL exits. NELL runs after her as...

SCENE TWO

The atmosphere changes as MRS FARLEY enters. A summer's day on a London street near a tavern. MRS FARLEY speechifies in religious tones.

MRS FARLEY And lo,

It is written in our lord's book

That this time shall come to pass.

And ye have only to look about ye and ye will see

That it hath come to pass

Yes, it hath.

NELL enters as if from a pub doorway. She carries a jug.

NELL *(calling in)* All right. All right! In a bleedin' minute.

She sits down to rest.

MRS FARLEY England has taken the royal serpent to its bosom and there it suckles.

The stink of brothel and alehouse corrupts our air and now the theatre lends its pestilential odour.

All is filth, smut and scandalous entertainment!

Ye shall find all men to be cheats and their hair to be lice-riddled.

Yeah, ye shall discover even the women at your hearth to be fornicators!

NELL *(calling in)* I'm having a fucking break!

MRS FARLEY And a great plague of locusts will settle in the fields and pester your cows...

She starts to cry.

NELL You crying? Don't take it personal. I always shout.

MRS FARLEY Usually I take round the hat. Just then I was making it up. Could you tell?

NELL Seemed all right.

MRS FARLEY He was my dad, the preacher. It was last rites all summer with the plague. He said God was protecting him. And then, last week, when it seemed to be over, the boils came up. Purple, behind his knees. This morning I thought I better just carry on, you know. This was one of our spots. There's a lot of work to be done. Stamping out heathen decadence.

NELL How much did you get today then? Stamping?

MRS FARLEY Nothing. What am I going to do? I could starve!

NELL That's cos you don't know how to work a crowd. I sold oysters with me sister. We had a patter. Crowds like patter.

MRS FARLEY A patter?

NELL You know 'Oyster sucking is better than....'

MRS FARLEY *(interrupting)* We spread God's plain and holy word.

NELL It's like you've got to have a bit of cunning.

MRS FARLEY Cunning?

NELL To get what you want.

MRS FARLEY I'm not sure. I think cunning is against my religion.

NELL God helps those who help themselves. I got meself this job at the Cock and Pie.

MRS FARLEY I've heard about places like that.

NELL I serve strong waters to the gentlemen.

MRS FARLEY I've heard it's the devil's own armpit.

NELL It has a decent, reg'lar sort of clientele.

(A bellow is heard from the Cock and Pie.)

On the whole. You do get the odd difficult customer. There's a bloke in there won't take no for an answer. I told him I wouldn't go with him. Not for sixpence. I know where he's been.

MRS FARLEY Where's that?

NELL With me sister, and she'd do anybody.

MRS FARLEY I'd better go. It's four o'clock. That's when I wash my dad's collars.

NELL No point washing 'em now. You never liked washing 'em, did you?

MRS FARLEY No. *(They laugh.)* It's only I can't think what else to do.

NELL Do you know poetry? I'll give you sixpence if you teach me a bit poetry.

MRS FARLEY Poetry?

NELL Can you say it?

MRS FARLEY 'The angel of the Lord came down and glory shone around.'

NELL Brilliant. *(NELL gives her sixpence. MRS FARLEY takes it.)* That a deal then? You won't starve now.

MRS FARLEY Not today. Why do you want to know poetry?

NELL For a job. Across the street. You turn up, show your legs and say a poem. The Playhouse.

MRS FARLEY That den of defilement! That pit of pestilence!

NELL I've seen the ladies. They've got lovely dresses.

MRS FARLEY Have they?

NELL I've crept in the back. I've seen them. Glittering buckles on their shoes. The candlelight shines on their hair so their hair seems like flames. Gold lace collars...

MRS FARLEY Lace! Do they fornicate?

NELL Fuck knows. They speak poetry and walk about.

(She demonstrates speaking in a posh voice)

'Oysters, oysters, by the shell or by the cup

Slide them down your gullet to keep your pecker up.'

MRS FARLEY And they want ladies?

NELL Just one.

MRS FARLEY Just one?

NELL Yeah

MRS FARLEY Oh.

NELL I heard them talking. In the pub. It's my opportunity. Teach me now.

MRS FARLEY I've a book with an excellent poem. At my lodgings. I'll go and fetch it.

NELL I'll come with you.

MRS FARLEY No. It's not far. You wait. I'll meet you back here.

She goes to exit.

NELL I'll wait then. *(Calls after her)* Here, I don't know your name.

MRS FARLEY Elizabeth. Elizabeth Farley.

NELL And I'm Nellie. Nellie Gwyn.

MRS FARLEY exits.

NELL goes over to the pub and shouts in.

NELL You can stuff your poxy job! *(She waits. To herself)* They want a lady. Lady Nell. Oysters... oysters... and glory shone around.

You need a patter. It's like you have to have a bit of cunning. Cunning? *(She jumps up and looks about her.)* Cunning cow. She'll be at the playhouse by now. Fuck. I've been bleedin' had!

NELL runs off after MRS FARLEY.

SCENE THREE

DOLL enters.

DOLL *(addressing the audience)* I wouldn't be a liar if I told you this place used to be packed to the nines. They all sat squashed on benches, which greatly facilitated the wandering of hands down breeches and bodices. Often the talk was like the roar of water and drowned out the stage. In winter you froze and in summer you cooked. It was a foul place really, but the punters came back time after time, louts and lords, lords and louts; who could tell the difference? Once they burned these places to the ground and pissed on the ashes. Swore they'd seen the last of them. But they sprung up again like mushrooms.

NELL enters.

NELL *(singing)* Sixpence each.

Will you be enticed?

Round and juicy

Cheap at the price.

DOLL It was a moral cesspit.

NELL Oranges, Doll, I'm talking about oranges! *(She produces some oranges.)* Anything I get over the sixpence I keep meself. I get tips cos of my song. I made it up.

DOLL I don't like it.

NELL You don't like nothing.

DOLL I'm bitter I sold every tooth in me head.

NELL What's the play today?

DOLL 'The Fatal Maiden' or something or other.

DOLL goes off.

NELL *(rapturously)* 'The Fatal Maiden'!

NELL exits.

The lights come up on MRS FARLEY tied to a tree. She looks very glamorous compared to the last time we saw her. She has been 'despoiled'. She poses and sighs pitifully.

MRS FARLEY O piteous fate, O horrid crime
Which none can heal, not even time
He tied me to this willowy tree
I struggled but could not get free
I felt the heat of loins afire
He panted with his foul desire
I am despoiled, so must expire!
Ah!

She dies.

MRS BETTERTON and MRS MARSHALL enter. They are two restoration actresses dressed as Amazons. They carry bows and arrows which they fire simultaneously into the wings.

DOLL's cry is heard off stage.

AMAZON ONE We have avenged you, alas, too late.

They indicate MRS FARLEY. They gather round the tree.

They recite a poem, taking turns.

AMAZONS In these wild woods we sadly gather
With our bows and shields of leather
Here we espy the sorry sight
Of our late queen whose piteous plight
Doth leave her here tied to this tree
O Penthisilea, we weep for thee
And bare our breasts after three.

They beat their breasts three times and after the third beat they bare a breast each.

For Amazons we still remain
And live without the rule of men
Fierce warriors both we be
And will go down in history.

ALL And so the curtain falls at last

On this our tragedy that's past.

They take their bows and exit. MRS FARLEY is the last to go. As an actress she is transformed from the first demure sighting of her.

As MRS FARLEY exits, NELL approaches her.

NELL Liz! Liz?

MRS FARLEY I'm Mrs Farley to you.

NELL Mrs Farley, then.

MRS FARLEY What do you want?

NELL It's the same thing as before, Lizzie. Mrs Farley.

MRS FARLEY Not that again. I've told you you've got to have the right way about you and you just haven't got it.

NELL What way?

MRS FARLEY Elegance, class, dancing. You've got to have a bit of breeding. You're selling oranges. What more do you want?

NELL I hate oranges. What about me poem?

MRS FARLEY You're never satisfied. That's your trouble. My advice is to forget it. You don't want to lead a life of disappointment do you?

NELL I'm going to ask Mr Betterton. I'll get someone else to tell us a poem, and I'll say that and show me legs.

MRS FARLEY Mr Betterton has all the girls he needs. He took on two last week. Extras.

NELL You never told me.

MRS FARLEY He can't see everyone. Otherwise he'd spend his whole life auditioning. It's a popular profession with considerable advantages.

NELL I know. You don't want me to be one – an actress.

MRS FARLEY The theatre has to have some standards. If it didn't, where would we be? Begging or starving. Now, I've got to get on. I can't stand here all day chatting. *(Pause.)* You'll thank me one day.

She exits.

NELL I bloody won't.

SCENE FOUR

A tableau.

MRS BETTERTON appears as Shakespeare's CLEOPATRA. DOLL appears as a statue, holding a bowl. MRS MARSHALL appears as CHARMIAN, MRS FARLEY as IRAS.

CLEOPATRA Give me my robe, put on my crown; I have
Immortal longings in me now no more
The juice of Egypt's grape shall moist this lip
Yare, yare, good Iras; quick. Methinks I hear
Antony call; I see him rouse himself
To praise my noble act; husband, I come
Now to that name my courage prove my title!
I am fire and air; my other elements
I give to baser life. So; have you done?
Come then, and take the last warmth of my lips.
Farewell, kind Charmian; Iras, long farewell.
(She kisses them. IRAS falls and dies.)
Have I the aspic in my lips? Dost fall?

CHARMIAN Dissolve, thick cloud, and rain; that I may say,
The gods themselves do weep!

CLEOPATRA This proves me base
If she first meet the curled Antony,
He'll make demand of her, and spend that kiss
Which is my heaven to have. Come, thou mortal wretch,
(To an asp, which she applies to her breast.)
With thy sharp teeth this knot intrinsicate
Of life at once untie poor venomous fool
Be angry, and dispatch.

CHARMIAN O Eastern star!

CLEOPATRA Peace, peace!
Dost thou not see my baby at my breast,
That sucks the nurse asleep?

CHARMIAN O, break! O, break!

CLEOPATRA As sweet as balm, as soft as air, as gentle,
O Antony! What should I stay –

She falls and dies.

CHARMIAN In this vile world? So, fare thee well.
Now boast thee, death, in thy possession lies
A lass unparallel'd. Downy windows, close;
And golden Phoebus never be beheld
Of eyes again so royal! Your crown's awry;
I'll mend it, and then play.
(She applies an asp.)
O, come apace, despatch, I partly feel thee.
It is well done, and –

A voice shouts from the audience 'Filthy whore'.

MRS MARSHALL *(whispering)* Did you hear that?

MRS BETTERTON *(whispering)* Ignore it.

MRS MARSHALL *(whispering)* I'm going to say something.

MRS BETTERTON *(whispering)* No.

MRS MARSHALL harangues an unseen member of the audience.

MRS MARSHALL Bastard! Poxy prick! You are no gentleman.

MRS BETTERTON Doll!

MRS MARSHALL Is there no one here who will run him through! I've a mind to see his guts!

DOLL Shut up!

MRS MARSHALL He started it. Pointing at me. Slandering me!

MRS BETTERTON I expect His Lordship's a little inebriated.

MRS MARSHALL He's pissed as fuck.

DOLL We don't want trouble.

MRS FARLEY You're making a show of yourself.

MRS MARSHALL Miserable cheating impotent swine.

DOLL Good evening.

They exit forcibly escorting MRS MARSHALL.

SCENE FIVE

THE TIRING ROOM.

The actresses are gathered. MRS BETTERTON addresses them.

MRS BETTERTON First pot.

DOLL I emptied it Tuesday.

MRS BETTERTON And it is now Friday. Mr Betterton's wishes are that it is to be emptied on a daily basis. He is the senior actor here and his orders come from higher up. From Mr Killegrew and beyond him, King Charles the second of England, Ireland, Scotland and the imperial conquests.

DOLL What's he care about a piss pot?

MRS BETTERTON Am I to be contradicted?

DOLL No ma'am.

MRS BETTERTON Good. Then I will proceed with precipitation.

DOLL picks up the pot and empties it unceremoniously just off. She almost bumps into MRS FARLEY.

MRS FARLEY Careful!

MRS BETTERTON *(reading)* The forthcoming season of works to be performed by the King's Company in the summer of this year sixteen-sixty-nine shall be as follows. Item, *Sir Fopling Flutter*, a comic drama by Mr Etherege in which a modern girl desires and achieves a husband of her own choosing. An unlikely play set in town. Item, *The Reluctant Shepherdess*, a pastoral epic of small moral dimension for which we shall hire extra ribald shepherds. Item three, four and five, *Macbeth the Murderer, Othello the Moor* and *Hamlet the Ditherer* by our own Mr Shakespeare. Desdemona to be played by Mrs Marshall. Ophelia by Mrs Farley. Lady Macbeth by myself, Mrs Betterton. Mr Betterton will of course play the Thane, the Moor and in the absence of Mr Hart, the Dane. In the event of an actress failing to attend a performance, management retains the right of instant dismissal or on production of a decent excuse, confiscation of wages. And while we at the King's would wish no great catastrophe upon our rivals at the Duke's, neither will we be praying that funds be forthcoming for the repair of their roof.

ALL Amen.

MRS BETTERTON As to the incident following our final performance of Antony and Cleopatra, Mr Betterton has decreed that no more is to be said on the matter. Not a word. Is that understood? *(Pause.)* May the muse attend us.

She exits. The actresses wait till she goes.

MRS MARSHALL Whore, he called me.

DOLL It's his vengeance.

MRS FARLEY Vengeance?

MRS MARSHALL But it's me that should have the vengeance.

DOLL Earl.

MRS FARLEY What?

DOLL You often get that sort of behaviour off of an earl, I've noticed. It's just their way. He'll keep on at you and on at you. Like a wolf at a carcass. He'll never let up.

MRS FARLEY Why was he shouting?

MRS MARSHALL He used to come in here. He paid. To watch us changing.

DOLL Not me. I ain't taken nothing off for ten years.

MRS MARSHALL Then he wanted to have me.

DOLL She didn't fancy it.

MRS MARSHALL He was a dog. But he persisted. So I said 'Marry me and I'll do it' thinking he'd go cock his leg up another tree.

DOLL But he agreed.

MRS FARLEY He agreed!

MRS MARSHALL So I borrowed a costume.

DOLL Desdemona, weren't it?

MRS MARSHALL And I met him at a church in a small country village.

DOLL Lewish-ham.

MRS MARSHALL And we were married by a priest. I thought if he's fool enough to make me his wife, I'll take him for what I can get. So he had his night... and when I woke up the next morning he was gone.

MRS FARLEY Gone?

DOLL Scarpered.

MRS MARSHALL The priest was no priest.

DOLL He was a bleedin' actor.

MRS MARSHALL I knew I'd seen his face.

DOLL Earls, they go to any length. They got time on their hands, see.

MRS MARSHALL I complained to the King. Lot of good it did.

DOLL Lie low, I said.

MRS MARSHALL And now I am publicly insulted.

DOLL Hounded.

Pause.

MRS FARLEY If I wanted to, could I borrow a costume? *(They look at her.)* I was only asking.

DOLL He could ruin you. Keep coming here, heckling. I seen it before.

MRS MARSHALL He'll get bored.

DOLL Will he?

MRS MARSHALL I could meet him, talk. Settle it.

DOLL You got trouble.

MRS MARSHALL I'll settle it.

SCENE SIX

Onstage before a performance.

MRS BETTERTON enters, tended by DOLL. MRS BETTERTON moves centre and begins to declaim in the grand old way. She is quite terrifying.

MRS BETTERTON I have given suck
And know how tender tis to love the babe that milks me
I would, while it was smiling in my face
Have plucked my nipple from its boneless gums
And dashed the brains out had I so sworn
As you have done to this.

DOLL Lord!

MRS BETTERTON A fellow began to shake. He was in the front row there. He shook from head to foot and crossed himself.

DOLL It's the way your eyes burn.

MRS BETTERTON Eyes are the windows to the soul. A lot of it's in the eyes. Mr Betterton swears by them.

DOLL What do you want doing today?

MRS BETTERTON Widow.

DOLL It's the black then. I'll get the black out. I don't like to say nothing but I feel I must. Our costumes ain't what they were.

MRS BETTERTON We haven't got money to cast to the four winds. This is the theatre.

DOLL But Mr Betterton had a new costume delivered Friday. With feathers.

MRS BETTERTON Mr Betterton has given his life's blood to this company, Doll Common, let me remind you.

DOLL I am reminded.

MRS BETTERTON He is entitled to a few feathers.

DOLL He's entitled to a whole pillow.

MRS BETTERTON Sometimes I wonder what would happen to a person if it was taken away. The thing one gives one's lifeblood for.

DOLL I've never had the chance to give nothing. I'm always the dead one under the cloak, or else I'm sweeping.

MRS BETTERTON I imagine it would be terrible. Terrible.

DOLL Still, I'm not complaining. What you've never had you can't miss. Well, we better go in and fix you up.

MRS BETTERTON Just another minute. Have you ever noticed how quiet it is in here, before? It's as if the air's resting.

The raven himself is hoarse

That croaks the fatal entrance of Duncan

Under my battlements!

NELL enters from the shadows.

NELL I want to do that.

DOLL Who's there?

NELL Will you show me? How to do it?

DOLL It's Orange Moll. Mrs Betterton hasn't got time to waste on the likes of you. Get going!

NELL I said a poem. I said it and Mr Betterton said I was to have a go. Saying something.

MRS BETTERTON A line?

NELL Yes.

MRS BETTERTON He never mentioned it to me.

NELL 'A line', he said.

MRS BETTERTON I suppose there's a few lines going.

DOLL Nothing fancy.

MRS BETTERTON I've only got fourteen myself. Have you any rural experience?

NELL Me mum kept a hen.

MRS BETTERTON Well then, there's the lusty shepherdess.

NELL I'll take anything.

MRS BETTERTON *(saying the lines)* 'Here stroll I the live long day
Watching my fellows fork the hay.'

NELL Here stroll I...

MRS BETTERTON And now I must prepare myself.

DOLL Some of us have preparation to do!

DOLL and MRS BETTERTON go to exit. NELL attempts her line as they are leaving. It is very flat and mumbled. It stops MRS BETTERTON in her tracks.

NELL ...the live long day.

MRS BETTERTON Never underestimate the value of opening one's mouth while speaking. One may go a long way in the theatre with an open mouth.

DOLL And not just in the theatre.

NELL opens her mouth but gestures wildly.

NELL Watching my fellows fork the hay.

MRS BETTERTON A word. Stillness.

NELL Stillness?

MRS BETTERTON *(with stillness)* 'Here stroll I the live long day
Watching my fellows fork the hay.'
See?

NELL Oh yeah. That was excellently still.

MRS BETTERTON A simple technique which may upon occasion be used to stunning advantage. As a child I was encouraged to sit still for long periods of time. I've found that invaluable.

NELL I never sat still, I had worms.

MRS BETTERTON You may also have noticed that my head was at ten to eleven.

NELL Your head?

MRS BETTERTON If you imagine the stage as a clock. I shall demonstrate. *(She demonstrates putting her head in the correct positions.)* Submission is well expressed at six o'clock. Shame at twenty to seven. Despair at five past twelve; not to be confused with heavenly abandonment at midday exactly. Death by strangulation is one of the only occasions on which an actress may employ a quarter past three.

NELL I see.

MRS BETTERTON The best way for an artist to improve their craft is by careful observation of a seasoned and expert colleague. You may observe me.

NELL Thank you.

MRS BETTERTON Follow on. You are honoured in joining a profession of much heart and great decorum.

She exits. DOLL does not let NELL follow her directly.

DOLL After me. And just remember, for every queen there are thirty friends at the banquet...

SCENE SEVEN

THE TIRING ROOM.

MRS MARSHALL and MRS FARLEY do each other's laces.

MRS FARLEY I laughed and laughed and laughed. I couldn't stop laughing. He drank down a whole flask, and the rest of them beat the tables with their fists, and the noise was deafening, and this woman came in, and you should have seen the state of her; she had a black eye and her hair was matted, and she had bare feet, and they got her to sing in front of the King; only she couldn't sing a note, and I laughed so much I cried; I don't know where they got her, off the streets – I think – and I never went home last night – I stayed away all night. What did you do?

MRS MARSHALL Nothing. I waited in. I sent word to the Earl of Oxford, asking for a meeting.

MRS FARLEY And?

MRS MARSHALL I got bored and went out. To a salon.

MRS FARLEY A what?

MRS MARSHALL Salon. A collection of people in some very nice rooms, but interesting people; philosophers, wits, poets. You drink coffee and you talk.

MRS FARLEY Talk? What about?

MRS MARSHALL Ideas. Discoveries. They now know that the human heart has four separate compartments.

MRS FARLEY Ugh.

MRS MARSHALL It's science.

MRS FARLEY What do they want you there for?

MRS MARSHALL I'm an actress. They've never had one of those before. I'm a novelty. They ask me things.

MRS FARLEY Ask you things?

MRS MARSHALL About plays. About me. About life here. How we strut and fret our hour upon the stage. I like it there. It's the sort of place you can say anything. I've said things I never even knew I thought. And people listened.

MRS FARLEY I never went home last night. I went somewhere else and I'm going there again.

MRS BETTERTON enters with NELL and DOLL. NELL stands amid the actresses.

MRS BETTERTON Go ahead.

NELL I am new.

MRS BETTERTON Speak up.

NELL I am new.

They look at her.

MRS FARLEY You!

MRS BETTERTON Engaged by Mr Betterton for a try out.

MRS MARSHALL She's not on with me, is she?

MRS BETTERTON *(introducing)* Mrs Marshall, Mrs Farley, Mrs Gwyn. *(Pause.)* The latter follows on the former. It is all easily done. *(Pause.)* Well, well.

MRS MARSHALL She'd better be proficient.

Noises are heard off stage.

MRS BETTERTON See to that, Doll.

DOLL goes over to the door.

An audience's place is in the auditorium. Goodness only knows what the attraction is back here.

MRS MARSHALL One can only wonder.

DOLL Like flies round....

MRS FARLEY A honey pot.

DOLL *(to door)* Bugger off! You're not coming in. There's ladies changing in here. *(Noise surges.)* You can wait till after and it'll cost ya. *(Noise surges again.)* They won't listen to me. They've no respect for a body.

MRS MARSHALL goes over.

MRS MARSHALL Shut up, you rollicking load of ball-driven fuckwits.

Noise stops; MRS MARSHALL resumes her preparation.

NELL I got a good one. For swearing. *(They all focus on her.)* We had it where I used to work. *(Pause.)* Turnip bollocks.

This falls flat. They resume tasks, except for MRS FARLEY. She beckons NELL over.

MRS FARLEY Come here. *(NELL moves to her.)* Show me your petticoat.

NELL What for?

MRS FARLEY Show me.

NELL lifts up her skirt to reveal it. Grey. MRS FARLEY laughs.

MRS FARLEY What a rag.

NELL What's wrong with it? *(MRS FARLEY pulls up a skirt to reveal her petticoat.)* That's beautiful.

MRS FARLEY A gift. From an admirer.

NELL It's fucking beautiful.

MRS FARLEY You could wear this in a palace.

NELL Yeah.

MRS FARLEY points to NELL's petticoat.

MRS FARLEY People don't want to pay to see that. That's like paying to see a dishcloth. An actress has to have the correct *accoutrements*. That's French.

NELL Blimey.

MRS FARLEY Didn't he tell you about *accoutrements* at the audition?

NELL No.

MRS FARLEY He did me. Liar.

NELL What?

MRS FARLEY You never had one, did you? Did you?

NELL No.

MRS FARLEY You wouldn't listen to me, would you? We work hard for what we've got. We don't need amateurs to ruin it for us.

NELL I won't ruin it.

MRS FARLEY You don't know what it's like – hundreds of faces looking at you. You don't know what the silence is like before you speak. The King's in today.

NELL He's not?

MRS FARLEY Yes. He's come to see me. He thinks I look continental. He gave me this. *(She signals her petticoat.)* I've been to the palace. There's special stairs round the back. They give you a candle and up you go. Next, I'm getting shoes.

NELL Shoes... are you going to tell on me?

MRS MARSHALL approaches.

MRS FARLEY Too late. You're on.

MRS MARSHALL *(to NELL)* You know what you have to do. Follow me on shortly. Don't muck it up. You look like a bleedin' ghost. Come on. *(Pause.)* Well say something.

NELL Turnip bollocks.

MRS MARSHALL God.

They exit.

SCENE EIGHT

MRS MARSHALL alone on stage, performing.

MRS MARSHALL Here have I flown to this lonely forest
Fled shame, dishonour and a passion torrid
Will I ever leave this wilderness?
What my fate will be I fear to guess.
My heart is beating strangely fast.
Shall I find relief at last?
(She draws out a dagger.)
This dagger I may employ to end my sorrow
Yet pity says wait until the morrow.
For surely salvation swift may come
With the sweet and rising sun.
(An idea strikes her.)
I shall call upon the Muses three
To aid me in my misery.

DOLL, MRS BETTERTON and MRS FARLEY enter as Muses.

MRS BETTERTON Who calls us from our heavenly nest?

MARSHALL Tis I.

MRS BETTERTON Then ask what you will of the Muses three, of music–

MRS FARLEY Dancing–

DOLL And poetry.

MRS MARSHALL My life is nothing to me now.

MRS BETTERTON Do not bend beneath your woe
Seek out friendship, hope will flow.
Now look, here comes a shepherdess
She will give succour to your distress.

NELL enters. She comes closer and stares at the audience. Terrified.

MRS MARSHALL Good lady, I have some small request
May I take shelter at your bower
And while away the cold night hour?

There is a dreadful silence. NELL gives a wail.

MRS BETTERTON Alas we can no longer stay
Sisters away, away, away...

MRS BETTERTON, DOLL and MRS FARLEY exit.

MRS MARSHALL May I take shelter at your bower
And while away the cold night hour?

NELL is frozen.

MRS MARSHALL exits.

NELL still seems frozen. After a bit she begins to dance a jig. She gets livelier. Warming to her task. The audience warm to her. She dances off, triumphant.

SCENE NINE

THE TIRING ROOM.

MRS BETTERTON, DOLL, MRS FARLEY enter shortly followed by MRS MARSHALL.

MRS BETTERTON *(scandalized)* Mrs Marshall!

MRS MARSHALL I just left her out there.

MRS BETTERTON Shameful!

MRS MARSHALL I said my lines and waited for hers. She just stood rooted to the spot. People shouting, hissing! She kept doing funny things with her head.

MRS BETTERTON She should have been at twenty to six.

MRS MARSHALL What?

MRS BETTERTON Mr Betterton has made a rare error in choosing her.

MRS FARLEY No, he hasn't.

MRS MARSHALL You can hardly call her a natural.

MRS BETTERTON It seems so. She has allowed personal feelings to destroy her performance. Mr Betterton once led the entire English army with a thorn in his foot. He never manifested a twinge. Later I had to dig it out with a cheese knife.

MRS FARLEY He never chose her. You did.

MRS BETTERTON I?

MRS FARLEY She lied. She never saw him.

MRS BETTERTON Never saw him? She said she was to have a line. That is what she said. Didn't she?

DOLL I took it with a pinch of salt.

MRS BETTERTON I am thunderstruck! Mr Betterton!

MRS MARSHALL *(to MRS FARLEY)* You could have said something.

MRS BETTERTON I have gone over his head by misadventure. Lord! Lord!

DOLL And with royalty in.

MRS MARSHALL It's us that look like fools.

MRS BETTERTON Terrible. A line. She said.

NELL enters slowly, dazed. They all watch her.

MRS MARSHALL You showed me right up, you silly cow.

MRS FARLEY Beg your old job back if you don't want to starve.

MRS BETTERTON I am afraid you will not do.

NELL seems in a trance.

MRS FARLEY I told you, didn't I?

NELL Everything swayed as if it was wind in a forest and people were hissing and that was like the sound of wind. And I felt like a small thing that the wind was carrying, carrying somewhere, away, far away... then a thought came into my head like a shout. It said do something and fucking hurry up about it. So I danced a little jig which I made up on the spot out of my head and slowly all the whistling, hissing stopped and someone started to clap, and then they all clapped. Laughed and clapped.

MRS MARSHALL They laughed and clapped?

NELL I felt like I had fire inside me, or whiskey.

MRS BETTERTON A reprieve! He may even keep you.

NELL Will he?

MRS FARLEY There's no accounting for taste.

MRS BETTERTON All for jig. Well, well, it has not turned out too badly.

MRS MARSHALL For her. I'm sure I've appeared to greater advantage. *(to DOLL)* Give us a rip. *(She takes her handkerchief from around her neck and gives it to DOLL.)* I get taken against my will in the second half.

DOLL Anything to oblige.

MRS MARSHALL Ta.

Sounds from outside.

DOLL That's what they're like, animals. *(She nods towards NELL.)* They get a sniff of it and they go wild.

MRS MARSHALL I'll see to it.

MRS MARSHALL exits.

NELL *(to MRS FARLEY)* I didn't mind the faces. I liked them. Like warm moons shining at me. And in a special box, a man in glitter, cheering.

MRS FARLEY A man in glitter?

DOLL The King.

MRS FARLEY He couldn't have been cheering. How's my face?

DOLL It's the same one you went on with.

MRS FARLEY Is it smudged?

DOLL Me eyes are bad. I can't do detail.

MRS MARSHALL enters. She is covered in muck - especially her hair.

MRS MARSHALL Stink! Stink! *(They stare.)* In my hair. Crap from the road. Get it off me!

MRS FARLEY Ugh!

MRS BETTERTON This is real!

DOLL *(sniffing)* Certainly.

MRS MARSHALL Outside. Two men. He sent them. Bastards. Thugs. Pulled me out. 'This is from the Earl of Oxford', they said. Then they rubbed shit into my hair. 'To teach me my manners.' He sent them.

NELL It's all in her hair.

MRS MARSHALL Get it off me!

MRS BETTERTON *(to DOLL)* It must be washed off.

DOLL What did I say? At you and at you like a wolf!

MRS MARSHALL gives a cry of frustration. DOLL leads her away, followed by MRS FARLEY. They exit.

MRS BETTERTON *(whispering to NELL)* Did you observe?

NELL Observe?

MRS BETTERTON Her head. Half past six, child, half past six. Anger. Anger and the desire for vengeance.

SCENE TEN

THE TIRING ROOM, the next day. Sunday.

MRS BETTERTON is rehearsing with DOLL. She hands DOLL her part.

MRS BETTERTON I am Widow Welfed. It is a small part with quite a lot of belching. *(to DOLL)* Are you ready?

DOLL I'm not doing any funny voices.

MRS BETTERTON I don't require any.

DOLL begins as Squire Squeamish.

DOLL Good day, Widow Welfed.

MRS BETTERTON Good day, Squire Squeamish. *(She belches throughout at short intervals.)* Please excuse me, it is rarely past midday and I have already consumed several birds of rare plumage. The last put up quite a struggle and would not go down. Squire, Squire, you grow quite pale and seem to require salts.

DOLL Salts! You would not eat me?

MRS BETTERTON Oh Squire, I would never consider the consumption of my own species.

DOLL Pray, madam, what species is that?

MRS BETTERTON A widow, Squire. A widow with appetite! Do not tremble, nor rattle the door in a vain pretence of escape. I am no mere morsel! I am a red blooded creature. Take your chance now while the servants are at market.

DOLL He gives a loud cry and leaps out the window. I can't do cries. I'd show myself up.

MRS BETTERTON *(taking DOLL's script)* That was quite satisfactory.

DOLL How could she stoop to that Squire?

MRS BETTERTON It is the task of an actress to discover the humours latent in every role.

DOLL But he's a row short of a full house. I wouldn't have touched him, not if his arse was hung with diamonds.

MRS BETTERTON Quite.

DOLL This is our seventh.

MRS BETTERTON Seventh?

DOLL Widow. I've been counting.

MRS BETTERTON You've no business counting. Did you have permission to count?

DOLL No, ma'am.

MRS BETTERTON No, in any case it's six. Six widows.

DOLL Seven, if you count the feeble brained spinster.

MRS BETTERTON Well, I am not counting her. She is an altogether different matter.

DOLL When are we doing the queen again? The Scottish one.

MRS BETTERTON Soon, soon. Rest assured.

DOLL I like her. She's horrible.

MRS BETTERTON If I asked you a question would you give me an honest answer?

DOLL Cross my heart and spit on a corpse.

MRS BETTERTON Am I old?

DOLL No.

MRS BETTERTON Good.

DOLL Not compared to me.

MRS BETTERTON Mr Betterton said 'We are getting older'. I could hardly believe he was talking to me. *(She brings out a candle.)* This is the most wonderful scene. The queen holds a single candle... why did she go mad, Doll?

DOLL She killed a couple of geezers. It done her head in.

MRS BETTERTON Could be. Could be.

MRS MARSHALL enters.

DOLL What you doing here? It's Sunday.

MRS MARSHALL *(referring to the candle)* I need that.

DOLL It's a company asset.

MRS MARSHALL Give it to me.

MRS MARSHALL attempts to take the candle but DOLL refuses to hand it over.

DOLL Don't get vicious. *(She hands over the candle. MRS MARSHALL takes it and begins carving with a small knife.)* What you doing?

MRS MARSHALL Nothing.

DOLL Looks like nothing.

MRS FARLEY enters.

MRS FARLEY I didn't think there'd be anyone here.

DOLL Me and Mrs Betterton have been practising. *(referring to MRS MARSHALL)* And she's taking a knife to theatrical property.

MRS FARLEY begins to hunt about for bits of costume in order to add to her own for glamour's sake. She picks up a shawl.

MRS BETTERTON I hope you're not entertaining the notion of leaving this establishment attired in thespian habiliments.

MRS FARLEY What?

DOLL In your costume.

MRS BETTERTON Mr Betterton has prohibited the wearing of such apparel outside of working hours due to the fact that they are returned lamentably besmirched.

MRS FARLEY I've got a rendezvous. An extremely important rendezvous. I can't go in rags.

DOLL Shall I get it off her. I have three long nails.

MRS BETTERTON No, no. Such a strategy may entail further damage to company property.

MRS FARLEY I'm surprised we don't go around naked on the pittance we get here.

MRS BETTERTON Pecuniary considerations should hardly concern us.

MRS FARLEY Why? It's not as if it's a part-time occupation. If I'm not performing, I'm learning lines. Two plays a week.

MRS BETTERTON Of course. We are artists. Artists work for the love of their craft. Artists would work for nothing.

MRS FARLEY Nothing!

MRS BETTERTON It's a calling.

MRS FARLEY You can't live on a calling. Air's the only thing that's free and you can starve on that.

MRS BETTERTON People come here, highborn and low. They come to our theatre to partake in the Sublime. To be part of that peculiar something that uplifts and transforms. To see real actors perform.

MRS FARLEY Real actors? I'm real aren't I?

MRS BETTERTON You! You are free to spend your free time as you choose. But not in our costumes. So, kindly remove them now.

MRS FARLEY You can't tell me what to do.

MRS BETTERTON This is tedious.

MRS FARLEY They don't come to see you. They come to see us.

MRS BETTERTON Us?

DOLL Don't take no notice of her.

MRS BETTERTON Us?

MRS FARLEY The young ones. With decent legs.

MRS BETTERTON Legs.

MRS FARLEY They can't get enough of it. Of us. They don't even see you. Not really see. Everyone knows.

MRS BETTERTON They see me. *(Pause.)* Of course they do.

DOLL Don't listen to her. What does she know? Mrs Betterton has come here every day of her life. Even when it was closed down. She does exercises with her tongue, to make the words better. I seen her. I seen her up all night with lines. I seen her wash her hands a hundred times so she could say it onstage and you'd believe her.

MRS BETTERTON It's all right, Doll. I am aware. I am aware that there are those types. The types that come for flesh. But I am dumbstruck for you. Sorry for you.

MRS FARLEY Sorry for me?

MRS BETTERTON If you have not had the joy.

MRS FARLEY I'm going now. There's a carriage waiting for me. I've got a rendezvous. You've probably never had one of those.

As she goes to exit, NELL runs on.

NELL Liz!

MRS FARLEY Not now, I'm late.

NELL But Liz.

MRS FARLEY I can't stop now.

NELL I was told to give you this. *(She hands MRS FARLEY a single coin.)* A man gave it me, to put into your hands.

MRS FARLEY A man.

NELL A messenger. He said to tell you 'parting gift'.

MRS FARLEY Parting gift – and that's all he gave you? This coin?

NELL That's all.

MRS FARLEY sits down.

MRS FARLEY Parting gift. Are you sure that's what he said?

NELL Yes.

Pause.

MRS FARLEY And that's all he gave you?

NELL Yes. *(Pause. MRS FARLEY is devastated.)* Never mind.

MRS FARLEY What do you know!

MRS MARSHALL stops her carving.

MRS MARSHALL There. *(She holds it up.)*

NELL What is it?

MRS MARSHALL Have a look.

NELL Ain't it good? A little man. A little wax man.

MRS MARSHALL Homunculus.

NELL He's got a little mouth. His mouth is open like a cry.

She offers it to DOLL.

DOLL I'm not touching it. It has hair melted on the top.

MRS MARSHALL I had a lock of his hair. The earl of Oxford. He gave it to me. A love token.

MRS BETTERTON also looks.

MRS BETTERTON Rebecca Marshall, that is evil. What are you doing now?

MRS MARSHALL I'm sticking a pin in the bastard's neck. *(They wince.)* That is for the shit rubbed into my hair.

NELL It has gone right through!

MRS FARLEY Will he feel it?

MRS MARSHALL sticks another pin in.

MRS MARSHALL This is for being an arrogant, villainous rogue.

MRS BETTERTON He will be in pain.

DOLL He will be in bleedin' agony.

MRS MARSHALL That is for crying 'whore'!

Another pin goes in.

NELL That's his bollocks.

MRS BETTERTON It is witchery!

MRS MARSHALL holds up the doll.

MRS MARSHALL Round about the cauldron go
In the poison'd entrails throw
Toad, that under cold stone
Days and nights has thirty-one
Sweltered, venom, sleeping got
Boil thou first in the charm'd pot.

MRS BETTERTON Fillet of a fenny snake
In the cauldron boil and bake.

MRS MARSHALL Eye of newt and toe of frog
Wool of bat and tongue of dog

MRS BETTERTON Adder's fork and blind worm's sting.

MRS FARLEY Lizard's leg and howlet's wing.

MRS BETTERTON For a charm of powerful trouble
Like a hell broth boil and bubble

ALL Double double toil and trouble
Fire burn and cauldron bubble.
(NELL does a demonic version of her jig.)
Double double toil and trouble
Fire burn and cauldron bubble.
(Chant grows to a crescendo.)
Double double toil and trouble
Fire burn and cauldron bubble.

MRS MARSHALL throws the doll to the floor and tramples it underfoot.

MRS MARSHALL Never prosper! *(She spits on the doll.)* He was my keeper. Now look at him.

MRS FARLEY You need a keeper.

DOLL You won't get another one.

MRS MARSHALL I don't want another one. I had a husband once. You wouldn't have known me. I used to creep about. He liked me to be quiet. (*She picks up the pieces of the doll.)*

MRS FARLEY If he don't want me someone else will. Won't they?

DOLL 'Course.

MRS FARLEY I want a drink.

MRS MARSHALL I went out last night. To a salon. Someone remarked that he'd never known of so much interest in the theatre, not since we actresses had arrived. Could I corroborate that? Oh yes, I said. I'll certainly corroborate it. 'You'll be wanting to own the theatres next,' he said, 'profits and all'.

MRS BETTERTON Shares are for leading actors. Mr Betterton has shares.

Pause.

MRS MARSHALL I'll have a drink too. *(to NELL)* You coming?

NELL In a bit.

MRS MARSHALL Anyone else?

MRS BETTERTON *(exiting)* I shall not be joining you. We have old friends for supper.

MRS MARSHALL and MRS FARLEY exit.

DOLL I fancy a bit of sweeping.

She begins to sweep.

NELL I had a message, too. From the man. He said there is a carriage outside and I may use it at my own convenience. The special stairs... *(Pause.)* What do you think, Doll? The King.

DOLL Life's like a storm, that's what I think. Don't get in its way. That's what I think. It don't matter what anyone does, we all end up dead meat, don't we?

NELL You look on the bleedin' dark side, Doll, that's your trouble. Anyway, I decided. I'll go. Just this once, mind. I'm an actress, not a tart.

NELL exits. DOLL sweeps.

Curtain.

ACT TWO SCENE ONE

A performance is in progress.

NELL and MRS MARSHALL are in breeches, sparklingly confident. Each with a sword.

NELL How now, sir. You're in my path!

MRS MARSHALL Nay, you are in mine, sire!

NELL I take exception to that.

MRS MARSHALL And I too. Will you not step from my course?

NELL I'm buggered if I will.

MRS MARSHALL Then I take you for an intolerable, plaguey rogue.

NELL And I take you for a right ambling Harry.

MRS MARSHALL Will you draw sir?

NELL Certainly. *(They draw their swords.)* Prepare to gasp your last.

MRS MARSHALL Say farewell to the sun. *(aside)* Mind he has a fine pair of legs for one so foul lipped.

NELL *(aside)* I swear the oaf has a mouth the colour of cherries.

(They begin to fight with gusto.)

Are you willing to submit to a superior striker, sirrah?

MRS MARSHALL Sure, it is you, Sir Feeble, who must crumble!

TOGETHER *(aside)* Odd! I could swear there is something almost womanly in the deftness, grace and expert sword welding of this stranger.

(They fight some more. They come close together, their hats fall off.)

I declare!

NELL Sister!

MRS MARSHALL Friend!

NELL Both disguised.

MRS MARSHALL Accounting for such noble limbs and lustrous eyes.

TOGETHER Let us waste no time in further strife

And without delay make amends

It is far more profitable to be friends

For us women in a land of men

So let us share our victory

Enjoying our mutual company

They turn to the audience.

And while we're at it, playing for your pleasure
We'll ask shares in your payments for good measure
The price of our glorious forms you see
Is shares in this very company.

They laugh, bow, exit.

SCENE TWO

MRS BETTERTON comes forward and addresses MR BETTERTON who is unseen in the auditorium.

MRS BETTERTON Thomas? Thomas? It is the matter we discussed at breakfast. You remember. I am afraid it has come up again. I know there is no precedent for it, dear. But in answer to that I have been told to reply that indeed there was no precedent for a wig till the first man did wear one. And now. Lo! There is scarcely a fellow who does not sport one. Bristly or fluffy. You cannot step out of doors nowadays but you see a periwig advancing towards you at great speed and in danger of toppling. Sorry. I do digress. *(Pause.)* No, my dear, we were not referring to your particular wig. How could you think so? *(Pause.)* Dear Heart, they will have shares. Shares, shares, they talk nothing but shares. They say you have shares and they will have them too. Company shares and profits. You may say that they have got above themselves. What with all the fuss there is about them. Royalty and whatnot. Carriages and flowers, messages and hangers on. That may be the case. Indeed it may. But that does not alter the fact that they will not be dissuaded from their course. They say the town does not come to see fusty old men in squashed hats declaim Caesar but to see actresses in the flesh, living and breathing, the real creatures. *(Pause.)* Squashed. *(Pause.)* Yes, I explained that it was your lucky hat, my dear, passed down through the generations. *(Pause.)* I can't remember their reply to that. *(Pause.)* No! It is not that I am asking. I ask only because I am asked to ask. But still, it would seem unfair to me that the others should have shares and I none. Am I to sit in the tiring room and watch them count out their coins while I knit mittens? Why, I should not like that. Indeed, no. Also dear, we need a new cupboard for the cheeses especially, and if I have not asked you once for the means I have asked you a thousand times till I am quite worn thin with asking. And if I did have shares I should certainly know how to put the cash to good purpose. Besides, I should also like to venture a few small opinions of my own concerning artistic matters. Indeed, Thomas, you are the one that's partial to cheese.

DOLL enters.

DOLL What did he say?

MRS BETTERTON He says he will give it his consideration.

MRS BETTERTON takes out a long piece of yarn.

DOLL What's that?

MRS BETTERTON There are three colours in it. Three yarns. You twist them together. It takes hours.

DOLL It's nasty. What's it for?

MRS BETTERTON I don't know. It's just a long thing. However it keeps weary hands occupied during long plays when one's appearance is minor. Doll, do you ever hear things? Voices?

DOLL What sort of voices?

MRS BETTERTON Ethereal voices. They have told me the waiting will not be for much longer.

DOLL What waiting?

MRS BETTERTON For a part. A great part.

DOLL How do you know they're telling the truth? Voices can be tricksy.

MRS BETTERTON I have proof. See this.

She holds out her hand.

DOLL Wedding ring.

MRS BETTERTON One morning I woke up and for the first time it was not on my finger. They told me where to find it and they were right.

DOLL Where was it?

MRS BETTERTON In the slops bucket.

DOLL How'd it get there?

MRS BETTERTON I've no idea. Not to wait much longer they said. Not much longer.

SCENE THREE

THE TIRING ROOM. The actresses enter.

MRS BETTERTON Indeed, I have not passed four and a quarter hours more pleasantly since I can remember.

DOLL I am numb all over.

MRS BETTERTON I was much struck by Mr Otway's new play, such elegance of phrase, well modulated passion and soaring tragedy. But perhaps it could be a little shorter.

DOLL How may that be done?

MRS BETTERTON By the removal of words. And also lines, scenes perhaps.

MRS MARSHALL Acts at a push.

DOLL What if he needs every word.

MRS MARSHALL He may but we certainly do not.

NELL *(to MRS BETTERTON)* What's my part then?

MRS BETTERTON The saintly martyred Dorothea.

NELL But she's not funny.

MRS BETTERTON No, she's saintly.

NELL How do you play that?

MRS FARLEY I can imagine playing it.

MRS BETTERTON A prerequisite for playing any part is staying awake to hear it read.

MRS FARLEY Am I the one that gets eaten by a mountain lion?

MRS BETTERTON That would seem most suitable.

MRS FARLEY I don't mind being eaten, but I'd like a proper speech, it just says, 'ow'!

NELL I don't mind doing Dorothea if he takes out the saintly bits.

MRS BETTERTON That would leave her somewhat skeletal.

NELL Audiences like to see me being witty. If I don't get some jokes I'm not showing me tits.

MRS BETTERTON I don't know what you mean.

MRS MARSHALL She means her part is a tit part.

NELL And if I'm going to make a tit of myself I want a few jokes.

MRS BETTERTON This play is a serious indictment of primogeniture.

NELL It's tit after tit.

MRS MARSHALL *(reads)* Marcellus spies Dorothea asleep on a grassy knoll.

NELL Tit hanging out.

MRS MARSHALL Dorothea discovered praying in her boudoir.

NELL Other tit hanging out.

MRS MARSHALL Vincolo struggles violently with Dorothea in the lonely cloisters.

NELL Both tits out simultaneous.

MRS BETTERTON It is not for us to come between a poet and his muse. If it were, I would be the first to suggest the creation of a large and diverting part for a maturer woman.

MRS MARSHALL I've got an idea for a tragedy. The main part is a woman. Her name is... Monimia. She's married but she takes a lover.

DOLL Tart.

MRS MARSHALL She doesn't know she has. She's been tricked. She thinks it's her husband she's sleeping with but really it's his brother who's smitten with her. Should she tell her husband or live a lie?

ALL Live a lie/tell him.

MRS MARSHALL She tells him. He is furious. She's punished, blamed. She suffers. Give that to an actress and the play would never stop running. I'll have a word with Mr Otway myself.

DOLL He won't listen to her, will he, Mrs B? An actress.

MRS MARSHALL But he would to a company shareholder.

DOLL You ain't got shares yet.

MRS BETTERTON Enough with this airy conjecture. We have work to do. Rehearsal!

The actresses gather props and small items of costume. MRS FARLEY comes forward.

MRS FARLEY My laces, Doll. You've got to do my laces.

DOLL Patience is a virtue.

MRS FARLEY Pull'em tight, Doll.

DOLL I am pulling them.

MRS FARLEY That ain't tight enough.

DOLL Me poor old fingers are giving out.

MRS FARLEY You do it, and I'll give you threepence.

DOLL Fourpence.

MRS FARLEY Done.

DOLL Mind, I'm not saying I can work miracles.

MRS BETTERTON, MRS MARSHALL and NELL come forward. They rehearse an extract of 'The Provoked Wife'. MRS MARSHALL as LADY FANCIFUL, MRS BETTERTON as CORNET, NELL as MADEMOISELLE. MRS FARLEY as PIPE, waits to the side.

LADY FANCIFUL Cornet! Cornet!

CORNET enters.

CORNET Ma'am?

LADY FANCIFUL How do I look this morning?

CORNET Your ladyship looks very ill, truly.

LADY FANCIFUL Lard, how ill-natured thou art, Cornet, to tell me so, though the thing should be true.

MADEMOISELLE My opinion be, matam, dat your ladyship never look so well in you life.

LADY FANCIFUL Well, the French are the prettiest obliging people; they say the most acceptable, well-mannered things, and never flatter. Get out of the room, Cornet! I can't endure you, you look so insufferably ugly.

CORNET Ma'am.

She curtsies, and exits.

MADEMOISELLE Ah, madam, I wish I was fine gentleman for your sake. I'd do all de ting in de world to get a leetel way into your heart. I make song, I make verse, I give you de serenade, I give you great many present; I no eat, I no sleep, I be lean, I be mad, I hang myself, I drown myself. Ah, ma chere dame, que je vous aimerais!

LADY FANCIFUL Well, the French have strange obliging ways with 'em. You may take those two pairs of gloves Mademoiselle.

MADEMOISELLE Me humbly tanke my sweet lady.

CORNET enters.

CORNET Here is Pipe, ma'am, to sing you a song.

PIPE does not enter.

Here is Pipe ma'am. To sing you a song.

Pause.

NELL Pipe! We ain't got all day.

MRS FARLEY enters as PIPE. She is now visibly pregnant. She begins to sing.

MRS FARLEY Fly, fly, you happy shepherds, fly... *(She tries. Tries again)* Fly, fly.

MRS MARSHALL You're nothing like a pipe.

MRS FARLEY I can sing, can't I?

DOLL You're showing.

MRS FARLEY It's not that bad.

MRS BETTERTON Someone else will have to be Pipe.

MRS FARLEY Who?

MRS BETTERTON I expect Mr Betterton will see to it. Some new girl.

MRS FARLEY I am Pipe.

MRS BETTERTON You will not do. Not in your present way.

MRS FARLEY I'll tie my lace tighter.

DOLL You and whose army?

MRS FARLEY I am not on long. Let's get on with it. *(She sings.)* Fly, fly... come on!

MRS BETTERTON It is impossible. Mr Betterton will not have it. He cannot. We could lose our licence. To be that way on a public stage. There are laws.

MRS FARLEY Laws!

MRS MARSHALL You knew about them. If we were all as careless as you, the theatre would have to close down.

MRS FARLEY It's not my fault.

MRS MARSHALL Whose fault is it, then?

MRS FARLEY I went back looking for the special stairs but I couldn't find them. They took me there before and it was easy, but when I went back I couldn't find them. It was like a maze. I wandered and wandered. You get tired. Where will I go?

MRS MARSHALL You should have thought about that.

MRS FARLEY Please.

MRS BETTERTON There's no choice in the matter.

DOLL You've been lucky hanging on this long.

Pause. MRS FARLEY turns to MRS MARSHALL.

MRS FARLEY Help me.

MRS MARSHALL What do you mean?

MRS FARLEY You know.

DOLL You don't want to do that.

MRS FARLEY Who asked you? *(to MRS MARSHALL)* I want you to do it.

MRS MARSHALL No.

MRS FARLEY You've got to. Please.

DOLL I know a woman who rotted inside, after.

NELL Shut up, Doll.

MRS FARLEY It's not too late is it?

MRS MARSHALL It's never too late. Have you seen it done before?

MRS FARLEY No.

MRS BETTERTON I've seen it done.

MRS MARSHALL Sit down. *(MRS FARLEY sits.)* Get a cloth.

DOLL gets a cloth.

MRS FARLEY Is that for blood?

MRS MARSHALL No. You put it in your mouth and bite on it.

DOLL You need something sharp. Long and sharp.

MRS BETTERTON fetches a costume brooch with a long pin.

MRS BETTERTON Here. A queen's brooch.

MRS MARSHALL takes it.

MRS MARSHALL Give us your arm.

She takes MRS FARLEY's arm. She sticks the pin into it. MRS FARLEY cries out.

MRS FARLEY Ah!

MRS MARSHALL That's nothing. Still want it done?

MRS FARLEY nods. The women close round her.

MRS FARLEY Hold my hand someone.

NELL holds her hand. They begin. MRS FARLEY gives a more awful cry. Then a worse cry.

MRS FARLEY No! *(She takes rag from her mouth.)* I can't. I can't.

The women move away from her.

MRS BETTERTON It doesn't always work.

Pause.

MRS FARLEY Before I go, would any of you ladies care to purchase a petticoat? Well fashioned and stitched. It's pure silk. French. *(She lifts her skirt to show petticoat.)* An absolutely invaluable accoutrement. *(She takes it off and holds it out.)* Well?

MRS BETTERTON It's very pretty, but not to my particular taste.

DOLL I'd only use it as a snot rag.

MRS MARSHALL How long can you live off a petticoat?

MRS FARLEY It's hardly worn. What's the matter? *(She waves the petticoat closer to the women. They back away as if not to be touched by it.)* Superstitious? I said 'it's hardly worn'!

NELL I'll buy it.

NELL gives her money.

MRS FARLEY Thanks.

She offers NELL the petticoat.

NELL You keep it.

MRS FARLEY keeps hold of it.

MRS FARLEY Maybe you should have a care. Maybe your luck will run out.

She exits.

SCENE FOUR

THE TIRING ROOM. NELL enters, singing to herself.

NELL Cease of cupid to complain
Love's a joy ev'n while a pain
Charming raptures, matchless sweets
Love alone all joy complete
Moving glances, balmy kisses

Oh then think how great his bliss is.

DOLL enters dragging a sack of props.

DOLL Don't mind me.

(NELL continues to sing.)

What a bleedin racket.

(NELL hums.)

What you dressed up for? We're only sorting.

(MRS BETTERTON enters, sits quietly. DOLL drags things out of her sack.)

Three dutch collars. Patching.

MRS BETTERTON Here.

She takes them. She starts to inventory items.

MRS BETTERTON Three dutch collars.

DOLL One spoon. Bent. In need of straightening.

MRS BETTERTON See to it Doll.

(DOLL bites it straight.)

One spoon.

DOLL One eaglet. In need of beak and feathers.

NELL We can't work miracles.

DOLL pulls something else out of the sack.

DOLL One maggot ridden corpse's finger.

NELL Oh god.

DOLL My mistake. It's an old bread roll. I've been looking for that. One crown. Kings. Requiring spit and polish.

NELL I'll do that.

She takes the crown. Drops it.

MRS BETTERTON Have a care. In the theatre we're not superstitious for nothing. One crown.

DOLL hands it to NELL.

DOLL I saw the old King. I saw him put his head on the block. Then whoosh.

NELL What was it like?

DOLL Well it sort of rolled off.

NELL Not that. The occasion.

DOLL Crowded. One soiled jerkin.

MRS BETTERTON That's not ours.

DOLL Ain't it?

MRS BETTERTON No it's one of theirs. From the men's tiring room. They slipped it into our sack.

NELL Bleedin' cheek.

MRS BETTERTON It's an old trick.

DOLL I'll soil it some more and slip it back.

NELL I would.

MRS MARSHALL enters.

MRS MARSHALL Nell, we are no longer hirelings.

DOLL Starlings?

MRS MARSHALL Hirelings. Hirelings. *(reads, to Nell)* The shareholders of the King's company do herewith agree that henceforth their number shall include... me and you, Nell. We are shareholders.

NELL Fuck!

MRS MARSHALL It has been agreed. We have shares.

DOLL I thought you said 'starlings.'

NELL Sharcholders?

MRS MARSHALL Shareholders!

NELL They saw sense then.

MRS MARSHALL Next time I see that fucking Earl, I'll tell him piss off! I've no need to shag arseholes now I have shares. Shares don't pretend to be your husband, abandon you, rub shit in your hair. I get all the love I want on stage and then go home safe and count my money.

NELL We'll drink to that tonight.

DOLL A scrap of fur. Two beads. That's the lot. The rest is curtains.

MRS BETTERTON From today I shall not be attending the theatre on a regular basis.

DOLL Gawd.

MRS BETTERTON Mr Betterton has talked to me.

DOLL You never said.

MRS BETTERTON Some younger actresses must be given a chance. People like to see them.

DOLL Gawd.

MRS BETTERTON They will partner Mr Betterton. We were partners for many years. Many years.

She sits still.

DOLL Mrs B? Mrs B?

NELL Mrs Betterton?

MRS MARSHALL She'll come to herself.

MRS BETTERTON I used to help my husband with his lines and naturally, I learnt them too. Then one day, he was playing Othello and his Iago fell sick. He ate something that disagreed with him. A pork pie. Anyway, it was rotten. Mr Betterton was caught short and could not find anyone else at such little notice to do the part. Except me. I'd read it with him many times. We knew it could mean trouble if the bishops found me out, being a woman, but we were younger and reckless and we thought no one would ever know.

NELL What happened?

MRS BETTERTON We got away with it. We were very close, Mr Betterton and I, and it was as if I hung off his breath and he off mine, and the words flew between us. That was my first time. (*Pause.*) After that we did it on a regular basis. My Fool to his Lear, his Falstaff to my Hal. And then, of course, the day came when everything changed and for the first time we women were permitted by Royal decree to act upon a stage. A great stir it caused. And I was one of the first ever and when I spoke, a great hush descended on the house, and it was as if the men and women gathered there were watching a miracle, like water turning to wine or a sick man coming to health. (*Pause.*) It was then I knew that I had done a terrible thing and that nothing would ever be the same for me again. I had tasted a forbidden fruit and its poisons had sunk deep into my soul. You see, Iago is like a whip that drives the life around him, when Hal makes a choice the whole world holds it's breath. I never forgot that feeling. The poison's still in my blood. Like a longing... A longing. I looked for that poison everywhere and couldn't find it. Not in the Desdemonas or Ophelias. Only in her, the dark woman. (*Pause.*) We were partners for many years. And when he told me it was over, I swear he had tears in his eyes. I had never seen him cry before, except, of course, when the part required it.

Pause.

NELL You better go home, Mrs B.

DOLL Better wait at home. Not here. You don't want him finding you. He'll think you've gone funny.

MRS BETTERTON I never missed a cue.

MRS MARSHALL We know that. We know.

MRS BETTERTON I shan't miss this one.

She exits.

MRS MARSHALL The first time I was ever in a theatre I saw her. Somehow she just knew how to do things. Even the business with the bloody clocks.

DOLL Fate is a wicked thing. Time don't have pity on no one. No one.

SCENE FIVE

Outside the theatre, some time later.

MRS FARLEY is standing alone. She looks ill, dirty, bedraggled, weak. She is clad in her petticoat, which is dirty, ragged.

MRS FARLEY Two pennies. Two pennies. I do anything. You can punch me look! *(She shows her arms which are bruised.)* Nothing. Stood here all afternoon. Nothing doing. Should have washed my face. Tired. Too tired to do it. Might have done better business if I had. *(Pause.)* It's not me. It's them. They're not doing their job properly. The blokes aren't coming out excited. They're coming out limp. They're not coming out looking for it. I should be in there. Not outside. *(Pause.)* Thing is I'm better now. Better than I was. That's the pity of it. I've learnt things out here. The art of performance. You can't act tired, not for business purposes. You've got to act like you like it. Love it even. You learn that. Out here I'm a real pro. *(Pause.)* I left it. Had to. Little pale body. Laid it on some steps. What a cry when I left it. *(Pause.)* I'm going to find a gutter or a corner and lie down. Not in the streets! Yes, right here in the streets. It's getting dark.

She wanders off.

SCENE SIX

THE TIRING ROOM. DOLL and NELL are present.

DOLL I looks out the window. I sees her. Feeding off the leavings.

NELL Don't be morbid. Do my hair.

DOLL Do it yourself.

NELL You watch it.

DOLL It ain't for a part, is it?

NELL I'm going out.

DOLL Well, I ain't employed to tart you up for private shenanigans.

NELL I'll do it myself then.

DOLL Them new shoes?

NELL What you hanging round for?

DOLL Do things. For her. Errands. Things to collect up. Breaks my heart.

NELL *(gives her a cup)* Here.

DOLL What is it?

NELL Sherry.

DOLL You won't get rid of me by poison.

NELL Don't be daft. It ain't poison. *(She drinks.)* See.

DOLL drinks. MRS MARSHALL enters.

DOLL Here's her parts. *(She shows a bag of scrolls.)* I have to give em to her.

NELL Who?

DOLL Her. *(She shoves the bag at MRS MARSHALL.)* Here y'are. Assorted queens and wives. Faithful have a blue star, unfaithful a red circle.

MRS MARSHALL Mrs Betterton's parts?

DOLL She's had 'em years.

MRS MARSHALL They're no good to her now.

DOLL I helped her with them parts. I helped her so long I forgot I couldn't read.

NELL How do I look?

DOLL Thought you was only going once.

NELL You're not paid to think, are you?

MRS MARSHALL You don't have to go now.

NELL Don't have to?

MRS MARSHALL Your rendezvous.

NELL It's arranged.

MRS MARSHALL Things have changed, Nell. As fast as that. The point is you can choose. That's the point. You don't have to go.

NELL I want to bloody go. *(Pause.)* It's all his hair. That hair's real. Lovely black hair.

MRS MARSHALL Are you in love?

NELL Love? Going there – it's exciting. I'm sixteen. I want to try things. New things. I'm lucky. I've always been lucky. People say I'm beautiful but so are lots of girls. So why me? So why me and the King? Luck. That's all. I get what I want. I always have. I had me own oyster stall at eleven. I have this thing I do. I imagine. I imagine what I want and then I get it. Somehow I get it. It just seems to go on and on and on. And I became an actress and I got the King.

MRS MARSHALL I imagined things too, not having a keeper. Freedom.

NELL And you got it. We're different that's all. I'm free to do what I want, and you are too.

MRS MARSHALL Free. To play a faithful wife or an unfaithful wife. A whore, a mistress. We play at being what we are. Where's the freedom in that?

NELL How d'you mean?

MRS MARSHALL Now I'm none of those things, so what am I? Now we've got a chance to be something different, new, do you see?

DOLL She ain't got no chances to be nothing.

NELL Stay out of it, Doll.

DOLL No chances left. That's the point.

NELL *(to MRS MARSHALL)* Don't take no notice of her.

DOLL I got me faculties. I'm telling her.

MRS MARSHALL Telling me?

NELL She's pissed.

DOLL Someone has spoken out of turn. Said something. Betrayed you.

MRS MARSHALL Betrayed me?

DOLL He had a bad back and three teeth pulled. Lord knows the state of his bollocks. He knows about the little wax man. The witchery.

NELL Who does?

DOLL The Earl of Oxford.

MRS MARSHALL Who said something? You?

DOLL Me? I never said nothing. I never cried witch.

MRS MARSHALL Witch?

NELL What can he do? The Earl?

DOLL They're still up to burning people.

NELL Burning them?

DOLL Not a pleasant way to go.

NELL They wouldn't do that.

MRS MARSHALL Wouldn't they? He hates me. I have to go. I can see that.

NELL We got shares now.

DOLL Shares!

MRS MARSHALL I'll have to live in some quiet place. Hidden. Quiet. Keeping my mouth shut.

NELL It won't come to that.

MRS MARSHALL What will it come to? Just a flogging? That gets an audience. Would you stay for that?

Pause.

NELL Maybe you could start again someplace.

MRS MARSHALL Maybe. They found another word for me before I could find one for myself. If they don't get you one way they get you another. *(She picks up the bag with MRS BETTERTON's parts.)* Don't say I've been here.

DOLL Leave her parts, then.

MRS MARSHALL No, they're not having anything of me. *(Pause.)* Think of me.

NELL Good luck.

MRS MARSHALL I'll burn these.

DOLL Burn 'em?

MRS MARSHALL indicates parts. She exits.

NELL I better get a move on. I'm late.

DOLL Burn 'em she said. Can't be right. Mrs Betterton's parts.

NELL Stop bloody going on. You're pissed. Look out of the window. See if there's a carriage.

DOLL *(singing)* I wish, I wish, but its all in vain, I wish I were a maid again. A maid again I shall never be, till apples grow on an orange tree. *(She looks out of the window.)* Can't see a carriage. I can see orange.

NELL Orange? *(She goes to look.)* Fucking hell. That's fire, Doll, fire! She's burning the whole bloody place down!

DOLL Fire! Fire!

NELL Fuck.

DOLL Help! *(NELL gathers a few belongings.)* What'll we do?

NELL We got to get out.

DOLL Leave here?

NELL Get moving!

DOLL But where'll we go?

NELL I dunno about you, but I'm joining The Duke's.

NELL runs out.

SCENE SEVEN

NELL is on stage at The Duke's Playhouse, glowing. She dances a much more polished form of the jig which shows her new star quality. She finishes with:

NELL It ain't my fault that heaven made me

Start out a barmaid not a lady

So, let us let the bygones be

And raise the roof for darling Nellie!

Applause.

SCENE EIGHT

NELL is in her private tiring room at The Duke's. MRS BETTERTON and DOLL enter.

DOLL It's me an' her. We sneaked in round the back.

NELL Enter! Ain't you noticed? I'm on me own. I have my own room. To myself.

DOLL Ain't it lonely?

NELL No. It's private. I've come a long way, ain't I? *(She picks up some parts.)* Look.

DOLL What is it?

NELL It's a play. It has a part for me. Especially written for me.

DOLL What's someone want to write a part for you for?

NELL Because I'm the shining light upon our stage. That's what she said when she put the part into my hands.

MRS BETTERTON Who?

NELL Mrs Behn. She is the author.

MRS BETTERTON A part written for Nell.

DOLL You've started her off now. A lady did it.

MRS BETTERTON Can they write plays?

NELL Don't be old fashioned.

DOLL Mrs Betterton is old fashioned.

MRS BETTERTON That is correct. You may blame longevity. You know you have done quite well for yourself.

NELL Yes, I have.

MRS BETTERTON Quite well indeed. I should like to think that I had a hand in it.

NELL You did.

MRS BETTERTON That is like a chink of light.

DOLL That's nice. A chink of light.

MRS BETTERTON You are now opening your mouth with competence.

NELL I make half my lines up. They're quite funny.

MRS BETTERTON Let us commence.

DOLL We are commencing.

MRS BETTERTON Today's lesson – Affectation.

DOLL Come on, come on, where's her shilling? She ain't doing it for nothing.

NELL All right. All right. It's in me purse on the side.

DOLL Mrs Betterton is vastly experienced and won't do lessons for sod all.

NELL I always pay, don't I? You're getting above yourself.

DOLL You is above yourself. You are privileged to be in the presence of Mrs B's presence.

NELL Am I? I don't want any more lessons.

DOLL Yes you do.

NELL No I don't.

DOLL Yes you do.

MRS BETTERTON No, she does not.

Pause.

NELL He says he will buy me a house. A whole house. If I leave.

MRS BETTERTON If you leave?

NELL It will have a large park attached. Plus a couple of peacocks, a footman, cutlery, plate, silver salvers, a necklace, half a hundred weight of linen, best linen and the loan of a horse and carriage.

MRS BETTERTON That is a lot.

DOLL That is a fucking fortune.

MRS BETTERTON Yes, I can see that is a fucking fortune. It would be hard to turn down. I can see that.

NELL I'm not going because of what you think.

DOLL Ain't you?

NELL No. I had a feeling. I never had it before. In my gut. Like there was something curled there. Something ready to spread round my whole body. I never had it before. Not like that. A feeling.

MRS BETTERTON Fear.

NELL Yes. That's what it was. I woke up and suddenly I couldn't imagine what comes next. I tried to imagine but I couldn't. *(Pause.)* Nothing. If I stay here I'll just grow old and then what? *(exiting)* A house with a park. Children.

DOLL Bloody hell.

MRS BETTERTON gets up slowly.

DOLL You're not hearing them voices again?

MRS BETTERTON begins to recite Lady Macbeth's final speech. She does it wonderfully.

MRS BETTERTON Yet here's a spot. Out, damned spot! Out, I say! One, two why then 'tis time to do it. Hell is murky. Fie my lord, fie! A soldier and afeard? What need we fear who knows it, when none can call our power to account? Yet who'd have thought the old man to have so much blood in him? The Thane of Fife had a wife where is she now? What will these hands ne'er be clean? No more of that, my lord, no more of that; you mar all with this starting. Here's the smell of the blood still; all the perfumes of Arabia will not sweeten this little hand. Oh! Oh! Oh! Wash your hands, put on your night gown; look not so pale. I tell you once again, Banquo's buried; he cannot come out on's grave. Come, come, come, come, give me your hand what's done cannot be undone. To bed, to bed, to bed. *(Pause.)* I know why she went mad, Doll. It was the waiting. The waiting.

DOLL You've not gone mad, have you?

MRS BETTERTON Me? No. I'm just eccentric. Old and eccentric.

She exits.

SCENE NINE

The stage darkens. It is the nether world. DOLL warms herself by the fire.

NELL enters.

NELL Doll, Doll. Is that you, Doll?

Pause.

DOLL How was your house?

NELL Oh, you know. Lots of cushions.

DOLL Everyone said you was very happy.

NELL On the whole. We had our problems. Most couples do. Sometimes he'd go on and on about his dad. You know.

DOLL Well he would.

NELL Yeah. But it's not as if I ever met him. My mum died pissed with her head in a puddle. I don't go on about it, do I?

DOLL I can see your point.

NELL You expect more off of a monarch. *(Pause.)* I had me picture done. Stark naked. He'd sit and look at it for ages. Just him looking at me and the room'd turn dark. Hours, and the room'd turn dark. *(Pause.)* I couldn't sleep some nights. The house seemed empty.

DOLL Big places do.

NELL Sometimes I'd get restless. Restless. *(Pause.)* Still. I never did nothing I didn't want to. Did I? *(Pause.)* Eh, Doll?

DOLL You don't see nothing. Do ya? Playhouse Creatures, they called you. And them was the polite ones. Like you was animals.

NELL Animals?

DOLL Before this place turned playhouse it was a bear pit. My dad was the bear keeper. One day this bear turned on him. The whip came down and down on her but still she came. She slashed his chest, here to here. That night they took out her claws and teeth. Ripped em out. And she howled and screamed and rocked in pain. It woke me and I ran in. There was blood on the floor. 'No, Dad, no,' I says. And he said, 'You let one of them get away with it and tomorrow none of them bears'll dance'. The bear had gone still and her head was hanging and I said 'Why should you whip her?' He took my hand and put it in the blood that was on the floor and then he wiped more on my face. 'She dances and we eat meat,' he said. 'Never let me hear you speak on it again.' The blood was warm at first and then it started to go cold on me and it seemed to turn me cold. I never did say nothing again. *(Pause.)* 'Playhouse Creatures' they called you, like you was animals..

NELL But we spoke and we was the first!

DOLL And where did that get you?

Pause.

NELL I'm going to do an epilogue. Do it with us? For old time's sake?

DOLL I can't remember no epilogues. My minds's prone to wander.

NELL We'll make one up. Go on, Doll. I'm going to dedicate it to Mrs Betterton.

DOLL Mrs B?

NELL Yeah.

DOLL She'd have liked that.

NELL Yeah. Look around. There's no-one here, Doll. Just us. Those promises we made. They're old. Dust. Now we can say what we like.

DOLL What will we say?

NELL Anything. Now we can say anything.

They come forward together as if to begin an epilogue. The lights go down.

Curtain.

The end.

PREFACE TO GOLIATH

Making *Goliath* was a joy. Beginning with Beatrix Campbell's book of the same name, I got to construct testimonies of 19 or so characters.

I worked with Female Titans. Beatrix, director Annie Castledine, Kendra Ulyart, Jenny Kagan, lone male Mic Pool, the many women and men and policeman desperately trying to look out for the disillusioned and disaffected young men in Cardiff, The Blackbird Leys Estate, Newcastle, and playing EVERYTHING... the incomparable Nichola McAuliffe.

It played venues all over the country and finished at The Bush. I remember thinking "the spaces we get are all approached round the side. Our audiences never get to come in through the front door..." It was fuelled by fierce collective white heat rage.

Bryony Lavery

Nichola McAuliffe in *Goliath* by Bryony Lavery
Photo © Simon Annand 1997

GOLIATH

BRYONY LAVERY

Goliath was commissioned by Sphinx Theatre Company. It made its debut at the Gulbenkian Studio, Newcastle Playhouse, on 13 February 1997, as part of a National Tour.

Director	Annie Castledine
Designer	Kendra Ulyart
Lighting	Jenny Kagan
Sound design	Mic Pool
Performed by	Nichola McAuliffe

Based on the book *Goliath: Britain's Dangerous Places* by Beatrix Campbell.

All roles can be played by a solo performer.

PROLOGUE

We are in Great Britain somewhere. Somewhere poor. Where urban meets rural. Buildings... their innards and carapaces. Walls low and high, a patch of scrubby grass, a small piece of sky... Water, Air, Metal, Fire, Wood present.

Night is falling...

CHORUS *(sings) 'This Scept'red Isle'*

A woman, alone, in a glass building...

Listens with careful attention to... pre-recorded voice.

GAUNT This royal throne of kings, this scept'rd isle,
This earth of majesty, this seat of Mars,
this other Eden, demi-paradise,
This fortress built by Nature for herself
Against infection and the hand of war,
This happy breed of men, this little world,
This precious stone set in the silver sea,
Which serves it in the office of a wall,
Or as a moat defensive to a house,
Against the envy of less happier lands;
This blessed plot, this earth, this realm, this England,
This nurse, this teeming womb of...

Breaks off. Listens... far off, the approaching sound of a fast driven car... as...

A SCANNER

The uncertain levels, uneven audibility, crackles...

Listens again to...

SCANNER It's a fucking dark fucking night...
on the job, Sarge... we're on...
what's that... Albion... Albion road, Sarge...
A193... it's the A193... It's a red Cosworth...
guess what another fucking Cosworth!!!...

trying to get... cccccccccc... catch up... they're
doing about 90, man... fuck... fuck... Dave...
can you... *chase* the cunts... shlllllllll...
we're on Tynemouth... oh... oh... oh... I can
see a number... it's... M reg... Dave, fuck... 234...
Apple Delta Orange... got that control...
they're looking to... Dave, they're...
they're going left fucking cunt
are goingggggggggchhhhhhhhhhhh...
they're heading for the Marden...
Dave, they're taking the coast road – they're
they're heading for Whitley Bay... fucking cunts
are taking us for a fucking day trip tonight to the fucking seaside!!!!
That's cheeky... that's very cheeky...
yes, sarge?... Monte 234 Apple Delta Orange...
yeah... yeah... it's stolen?... weeelll...
(Bad Cilla Black impersonation...)
"Surprise Surprise!!!"
Oh, shite, they've got a straight road they've got a straight road frrrrrrcccccccccccc...
Haway, Dave, let's race the cunts!
they're going to be in fucking Northumberland!!!!
...it's got to be our collar... No other manor's going to cop for ittttt... fuck! look at the dial, man!
fuck! one hundred and twenty nine, man!
one hundred and twenty nine!
Fuck!
Wey-hey-ye-a
Wey-hey-ye-o!!!!
they're fucking giving it!
Stay with them, Dave...
stay... aw, man, this is the *business*!

Whoomph of loud explosion.

They've *crunched*!

they've hit a... lamp-post!
they've hit a lamp-post!
car's spun...
they've hit a wall...
it's bounced...
fuck...
we've got them...
we've got the cunts!
we've got a Result!!!!!

"Whoomp" of another explosion... lit by burning red flames.

Fucker's gone up!
Fucker's exploded!
Christ!
Sarge... the vehicle's met with a...
fuck
fuck
fuck!!!!
it's on fucking fire!... yeah...
get the... Sarge get the...
fire service, yeah...
ambulance, yeah...
two, I think...
two, yeah...
two of em yeah...

The woman slowly becomes...

THE DRIVER

A young man, Gary, newly dead.

DRIVER tha lamp-post stops the car dead
but ah keep going!
Through everything!
Fucking speed...
Fucking hundred and twenty miles per hour!

Fucking speed's in me!
Ah'm fucking flying! Fucking Superman!
"You'll believe a man can fly!"
Ah'm air and moving and speed!
Ma neck breaks.
Whack!
Fucking deadly whiplash, man!
Did ya "Belt up"? Did ah fuck!
I'm still gannen forward at a hundred and twenty...
Steering wheel sinks a punch through
ma ribs fucking Chris Eubank...
fucking Mike Tyson. Yessss!
Ah hit the Cosworth the Cosworth hits wa
Heavyweight Contest!
The impact dislocates ma wrists yeah
and ma ankles yeah ah'm Andy fucking
Pandy man no no no Thunderbirds Are Go
Ah'm fucking Parker getting oota tha Roller!
(*Parker impersonation...*)
"Haway, Lady Penelope, shag this!" Ma legs have come up bent...
ah've kneed the dashboard...
them Cosworths are fucking well-built, man... ma knee caps crumble...
it's like hitting fucking
digestive biscuits with a hammer!!
Oooooooffffffp
Something sharp... ah cannet see...
has gone into ma heart...
there's blood... [everywhere...]
there's something everything leaking out of wa...
blood and piss and shite and something oozing oota ma ears something burst there...
and something's leaving wa...
something's off away... [up]
and...

and...
and...
(A huge sound of air.)
(A huge realisation enters him.)
Ah'm fucking dead!
(Pause. He is immobilised by the thought. It will not enter him. So...)
Then... shooom!... Cosworth's a fucking
firework display...
ah can smell maself burning
ah smell like pork.
Ah'm a fucking Sunday Joint.
(Pause – Still the thought will not enter him.)
(Another escape of air.)
Now, it gets geat weird!
Ah'm oot the car
and ah'm sort of... [up]...
and ah can see... me... there still...
but ah'm outside wa...
look at that look at that
that's what ah look like!
(He looks with intense interest.
He is up above somehow.)
Ah'm bigger than ah thought. Ah'm older.
Ah'm canny.
Coppers are pulling someone oota tha passenger seat... it's...
its...
oh...
it's...
my...
No. Shhhhh.
Ah don't think about that.
(Shakes his head fiercely.)
So.

They cannet pull wa oot.
Me and the car's inseparable.
Ma mouth's open
like a geat bairn
ah'm shouting
ah'm shouting
ah'm shouting
"Maaaaaaaaaaaaaaaaaaam!!!!"

The sound of babies crying all over the space.

GAUNT This land of such dear souls, this dear dear land
Dear for her reputation through the world...

England, bound in with the triumphant sea
Whose rocky shore beats back the envious siege
Of watery Neptune, is now bound in with shame

That England, that was wont to conquer others
Hath made a shameful conquest of itself...

END OF PROLOGUE.

Beautiful, sad music...

The woman becomes, turn by turn, the following characters...

ACT ONE – ELY CARDIFF

A RETAIL DISPUTE.

RASUL, a polite, very tired, very angry Asian man in his thirties. Strong traces of Pakistani accent. He is in his grocer's shop.

RASUL I am successful business man.

I have a grocery shop in Watson Road
wise capital investment has allowed me
chilling and freezer equipment large stock
good turnover
I am doing okay
I have also
fortified my shop because of incidents
incidents such as....

He has a dog-eared notebook to which he refers now and then...

1987 – van set alight
such as
same year – abused by young men
such as
1988 – abused by drunken customer
such as
1989 – annoyance cause by youths
such as
1989 – my car set alight
1989 – my arm broken
(He may favour this arm and flex it at times...)
1989 – lock of my shop door superglued
1990 – eggs thrown at shop
1991 – 1 January - windows broken

3 January – annoyance by youths calling names, causing aggravation in shop.

17 May – petrol bomb thrown at my shop after it had closed, at 11.15pm...

these are incidents I report to the police...

others...
(He shrugs.) I have
shutters
an alarm
an anti-theft device which allows me to detain a shoplifter by throwing a switch under the counter,
which locks the door.

I live above the shop in my flat.
next door, from two years ago, is a newsagent.
white.
Mr. Colemmis.
I do well
He does not.
(RASUL holds views on why this is.)
I am abiding by a restrictive covenant
from the original owner,
which says what we can and cannot sell.
Newsagent cannot sell food!
Soon as he comes here, Mr. Colemmis starts selling food
as well as newspapers
sweets
cigarettes
I protest...
he takes his case to the Racial Equality Council
his complaints about *business competition* to a racial equality forum!
(He shrugs... where else?) I am encouraged by the leaders of my community to make sure I do not
by my own behaviour,
expose myself to criticism
the newsagent is encouraged to challenge the covenant in court
he continues to take his complaints to the Racial Equality Council...
his economic grievances!
he is never racist

it is never racist

no

Tuesday, 27th August...

the court finds in my favour and upholds the covenant!

I am granted an injunction preventing Mr. Colemmis from selling groceries.

He is ordered to pay me £3000

compensation for lost trade.

I am vindicated.

THE SMALL BUSINESS

NAN COLEMMIS, a slightly-drugged down looking Welshwoman. Light Cardiff accent. Dull delivery of one picking thoughts carefully.

Wife of MAX, newsagent, of Watson Road. She is in "Nan's News", her newsagents shop.

NAN Oh no!

No!

No way!

You can't pin that one on us! This isn't a race thing!

My *husband's family's* originally from *Cyprus*!

They wasn't born yere! S'not racist this.

We're just trying to make a decent living!

You try making a small business like this go!

You've got to diversify...

otherwise people just get everything up town!

Folk *want* us to sell bread and milk here.

They *prefer* to have a choice of shop.

That's not racist, that's free enterprise!

That's competitive!

You've got to make it work anyway you can!

£3000 Fine. That's out of order.

Where are we going to get £3000?

We haven't got that kind of money. Everybody's furious!

Everybody!
Max's cousin Megan said "That's it!
I'm getting up a petition!
They can't do this. Not yere!"
She's round the estate, knocking on doors...
Max is wild. Wild.
Today...
He says "Give us a felt tip!
writes on a piece of card
sticks it in the window!
"because of our good neighbours next door,
from 27th August
we regret we can no longer sell you bread,
milk, or other food."
Then everybody knows what's going on!
E's restricting our freedom!
Everybody's on our side in this one...
Everybody.

You watch!

ANOTHER HOT, HOT DAY.

RASUL, in his shop, hot August day. His notebook.

RASUL Wednesday, 28 August.
Another hot hot day.
I catch a thief
I lock the door
flick the switch under the counter
wait for the police to come

the thief
youth
in his twenties
can of beer, drunk
shouts racial abuse
(RASUL shrugs, what else?)
then he escapes from me...
but he throws himself through the plate glass door...
police arrive
while they are interviewing me
their car is stoned
a gang outside shout at me abuse
police call for reinforcements
no arrests

until late at night
from my flat....
I hear glass breaking downstairs

my wife is terrified
children cry
can't sleep

Thursday

a gang gather outside my shop
people come into my shop
spit at me

complain about "greedy Paki bastards" say
"Why can't white men sell bread when you can?"

Friday morning...
The police urge Mr. Collemmis to remove his cardboard notice
although it does not constitute an offence under the public order act
it is felt to be provocative...
they check out on their radio
whether it is incitement to racial hatred...
they conclude it is not.

just before eight pm...
my windows smashed.
I call the police again say
"They smashed my windows last night and they are doing the same tonight!"

10p.m.
I close the shop.
A crowd of about thirty people hanging around outside...
It is not safe to sleep upstairs.
I need a police escort to get out...

Crowd of young white men outside the pub drinking
jeer at the police car... we just drive past them... away...

I am tired.

EQUAL UNDER THE LAW

Donald Turvey, ex-policeman. Late fifties. Out-of-condition, smoker, overweight, deliberate, heavy. Ponderous, almost continuous speech. Retired, but bored... He has plenty of time for opinions...

DONALD TURVEY Well I think in the police force you find a complex of prejudiced minorities. For example you might find that a certain number of police officers would be prejudiced against taxi drivers, bus drivers or against Jewish people.

But I think that colour prejudice is virtually absolute. In other words, it extends to probably 99% Senior officers...? No they didn't counteract it... either they were unaware or they just chose to ignore it... When we talked among ourselves about coloured people... I suppose our general attitude was one of looking on them as inferior people...

There's this sort of hardman cult which exists among the lower ranks and this requires a young man to prove himself in many ways... mainly it requires him to prove himself by the number of arrests he makes...

in relation to coloured people the old tradition would be that the coloured man is not fully aware of his rights as a white man would be and on this assumption I suppose he would be more vulnerable...

How do I feel about that?

...well, it's very difficult to preserve any individual views that one might have at the outset. It's uh you get carried along with the tide. Very difficult.

I mean, yeah, you feel like objecting; I don't know. I can't speak for everyone, but I felt like objecting on a few occasions, but it would have been out of the question.

It would have been socially unacceptable within the police force...

"BOWLAIS TWINNED WITH BEIRUT"

SUE PARRY, shopper, mother of two young teenage sons... lives on the estate near Watson Road. Enjoying the constant sun and the vibrant excitement of having, in her view, a number of righteous causes keeps a vigilant eye from a low stool in her scrappy, threadbare front garden... The ugly, triumphant expression of one given a hearing for bearing hatred...

Sounds of an agreeing chorus of young boys occasionally back up her assertions...

SUE PARRY That shop'll go up
Thass history that shop.
Soon e's gone that'll be it
Soon e's gone that'll end it then
it'll stop that'll be it.
We bin waiting four days now. We can wait some more!
(As if asked the question "How do you feel about that?" from somebody near right.)
they deserve everything they get far as I'm concerned
Loaf a bread at Nan's five pee cheaper than at his...
makes a difference to your pocket!
nobody round yere's got much money see, e's not been
yere in this country long enough to understand that, see...
not like Max...
Max been yere thirty year
been yere long enough to be
like us...
(As if asked about the crowds of kids hanging about...)
all these kids hanging around now
– they're all wasted –
thass not having enough to do...
(She points over left...)
two weeks outta six weeks
thass all that club's been open
two weeks outta six weeks!
this estate's gone back twenty-five years

we had cinemas
pool hall all closed...
it's like they're all across the road
they say we're off up The Raid!

that's what they do for boredom
bit of excitement

I think he'll go
he'll move
that shop will go up
S'only because the police are yere
there's no damage
his windows have gone
but thass nothing
s'not going to stop tonight
No way
Noooooooo!
Police doan say wass going on yere
We say wass going on yere!
(Shouts towards the parade...)
Pakis out!
Kill the pigs!
Fuck off back to Fairwater!
(She is immensely righteous, joyful, alive.)
Make my Saturday!
Blow it up!

"COOLING OUT"

RITU BARRY, REC Director, an ex-academic, bright, angry. She is worn out. She is constantly in contact with a telephone. Indian Brahmin intelligentsia...

RITU This is the part of my job I hate most,
the very moment I feel impelled to exert control
upon the black communities –
the phrase I use is "cooling out"
I know I am acting as an agent of control
on behalf of white agencies...
(Breaks off... speaks into the phone...)
...yes... yes... I understand but you see
I am keen that our young boys do not mobilise and fight back;
I do not want them ending up in court!...
yes, yes... you must tell them...
(Back to us... as she waits...)
It seems sensible
but I hate doing it
- telling Pakistani groups -
"Thank you, but don't come.
Stay off the streets.
Don't put yourself in the wrong."
(She sighs... immediately stops, talks to phone...)
you must reassure every group
that I have received assurances from
the police that they *will* record the incidents
as racially motivated...
they *will.*
this time they,
at least they are giving protection...
yes. I know
I know...
(To us...) The Pakistani Hockey team is in Cardiff

this weekend as part of a goodwill tour
and since the city is host to many
Asians arriving to watch the world champions...
we are fortunate
(Breaks off to talk into phone...)
I'm just saying
the Ethnic Affairs unit is on duty...
to make sure no-one gets involved in Rasul's troubles
(Breaks off... listens... then in Punjabi into the phone, urgently.)
Tandare! *[stay calm.]*
Tandare okay? *[calm down okay?]*
Miino pata tu ki sothidee herr...
[I know what you are thinking]
Mino pata. *[I know]*
Okay
Kosh na curi *[don't do anything.]*
Gerudi ah raccana law and order...
[It is important to maintain law and order...]
Okay.
(Back to us...)
I do what our brief seems to require
– to circulate within a black orbit –
– to create calm –
– to maintain a commitment to "law and order"

So, the black community is calmed.
The white community is not.
We manage our angry young men.
Who manages theirs?

CHOCOLATE BISCUIT BOY

CRAIG, a deeply-tanned, handsome, ordinary Welsh youth... full of uncomplicated testosterone... very lighthearted... as if he is a player in a hard-fought football match...

CRAIG I just come up to see what's going on!

(He looks around.)

I use the shop myself!

I've no views on the dispute!

I've been fishing all day Saturday!

Come up yere tonight...

Evrybody's just standing about!

Buying chips!

Cans from the offy!

Police are there

(About 200 yards away...)

We're here!

What they gonna do?

What we gonna do?

(It is Mexican standoff... very exciting. He is feeling very powerful.)

All they done so far is drive the Paki guy in and out...

An stand there eyeballing us.

Somebody behind me goes

"there's going to be a barbecue tonight

and there's pork on the menu.

You're going to burn, man."

Just lighthearted banter, like...

(He sees...)

...police car drives up...

parks by all the coppers...

so we're [chanting] "CID CID"

the driver goes...

(Beckoning motion with finger... police directing traffic-style...)

come over here

...this hard lad goes up to the car
"Don't talk to me, I don't want to know you"...
...the pig gets out of the car
"don't you fucking swear at me...
come here you, come here..."
... the hard lad just walks back and sits on the wall
... the old bill's tryna take him
... the hard lad's holding on to the wall...
then another copper comes and says
"leave him, leave him..."
they've gone back in the car.
someone's chucked a brick
then some bottles
and cans
and up go the riot shields
down go the helmets
there's *real* chucking now
some Big Cheese shouts through a loudhailer...
(Makes his hands like a loudhailer...)
"Go Home. Now. I am telling you to GO-HOME!"
(His face changes.)
We fucking *are* home.
(Pause. Stares aggressively.)
It's dark now.
(He rubs his belly abstractedly.)
I've got all me snap from fishing.
(To all about him...)
"Anybody wanna sandwich?
Smoky Bacon Crisps?"
I've got some chocolate biscuits left....
"Biscuit, anybody?"
(He holds out a chocolate biscuit wrapped on silver foil...)
the copper shouts

"metal objects.... put away the metal objects"
he's only talking about my fucking chocolate biscuits in
fucking silver paper...
(He jokingly demonstrates threatening with a chocolate biscuit.)
"bit of choccy biccy, piggy?"

and he's "Right fucker,
I'm having you"
And here they come
they're whacking us
giving it boot
two of them are pulling us towards the van...
one pushes his fingers up my nose
pulls my head back, going to the van...
Man...!
and the driver says "Fucking close the doors,
there's cameras out there! Let's go, let's go!"
...I'm not getting in that van...
they'll kill us so...
(He runs back.)
I'm running and
through the crowd and I see this fellow climbing...
I follow him up onto the roof of the chippy
(He does.)
and up here he's saying
"I've lost me son.
I've lost him in the crowd.
I've just come up here
So I can see where he is..."
the police are shouting "Get down here"
...this fellow has a wobbly... he can't move
...so we both sit down on the
(He makes a V of his fingers.)

this of the roof… police are going
"Come down"…
(Shout) "No, you'll beat us up" and then…
(Helicopter sound.)
Fucking blinding light…

Blinding light above. He looks up into it… shouts challengingly with all his voice…

Yeaaaaaaaaaaahhhhhh…
Bastards?????????

CHANGE OF MOOD

DEMMS WILLIAMS, toppish brass, police spokesperson… experienced policeman and used to speaking in public. Strong, confident, experienced… sometimes his lower-middle-class roots emerge…

DEMMS … can I assure you that it is my first priority

to have *no* police presence in Ely…
we are adopting a softly-softly approach…
with minimum uniform presence
and we have only used sufficient force as is absolutely necessary.
our tactics are fully justified
the helicopter is picking out
pockets of violence
back-up teams are waiting to move in

we've tried to police 'em conventionally earlier on.
that was deployed earlier this evening…
having said that…
once missiles started to be thrown…
at our officers
the commanders have no alternative but to deploy officers
in protective clothing but we hope.
that the officers will be able to contain it
but the mood changes
the mood changes very quickly

and it's extremely difficult for officers on the ground to judge when that change of mood is gonna take place...

the grocer's shop is no longer targeted
we believe that the crowd has lost sight of the original grievance...
it's just being used as an excuse
to carry on and cause trouble
by known trouble-makers...

Thank You.

A SECRET ADDRESS IN BIRMINGHAM

RASUL is out of his shop, out of his city...

RASUL Please don't give out this address.
My wife and children are in Pakistan
I have told them to stay there for their safety.
I may never be able to return to my home and business in Cardiff because the Ely community is against me...
Before Friday it was just a minority of three, four families who were against us...
But when you see a crowd of 400 or 500 people staying all weekend you know it is more than that

When we were in the flat
we could hear the crowd outside
banging on the windows and screaming
"Bomb the Pakis"

I feel betrayed.
I have two children to think of.
If I went back now I think all of our lives would be at risk.

I was happy in Cardiff but now I feel the whole
community has been stirred up and is against me

There were no Asians in that crowd.
The majority were white.
If the dispute had been between two Asian shopkeepers
or two white shopkeepers
this would not have happened.
(Pause. As if asked an expected question.)
I left Pakistan twenty-two years ago.
(Pause.)
I've nothing against Britain for what has happened
(Pause.)
I will read my country's newspapers
(He is trembling...)
I will read about the disturbance
my disturbance...
the white participants in this
will be given an alibi...
to dignify their actions
turn it into decent history...
their disgustingness will be turned into a *real* problem...
reasonable citizens rebelling against
an unreasonable trader
in a dispute over bread.

No racist undertones
dignity
history

Beautiful, elegaic music plays as...

END OF ACT ONE.

ACT TWO – BLACKBIRD LEYS, OXFORD

"ONLY MUGS WORK"

ANDY, sixteen years old, a weasely, ferrety youth whose pretensions to "toughness" and "gangsterdom" sit uneasily and comically with his soft Oxfordshire accent. He wants to show off his business acumen, gang-belonging and brilliant police-baffling activities... He wants to do all the activities he describes... expert in what is done rather than having done it.

ANDY There's always ways of having cash in your pocket.
Only mugs work.
When there's a burn we tell everybody
"there's gonna be a Display"
and we charge a quid to watch
two quid for outsiders
now we got our *manifesto...*
(Quotes or reads from it...)
"in taking performance cars and making them perform we
the joyriders demonstrate the proper use of all
technology... its use for fun!
To live as we choose we must suppress those who choose how we live..."
(He is incredibly impressed and uplifted by this...)
that's twenty quid...

Mostly journalists and them buy it
You want one you ask *us*
The Blackbird Leys Massives...
not The Posse
and *not* The Rizla Massives...
and that goes for videos
we do the videos so you can watch us
in the comfort of your own homes...
us!

you got stealers who go out
and steal the car
you break in with a centre punch or a screwdriver, rip off
the plastic round the ignition, hot wire the motor...
twenty seconds tops!
stealer goes out and maybe spends all day looking to get the cars
Ten times outta ten
the display driver is not him who got the car...

Then sometimes a hoarder keeps
a car hidden away for a meeting on another night.
but very often it's used that night...
the people who nick the cars get a buzz out of watching it
it's because people want to see the display they nick them
they come out to the shops and they say
“there's a car parked”
by the shops is good
because it's wide
and it's the main bit of Blackbird Leys

it gives everyone a buzz, a bit of
excitement.
What's the harm?
sometimes, if the car spins really well,
the driver gets out and bows to the crowd
then he walks away shouting
“I'm bad, I'm bad”
(This is incredibly worthy of respect...)
the motor is handed over to a driver
and he goes blaring the horn
and screeching the horn
and that's to bring the crowds
that's to let 'em know

there's gonna be a burn...

we don't do it at 3 o'clock in the afternoon...
(As if...)
because that would be dangerous
but we do it any time after ten o'clock.
Anyone who came into Blackbird Leys
after that would know as soon
as they hit the shops they had to beware
because a car could pop out of anywhere...
(Sound of car revving over this...)
it's not a no-go area
it's just that people know they've got to be careful and that
the driver is the one calling the shots...

The coppers call this place "The Jungle"
... soon as we hear that
we know they're coming

we know all about them
who what shifts
electric ears
mind readers
brain scanners

the "family" know they're on the way
before they're out of first gear...

A NEW BROOM

THE CHIEF CONSTABLE... new, nervy, education overlaying a simple country bobby. His "Izat" has been challenged. This is unacceptable, but entirely unacknowledged...

CHIEF We are responding to the criticism by
a Blackbird Leys member of the city council that
"the people of Blackbird Leys are coming
to the conclusion that the Chief Constable
has lost the ability to maintain law and order on the estate"
(He is furious at being criticised.)
I'm a New Broom.
I'll be Sweeping Very Clean!
We know these joyriders are just taking the mickey!

I have dispatched police
transit vans to the square
and apprehended participating youngsters
under the Public Order Act,
I am adopting a long-term strategy of working
with the community,
with the local council and with local agencies
and communicating to any person who we feel can help us

Statistics-wise...
In 1990, 2,395 cars were stolen
and 2,934 cars were burgled
in the first half of this year
car theft rose by 10%
theft from cars by 29%
Car thefts in Oxford are running at about
four thefts a day

we refuse to be drawn into high-risk pursuits
and these jokers exploit that fact!

We have received a lot of information
a lot of information
from people on the estate
that these youths are going to take retribution
for the earlier police action.
This information contains two factors.
One, that the police will be attacked and
Two, that petrol bombs will be used in the attack...
therefore I have no alternative but to instigate maximum uniform presence...

"LAW OF THE JUNGLE"

THE DON, unlike ANDY, is the driver. Arrives with all the presence of a top performance vehicle. Top cock of the walk. Immaculately dressed, very powerful, very confident. Full of energy, which he contains or unleashes at will. Oxford accent. Waiting in his stolen car.

THE DON You're afraid, fuzz
What can you do anyway, wanker?
Upper hand Plod.

you see a bad boy car and you say to yourself,
yeah, yeah,
I'll have some of that
I'll say to myself that if the police come
they can't catch me.
If I'm in a stolen car
the police have to be fucking good to catch me.
The police have chased me on many occasions.
(Presses a button, rap music plays as...)
ya cyan reach down pon Oxford
a driven a bran new Astra
Lef it pon de street
I man go tief it from you Rasta

A Golf GT wid a eris alloy wheel,
Bring it ere nub man an leh we see ow it feel
De M40 is de wrong place fuh you,
Luhn a fickle respeck or me go box yah face for you

Me nuh belong to de lef
Me nuh belong to de right
Drive tru de shit in de middle of de night
(He smiles)
chic dude
ironed tee-shirt
sharp crease in the sleeve
never a wrong wrinkle
trainers
accessories... scanner...
access to radio technology – yeah

young boy at de shop
doing a handbrake turn
pure display
de handbrake turn
but de A34 there's no handbrake turn
no spectactor fe look, an no fe he learn

I'll come out when I'm ready
say eleven o'clock
I can sit out there
and the Babylon come out there in force
but I can sit there till two or three o'clock
in the morning and then I can come out
and do what I'm gonna do...

at the end of the day
there is no-one who goes out to display
who does not believe, in themselves
that they will be getting chased
If you go out there you have to expect to get chased
it's a educated risk.

we can guarantee a police presence
we're irresistible
we just stay there till they come
the main thing is to get in there
and have one over on the babylon

lovely night
I'm the Don!
I am The Don!
I wear the trousers!
What I say *goes*!
everybody wants to be boss of something,
I want to be boss of Blackbird Leys!

He dresses for action... takes a dangerous catapult and loads it as...

REPORTER ...the incident which ignited the riots...
on the evening of Thursday, 29th of August...
was when police officers, led by Superintendent Parr,
went to the Blackbird Leys estate,
where there was a blatant display of joyriding.
When he got to the estate,
Superintendent Parr saw a young man
in his late teens pull something up towards his shoulder.
It was a catapult,
which fired a piece of flint
at the police car.
With stunning accuracy,

it went through his window
and hit another officer...

MARRIED WITH BABY DAUGHTER

TONY MOORE, police constable, St. Aldate's, early twenties, gentle, slightly, charmingly slow.

MOORE I was looking out the side window
and saw this person with the catapult.
The stone came through the driver's window
and then smashed through the passenger's window

I think I was lucky
– had it hit me on the temple
– it might of killed me.

This is probably the worst we have had
in two years I have been here.
We have got to the stage where we're
just targets for these rascals.
It is very disruptive for quite a few police officers who are
having to change their shifts and work a lot later...
I'm married with a baby daughter –
It must be on the cards that one day somebody is going to
get seriously injured or possibly killed
2,040 vehicles
worth a total of £10 million
were stolen from between St Aldate's manor and Cowley...
I calculate that those cars...
put nose to bumper...
would stretch the three miles
as the crow flies between the two stations!

we are talking about young people
who wear designer clothes

some of them already own quite fancy cars
– they use £50 radio scanners –
these people are not deprived!
they're not the sort who take to the streets
because they've nothing to lose...

We've a few tales of brutality ourselves!
Keith... wossisname... anyway... from Cowley...
was temporarily blinded when a paving slab crashed through the windscreen of his car
When police officers are met with violence
we are entitled to use a certain amount of force to effect an arrest!

you know anything
confidential information
special answerphone service
St Aldate's police station
Oxford 791006
that's
Oxford 791006

ONE WHAT I FOUGHT FOR

HAROLD is a doddery, friendly, very deaf man in his seventies, hearing aid which he adjusts. Fought in Burma. Wounded. He is erecting a deck chair...

HAROLD there's nothing else for the kids to do!
they're just interested in cars!
Not breaking into houses!

When it happens I go out and watch!
It's the curiosity of watching Nigel Mansell driving at 90mph
this estate isn't dangerous
it was built for car-workers from Rover Cowley
it's a nice estate

your lad that does these stunts...
he doesn't rob banks
he doesn't hurt old people
he doesn't do it for profit.
latterly, these lads would have been employed over there...
(He points over the fields, where the towers of Cowley Car Works can be easily seen.)
the lad they caught outside the pub...
they were...
(He mimes...)
beating him with long batons...
like in South Africa...
instead of handcuffing him
they were just hitting him
knocking hell out of him
time after time
across his back
in front of everybody
outside 'The Blackbird'
(Each detail is impossible... an affront.)
if that's *England*!
there's going to be trouble...
if that's what you call community policing...
well...

It was hot all night
there was everybody out in deckchairs in their gardens
with sandwiches and flasks
like the seaside...

apparently it was from a catapult...
a piece of flint
(He demonstrates its size.)
the size of... what would you say...

a brazil nut.
the police car driver sees him
pull something up to his shoulder...
stunning accuracy...
through the window
just missed the both of them.

there was a police car *rammed.*
Why this now?
(He watches. The sky grows dark.)

BRILLIANT ESTATE

TOSH, a middle-aged dog-walker, ex-car-worker... originally from South London... moved to Oxford for work in his teens. Speaks while controlling his dog. Car noises whiz and race around him.

TOSH These youngsters are making our lives a misery!

You lie in bed late at night
and hear the tyres *screeching* as they race past the house.
They drive up and down Cuddeston Way
then wang up Blackbird Leys road
then back along Pegagus
ripping along
at incredible speeds
... it's a wonder no-one's been killed yet.

If it wasn't for the police our lives
wouldn't be worth living.
These last twelve years this estate...
it's really gone downhill.

Most people who live round here are afraid to go out at night.
You can't walk your dog after 10.15pm around here.
I won't come out after then because
I don't want my house wrecked.

I've had four cars parked outside
my house damaged in the last few months...
and some of those causing trouble can't be more than 14 or 15...
just what do their parents think they're up to
when they're allowed out all hours of the night?
I think the police are doing a damn good job... fantastic...
but I think this should have happened 18 months ago...
before the joyriders it was a brilliant estate...

I've seen parents with young children
and picnic chairs on the side of the road!
I cannot understand the mentality
of people who take young children out
to watch trouble they know is brewing!
There is no reason for it
and there never was!
If it rained they would all go home!
it isn't joyriding
it's death-riding.

"SHEER FUCKING JOY"

JOYRIDER, young, unidentifiable because of his balaclava helmet...

JOYRIDER I just want to be in a car
driving
my thing is driving round
nicking cars
just driving till all hours with the lads

when you get in the car
you're hyper hyper
you can never say when you're going to do it
or when you're not going to do it
you don't know that you will *not* take

a stolen car
you might see a car and you just want to be in it
you get the urge
you get hyper
you don't know why
you see a *bad boy* car
and you think to yourself, yeah, yeah.
I'll have some of that
not mine
mine
rev
rev
go

I'm a high performer
in high performance cars
I throw it about
like money
no fucking old banger
no fucking family saloon
my fucking Dad *made* cars
I fucking *ride* them
something with
enough speed for the space
enough power in its pants
I've no job
no wage
no property
no car
no responsibility
one thing I've got
a reputation

I pick it up
give it a real burn
power
machinery
speed
transcendence
the howl of a handbrake turn
the scream of speed
gliding
dancing
skating
man tangos with machine
rude and red
the Maestro is my perfect dancing partner

it's doing it
they're impotent

it's not a star among cars
the Maestro
but it's strong
it can swing
mainstream motor
the performance is witty
as well as piquant
I make it more than a Maestro
I toss it into an *immaculate* handbrake turn
hit the horn
sweep into the wings
performance matters
mainstream motor
star performance
it's wild

it's Silverstone

Mecca

Cars

spinning around

smashing into walls

(goody-goody voice) “why don't we give these lads a dirty old car in a dirty old field?

let them drive around like that?”

who'd want to do that?

“TRAX” yoof initiative...

fuck off!

it's stardom

it's quality of life

what's joyriding about?

Joy

Joy

fucking cunting bastard Joy!

END OF ACT TWO.

ACT THREE – MEADOWELL CHORUS

(Sound of driving into...)
(Sung) Land of Hope and Glory...
Mother of the Free
Mother of the
Mother of the...
(Sound of driving accelerates into...)

GARY Fucking speed...
Fucking hundred and twenty miles per hour!
Fucking speed's in me!

SCANNER Ah'm fucking flying!
Fucking Superman...!!!
... A193 it's the A193... it's a red Cosworth
guess what, sarge,
another fucking stolen red Cosworth...
haway let's chase the cunts!!!!!
(Driving ends in huge explosion as...)
They've crunched!
They've hit a lamp-post!
car's spun

it's bounced

we've got them...
we've got the cunts!
we've got a Result!!!!!
(Another huge explosion as...)

SCANNER Fucker's gone up!
Fucker's exploded!
Christ!

GARY Ah'm fucking dead!!!!!
Maaaaaaaaaaaaaaammmmmmmm!

Maureen, Gary's mother, is sorting through his effects as...

VOICE Summer 1991.

Car crime rocketed.

In July the corpses of forty-seven stolen cars

ended up at Meadow Well estate, Tyneside.

In August the total reached fifty-two.

On Friday, September 6th two boys died

in a gruesome crash,

in a high-performance stolen car

after being chased by police along one of the coast roads.

They were consumed in flames

when the car crashed into a lamp-post at around

130mph and immediately blew up.

Their identities could be traced only through the teeth, keys

and jewellery

found among the remains...

Music over woman sorting through clothes.

A POTTERY SHEPHERDESS

MAUREEN, pregnant and married at sixteen, now in her late thirties, had a son, Gary, who was seventeen. Honest, loved her son who is a child to her, a bad lad to everybody else. Thin and vibrating with anxiety and depression. Woman of wood... stuck, harmless, kind, slow.

She is sorting out her dead son's effects. In her hands she carefully carries a rather pretty but awful pottery shepherdess ornament. She gives it a careful examination, turning it round, upside down...

MAUREEN Where did he get you?

You're a lovely lass but you've got "robbed" written all over you!

He comes in with it in a carrier bag

says "Happy Birthday, Mam"

and I'm pulled both ways like a turkey wishbone

he's remembered us birthday

but he's given us capo da monte knockoff!

I'm sure.

I said "Look me straight in the eye, Gary, and swear on
Nan's grave that you didn't steal Mam's present".
He looks me straight in the eye.
He says "Mam, I swear,"
cheeks don't flush up
looks as if butter wouldn't melt in his mouth
so I know he's lying.
I say "You're lying, Gary,"
he says "I'm not"
I say "If you just tell the truth, Gary, I won't be cross..."
He says "I am telling you the truth."
I says, "Well, I don't think you are."
He says, "Aw, well, if you don't believe us I'm fucking fucking off then"
and that's him gone...

She hears her own last word. It is unbearable.

CRAPPY PERSON

Saturday evening.

RUTH, a metallic, sharp woman, angular, late forties. Very clever but with no pleasure in her brains... they are merely utensils. Brisk and to the point. Woman of metal... sounds like knives sharpening, cutting and snipping... She is watching, waiting for something to happen.

RUTH Two of those daft hard buggers
Have got killed in a stolen bloody car...
and the whole estate is turning them
into bloody martyrs...!

It's hotting up....
there's lads hanging aboot
the Asian shops....
Mr. Singh at the chippy says
things don't feel right...
he's worried...

wa all using it as an excuse
to go on the *rampage*!
You watch!

I want my sons home!

Now!
(Think of something else...)
all this...

Before I come here
I'd no idea what poverty was...
I thought I was poor
but there's a difference between poor and poverty...
this is poverty here.

I started on things...
we did...
we do...
some of the women...
best thing we do is The Credit Union...
we formally launched it... 1984...
at the Advice Centre...
with a dozen members all saving £1 a week...
that's its only capital.

Members can borrow 20% above their savings
arrange their repayments with the loans committee...
me and other lasses.
We've done a survey on debt...
just in a couple of streets...
we calculate that an average of
£10 per week is leaving each house

in repayment of debt at rates that vary between 33% and 1000%!
We assume about half people's repayments went on interest.
That means an average of £5
leaving 2000 households
fifty-two weeks a year...
on interest alone!
Daylight bloody robbery!
We've started to turn all that around!

By beginning of this year...
Credit Union had about 400 members...
We're starting to make a difference to...
we organise stuff
Cedarwood Centre has washing machines
for folk to use...
a drop-in centre for lasses wi' bairns
we set up a Wellbeing Group
... local branch of Church Action Against Poverty
had a Women's Issues Group
and this came up with the idea of a food co-op!
From 1985 co-op's been going weekly to the Cash and Carry,
bringing back what basics we can manage and selling them...

and all this while contending with the lads locking us in
when we're havin meetings pulling the shutters down
lads shouting through the letterbox
"You can't get out unless you pay us £10,"
Whole estate's petrified, young and old... and...
it's *us*
lasses.

not *one* of them...
(Sudden shockingly personal change...)

The men never, never say they are proud of us!
My husband says "Who do you fucking think you are,
Jesus or somebody?
You think you can walk on water!
You just do it so people will think you are wonderful.
But you are just a fucking cunt, you neglect me, you neglect your kids, you neglect the house.
If you were a decent woman you would stay at home and look after me!"
He's a bloody *bairn*!

I get this all the time.
But he doesn't do any of it.
He complains about the bills.
They're *my* bills, he says.
I say yes, they are mine!
I use the washing machine,
I use the iron,
I use the cooker!

And now *this*...
and we're frightened...
he says...
"Now see what you've started..."

A disturbance... sound on tape... RUTH looks towards the sound, worried, as...

"THE LORD IS MY LOFTY CRAG"

Sunday evening.

HOPE, a calm black woman in her late sixties. Woman of water... forgiving, fluid, endlessly sympathetic... flowing, liquid speech patterns. West Indies lilt. Easy journey through a hard life. A Grandmother. She is listening to the radio... Evening Service.

HOPE "The Lord is my lofty crag
(Singing in a beautiful, quavery voice, The Song of David...)

my fortress
my champion
my God
my rock,
in whom I find shelter
my shield and sure defender
my strong tower
my refuge, my deliverer
who saves me from violence.
I shall call to the Lord
to whom all praise is due;
then I shall be made safe from my enemies..."
(She ponders the words...)
I don't think God gets up North much.
(A loud smashing of glass. HOPE looks through the window... cannot locate the sound but sees...)
That space there, that desert, that wilderness...
was once an old corporation depot
and it was a *disgrace*!
it was earmarked as a car park
it was earmarked as an allotment ground
it became neither
everybody tipped rubbish
I shouted and called and bawled so long and so loud that finally the girl from the Advice Centre said, "Well, Hope, you do something," so I did.
I created a Holy Trinity...
adults
advice centre
children
we asked everybody what *they* wanted
we surveyed the residents and found that 88% supported a play space.
So we launched a campaign.
All the schools supported us.
A group of girls from... I forget which school... designed a model.

Very clever.
And we rang and wrote and visited the council till eventually the council put up £140,000
for a glorious playground well equipped
good quality... *sturdy*... playground furniture... a playworker's hut,
and all of it surrounded by a fence.
The ribbon was cut just before the school holidays.
Summer 1986.
We thought we were in clover!
(She sighs, remembering...)
Top of the kids list of priorities
they wanted a parkie on the site...
they knew they would need protection...
we asked for money for a keeper to keep it safe.
No money, said the council.
(Girds her loins)
Well, never mind. We'll do it ourselves.
So, every day, on a rota,
we residents opened up the playground
and every night we locked it up.
Every Sunday we cleaned the site
Every Monday we discussed with
the council worker what needed to be repaired or replaced.
(Massages her tired face...)
After a year, we were tired.
Suddenly, the council employ a 'playworker'.
No consultation... no talking to us!
We felt taken for a ride.
Hurt.
Snubbed. Pride you know.
The council tried to patch it up.
Too late.
Sunday clean-up stopped.
Monday repair session ended.

Our lovely play site deteriorated.

The play organiser... nice young man... tried.
Organised swimming trips
competitions
parachute games...
but the bad lads... they tried to push him...
take his territory...
they set fire to his hut...
stole from it
stole from him...
he was defeated
(She thinks.)
we were defeated... by...
(Counts the reasons off...)
children's destruction...
damn poll tax cuts!
hopelessness.

It's like a wilderness now.

You're like everybody else, God...
You don't choose to live on
a council estate.
(A whoomph of an explosion... more glass shatters... Then excited cries of a crowd in the darkness...)
O lord, what are you letting them do now?

A POLICE MANAGER

ROWTON, a police officer... he is listening, slightly apart, to someone of lower rank dealing with phone calls from Meadowell... he is angry and impotent.

RUTH There's a great gang 'a lads gathering outside Collingwood Youth Centre...

will you send a police car or sommat.
(quoting) “Pigsville
The Bronx
Botany Bay
Vietnam...”
that's what my lads called Meadowell when I moved here...

HOPE I need to ax you for some help.
We have no lights.
An I can see something from my window...
I think something's burning...
Oh, dear God!
I think it's the barn, you know...
next to the Youth Centre...

ROWTON *(quoting)* “Meadowell?
We need to build a wall round
and throw raw meat over...”

SCANNER PC Sarge... we're withdrawing...
we're effecting a strategic withdrawal...
... cunts are stoning our fucking patrol vehicle...!

RUTH They're erecting barricades across Waterville Road now!
They've chopped down a tree!
What are you doing aboot it?

ROWTON *(quoting)* “A blot
A boil on the bum of the organisation”
that's what my lads called Meadowell
when I came here
“A boil on the bum of the organisation...”
and nobody was prepared to take penicillin
or go to the doctor about it...
So what happens?
the boil bursts...
(Urgent sirens scream across the space)

ROWTON (*to off)* The priority is to restore order... not make arrests!

(to us) There isn't a single copper hasn't had his nose twitching over this one...
It's been going off...
I've been smelling this for months!
I said back in *March*! we needed more lives on the ground....
needed somebody in there doing some *stroking*...
somebody to show the 5 per cent of Herberts who *do* want trouble that we're there for the 95 per cent who don't!
I said it!
Said we needed some *visible presence*,
couple of vans...
a few Pandas driving round the estate just showing we were *there*!
I said we needed to provide a service...
I filed a report!

Well....
Scrambled Eggs blocked it of course.
Suggestion was turned down at a higher level!
Meadowell was a problem,
But not a priority.
If you've got limited funds...
You only spend it on emergencies.
But not having the funds *makes* the emergencies...
Not providing the service *makes* the crisis!
It's cash
it's always cash
(An urgent phone ringing sound... perhaps a red light... as...)
Answer that!
Response!
Christ!!!!

RUTH This is the third time ah've called!

Where are the police?
Where are the police?

I've called three times!
Three times!
When is any of you lot coming to help wa?

I'm across from the shops...
there's folks gannen in and
haying stuff away!....

Interrupted by another line with....

HOPE ...someone thrown a petrol bomb now!
The Asian shop is burning!
everyone axing...
is the Sharmas still upstairs...???

ROWTON A riot...
you deal with it like a fire....
you seal it off you contain it
so it doesn't spread...
you cut off its supplies...
you hold it all in there until it burns itself out!

So I'm sitting here like a bloody wally
and I can't go in
while they torch and
smash and loot
teasing us
challenging...
saying "Come On Then, Take Us ON!"

and
I can't go in!
As a police officer,
your first priority is the safety of your men...
although they want to get stuck in...

our bloody psychopaths again their bloody psychopaths...
rapid response vehicles
big batons hard men big boots
"fan-fucking-tastic-Gov" !!!!!!

How am I going to be able to say
"Go out and be caring, lads" after this?
How are they ever going to see someone in uniform as same as them ?
How are they ever going to see
We're no different?
We're buggered!
(Urgent phone ringing, many lines. Red lights. He rushes towards them as...)
Someone *Answer* That!!!!!!

BINGO NIGHT

RUTH, in full "general in heat of battle" mode ... with a bottle of milk... tiny light in surrounding darkness. She is shocked.

RUTH Bingo night for pensioners
at the Community Rights centre...
I pop out for a bottle of milk...
and I notice lads lining the road down Waterville Road...

I just know this is it
I go back in and get all the pensioners out
I go home
I phone the police
I phone three times
I go down towards the shops
I can see men in their sixties crying.
People are saying
"Where are the police?"
I phone them again.
They say they cannat enter.

Lads are making sure they're cocks of the walk!
Then someone says
"Ridges substation's been petrol bombed!"
and... the whole estate goes dark.
Even the streets lights are oot.

people are shocked there's nae response.
I go trawling the streets to find
my family
my friends
everyone is fearful
flabbergasted

There's about two three hundred
up the shops
coming away with crates of beer!
you have to look sharp because
cars keep speeding in and oot of the area with nae lights!
(Helicopter sound.)
there's a helicopter circling!
(Furious contempt.)
they're looking at us from *high up*!
from a *long way away*!
wa must look like just a seething blob!
wa reduced to dark shadows seeping across the ground!
that's how they choose to see us!

Pause.

A bit after eleven
I meet my two bairns corning up Avon Avenue with Hope...
then
as if from nowhere
two police vans arrive
they're like the Keystone cops, man!

they jump out in riot gear
and go for two of our lads with their great truncheons!
We mothers say, "Haway, no man,
they're doing nothing..."
and the police shout
"Get in your fucking doors
and shut your windows...
Get in sluts!"
That's what we were hearing from them.
I say "That's not what you should be doing..."
naebody was cheeking, there was nae panic–
people were too frightened to panic
or ask questions
we accept everything
we just keep the peace.
we never ask questions
they were just being tough

I'll give em tough
Not one policeman has come by to say they're sorry...

WOR LATEST GAME

MAUREEN, more sorting. She finds an eternal-bow teapot.

MAUREEN He give us this.
Happy Wedding Anniversary, he says
Ah said, "Where's this from like?" He says, "A shop"
it's Eternal Bow
it's what ah've got everything in
but...
(Discovers a ghetto blaster...)
And *this* was on top of his
wardrobe underneath a jacket!
Now why's *that* d'you think?

ten he was...
this started...
one night he's in and oot tha kitchen
he opens ma purse
takes some money oot
says he wants to go oot for fish and chips
I say it's too late
his dad says nowt

he pesters and pesters
I gan
"Okay, but be back by ten"
and he was.
I said "good boy"

He's standing behind ma chair
Ah'm feeling funny
Ah say to my husband
"What's he daeing. like?"
His dad laughs and says
"He's pretending he's got a knife
and he's stabbing you in the neck."

I've found cider bottles under his bed
Ah think he had a drinking problem
on top of everything else!
he'd started being violent at home.
He hit wor.

Eleven
he wouldn't go to school
He was *my* problem

I took him to school
the head says “Oh, you're stopping?”
my lad says “No”
So the head says, “There's the door. Ooot”
Ah've tried.
Bloody school didn't.
Ah've learned him the most I could
how to read
how to write
how to tell the time...
hit wor and said I wor a grass.

I knew I was losing him to the streets last year

I discovered Gary in the *act* of breaking into
wor own newsagents...
where wor get wor tabs from!
I called the police from the call box.
They said “You're grassing your own son?”
I said “Yes”

They said, “We've picked up your son.
Are you coming to to get him?”
I said “No.
This is the only way I can think of to get help!”

It's done no good.
He was in and out of prison all the time.

I did love him.

"DAVID AND GOLIATH"

Monday evening. HOPE, in darkness, reading the Bible... the electricity and water supplies are off.

HOPE "They drew up their lines of battle,
the Philistines occupying a position
on one hill, and the Isrealites on another,
with a valley between them..."

oh, yes.
(Around her, the sounds, smells, sights of modem riot continue...)
"A champion came out from the Philistine camp,
a man named Goliath, from Gath;
he was over nine feet in height"

that's a big lad...
I wonder what his Mammy fed him...
(Reads from further down...)
The champion stood and shouted to the ranks of lsrael...
"choose your man to meet me
If he defeats and kills me in fair fight,
we shall become your slaves;
but if I vanquish and kill him,
you will be our slaves and serve us.
Here and now I challenge the ranks of lsrael.
Get me a man, and we will fight it out."

Philistines everywhere
Goliaths shouting and shouting
Where are you then, David?
(She stops and listens. She hears nothing. She looks round wildly for signs of God. She sees nothing. She quotes...)
"To the loyal you show yourself loyal
and blameless to the blameless

to the pure you show yourself pure
but skilful in your dealings with the perverse
You bring humble folk to safety
but humiliate those who look so high and mighty."
(In despair, she sings...)
Lord, you are my lamp;
my God will lighten my darkness.
with your help I storm a rampart;
by my God's aid I leap over a wall.

Philistines.
Israelites.
David.
Goliath.
You're all the same.
Lads with bricks!

Well, God, lad.
you should have been
my rock
my strong tower
my shield and strong defender

I've loved you all my life
always in my heart
Until you showed me what a godless place this is.

You don't listen to women, do you?
You don't like poor people.
I don't love you any more
I'm leaving you.

She is very frightened.

oh

oh

oh.

There is a massive, monumental explosion as the whole of everything blows up. All of Meadowwell, everything, blows up. Darkness.

END OF ACT THREE. Then, a new light...

AFTERMATH

ROWTON in the riot-torn space. Hopeless, ashamed, he picks things up, inspects them.

ROWTON Meadowell... exploded.

I went in for the aftermath.
I ordered an
Increased density of women police officers.
The organisation perceives that as their
strength
calming things down
tidying
cleaning
mopping up.

Smell of smoke everywhere
blackened buildings
looked like Belfast
or Beirut.

I accompanied some of the women to
the Community Rights Centre,
Avon Avenue...

we pass the Asian shops...
all wide open
they'd been looted most...
they'd clearly been a focus of attack...

the women open up the centre doors
they switch on
and
miraculously...
everything's working.
(A new, strong small light.)
they put the kettles on...
and people start trailing in for help.
people are in shock
they start turning up at the centre
saying they can't sleep,
terrified they'll burn in their beds....
place is like a war-zone
it was...

We are a concentrated, low-key presence
at Meadowell for two weeks.
Going from house to house,
everyone anywhere in the vicinity of the riots
got a visit from us.
We interviewed over six hundred people...
but we came away with only a handful of statements...
It's like most people said...
the riot was as much the police's fault as the lads...
I don't know....
CID was very disappointed
the evidence crisis was a strategic disaster
in July... at the trials...
nobody would testify...
and it turned out that the evidence-gathering camera
which had been logged as requested
put aboard the helicopter
at 22 hundred hours

on the night of the riot...
just hadn't been...
put aboard...
there was
therefore,
no independent police corroboration...

well...
my thirty's up next year...
I'm out of it.
I'll never make ACC.
Not "fast track".
No university degree.
I'll take early retirement...
take the time to...
take the time to...
spend a bit more time with my family...
my son's said a categoric "no" to a police career
I can't say I'm sorry...
I'd like to see him somewhere
he can be himself...
where he can be...
(Thinks until he has the word that means what he wants to say...)
effective

where his potential...
where he won't be...
wasted.
(The area, atmosphere, reminds him of something...)
"Then Mother said, "Right right young feller
I think it's a shame and a sin
For a lion to go and eat Albert
And after we've paid to come in..."

Then off they went to the Police Station
In front of the Magistrate chap
They told him what happened to Albert
and proved it by showing his cap.

The Magistrate gave his opinion
That no-one was really to blame
And he said that he hoped the Ramsbothams
would have further sons to their name...

At that Mother got proper blazing
"And thank you, sir, kindly" said she
"What, waste all our lives raising children
To feed ruddy Lions? Not Me!!!"

Lights fade slowly...

The end.

PREFACE TO THE SNOW PALACE

Imagine trying to enter a tangled mindset of obsession, passion, dedication and vision. Add to that an icy leaning towards self-punishment, justice and denial. Bring a razor-sharp intellect together with a damaged heart that refuses to allow mind and body to unite, as the ego hurtles this troubled soul to her own destruction.

Imagine writing, "the greatest analysis of the French Revolution," whilst allowing yourself to starve and freeze to death and keeping a scrupulous record of your own isolated demise. Imagine being consumed with love for an historical figure long since dead and a living father who has abused you.

Pam Gems set her unique mind to this jigsaw of Stanisława Przybyszewska and birthed *The Snow Palace*, giving this kaleidoscopic woman and her work a voice again.

I was the lucky actress challenged to stand this behemoth up off the page with the enormous support of Sphinx, Janet Suzman and a stellar company. Actually, three companies, as venues across the UK and Poland invited the work to travel and Dantons and Robespierres moved on to other jobs and Stanislava was the last woman standing and not done with me.

Witnessing the Polish audiences delight at having one of their heroines recognised from abroad was the reward; to help re-ignite this creative, mysterious woman's work and her battle-cry denouncing institutions that historically have failed to support the creativity of women or at worst actively neglected and destroyed it. A battle-cry that I suspect will still be valid for some time to come.

It was a privilege I treasure to perform a lion amongst women who had the fragility of a fawn, and on the stage in Lodz where Ira Aldridge (first Black Shakespearean actor) reportedly died whilst playing *Othello*. Janet and I searched for his grave and laid flowers there. It seemed to be a thank you to all brave souls who with integrity, and no matter what the cost, follow their bliss.

Kathryn Pogson

Justin Avoth and Kathryn Pogson in *The Snow Palace* by Pam Gems
Photo © Pau Ros 1998

THE SNOW PALACE

PAM GEMS

The Snow Palace premiered at The Tricycle Theatre (now Kiln) in London, in 1998, and subsequently toured to Warsaw and Lodz.

Director	Janet Suzman
Designer	Bruce Macadie
Sound	John A. Leonard
Lighting	Ian Scott
Cast	Justin Avoth, Kristin Milward, Kathryn Pogson, Kenn Sabberton, Jemma Shaw, Robert Wilcox

CHARACTERS

Minimum cast, three women, three men (excluding taped voices).

STANISLAWA
MOTHER/AUNT HELENA
FATHER/DANTON
ROBESPIERRE
SAINT-JUST
ANNA/LOUISE/WOMAN

And the Voices Of

ÉLÉONORE
DESMOULINS
LEGENDRE
COURTIS
PHILIPPEAUX
COLLOT
BARERE
CARNOT

ACT ONE

The interior of a wooden hut. It is extremely poorly furnished with almost no furniture. What there is, is broken or impoverished. There is a small black stove with a pipe and a window which is half-draped with a ragged orange cardigan. The small panes of the window are so thick with frost that the light from outside is obscured.

A WOMAN is writing at a small kitchen table. She is very thin, with darkish hair roughly cropped in the style of the 1920s. It is hard to tell her age. She writes swiftly, hunched over the table, her hands cramped with the cold. Voice-over on the P/A.

STANISLAWA *(V.O.)* ...Nonsense, a lie, untrue! ...to the contrary, I'm very comfortable. I have a small but charming room in the school grounds here... *(She looks round the room briefly with no indication that she does not find it so.)* ...true, my funds are small now that I've given up teaching, but dearest, will you stop worrying about my health and sanity! – I am, as the English say, in the pink, so less, less, less of the cat with the drowned kitten... on second thoughts, continue to be concerned for your highly intelligent, deeply talented and wholly adoring niece... Stanislawa. *(STANISLAWA finishes writing, puts down the pen then picks it up again to add a postscript.)* How is the old man, still dispensing charity to those above him? Damn him! – Buy the skirt! My heart is yours. *(She puts the letter into an envelope, makes to lick the seal, adds another postscript.)* I have begun... my new... play. The subject? My beloved Robespierre! – Who else?

She straightens up and stretches stiffly, pulling her arms wide and easing her shoulders, something she does throughout. She seals the envelope, addresses it, and, as another afterthought, turns it over and scrawls on the back.

STANISLAWA I – am – well.

She stands, the sealed letter in her hand, white-faced with the cold. Looks about vaguely then, propping the letter up on the table, crosses to the stove. Shivering, she picks up an old battered enamel saucepan from the top of the stove and crosses to the door. Opening it, we see white snowdrifts. She disappears outside, and returns with the saucepan piled high with snow. This she tries to melt on the stove but it is not warm enough. She finds a candle-end, looks for matches and lights it, with difficulty, with a twist of old newspaper poked into the stove. She puts the lit candle under a tripod, rests the saucepan on the top and looks for wood for the fire. She finds a few pieces and puts them into the stove. She returns and stirs the snow until it melts. She sips the water from the pan, wincing at the coldness, and walks about, pan in hand, sipping.

As she does so there is the sound of a woman laughing, low, on the P/A.

STANISLAWA paces, sipping. THE WOMAN laughs again, closer. Further off a man begins to protest mildly.

ROBESPIERRE *(V.O.)* Not now, Léo... no, no, no!... Éléonore!

THE WOMAN's laughter, low and close and seductive.

STANISLAWA *(V.O.)* Oh we know what *you* think, my dear Robespierre!

She imitates his dry voice and precise diction. ROBESPIERRE enters in dressing gown. Immediately STANISLAWA, without looking at him, stops pacing, goes to her table.

STANISLAWA *(V.O.)* "Manifestations of love during the daylight are in the worst possible taste!"

ROBESPIERRE Did I say that?

STANISLAWA bends over the table, writing rapidly.

ROBESPIERRE *(laughs gently)* Fine principles from a fit man. From a weak wreck, less persuasive.

STANISLAWA On the contrary, my dear, you're obviously recovering. Alas.

ROBESPIERRE You'd rather have me on my back?

STANISLAWA *(sadly)* At least I see you then *(looks at the page, pencil between her teeth)*... at least I see you then... I see you then... *(chews the end of the pencil).*

ROBESPIERRE My poor Éléonore...

At the loving concern in his voice, STANISLAWA half turns in her chair with an involuntary spasm of anguish. She pulls an ugly face, dismissing the feeling.

ROBESPIERRE My dear. I'm sorry *(with a groaning sigh).* I really believed it. A year of intense revolutionary work, then back to privacy and you... instead of which... instead of which I'm becoming nothing but a huge, inflamed Brain and – ach!

STANISLAWA nearly jumps out of her skin at a rat-a-tat-tat on her door. She swings herself back against the wall so that she cannot be seen by anyone looking in at the window.

ANNA *(calls from without in a child's falsetto, her form of greeting)* Ooo-ah! Ooo-ah!

STANISLAWA, rigid against the wall, pulls a vicious face. She edges further away. Sounds of scraping as ANNA gets a foothold, sounds of scratching as she clears a pane of glass, and peers in the window.

ANNA Hullo, Hullo... anyone in? It's Anna, your neighbour. May I come in?

STANISLAWA keeps still. Scraping sounds as ANNA keeps a foothold, then the characteristic knock once more... rat-a-tat-tat.

ANNA Hullo?

Silence. Then the sounds of ANNA's departure. STANISLAWA, bent double to stay below the line of the window, creeps back to the table and slides into her seat. But her concentration has been dented. She sits, raking her neck back and forth like an angry fowl, muttering to herself. She pulls herself together with a visible effort.

STANISLAWA *(through her teeth)* Not... important. *(Released, her mind drifts back to her work.)* Not important. *(She makes a sudden decision.)* Get her off. *(She picks up her pencil, bends over the page, mutters to herself.)* Farewell, Éléonore.

On the P/A the same rat-a-tat-tat at the door.

STANISLAWA And enter... the Angel of Death... the baleful... Saint-Just!

ST. JUST's voice becomes louder as he approaches.

ST. JUST *(V.O.)* Citizen Robespierre is out of bed? Excellent – my God, do I smell coffee?

His voice is close on the last word and STANISLAWA groans at the word `coffee'. She rises, crosses, burrows among empty tins. No coffee. She smells an empty tin for its fragrance, finds a heel of bread, wipes off dirt and wolfs it down absently, sliding back quickly into her seat, anxious not to lose her thread as ST. JUST enters.

ST. JUST *(turning behind him)* We should have arrested every malcontent, madman and rogue six months ago... as it is, God knows what's going to happen.

ROBESPIERRE enters again, looking frail. Like ST. JUST, he carries a lot of paper. They are dressed in a mixture of modern clothes and period.

ROBESPIERRE *(lightly)* I thought you'd abolished God – oh, now you're annoyed with me.

ST. JUST My feelings are neither here nor there, they don't enter into it, although I do, as you know, feel most strongly that we should remove every icon, totem and medieval magic from the people if they are to march forward –

ROBESPIERRE All right, all right, all right... sorry, I've been away from... from your wonderful energy, my dear.

ST. JUST It's been the devil without you. People slide! A few setbacks, all of a sudden this man's left Paris, or the country, others change hats, the pettiness of the squabbles you wouldn't believe! There's a weird cynicism about – well we all know where that comes from.

ROBESPIERRE Oh, not again!

ST. JUST You haven't been here... you've been ill. When I tried to tell you of new alliances, people switching sides overnight, you were jittering with fever. He never stops!

ROBESPIERRE But that is Georges! Like you, he has this wonderful vitality. I wish I'd half –

ST. JUST I am insulted to be coupled with Georges Danton.

ROBESPIERRE Anton. He is a colleague. A different sort of man, that's all. No less relevant, we all want the same –

ST. JUST No, no, and no. What he wants is your place. He's got the streets behind him but that isn't enough and he knows it. He needs the respect and trust that is yours, that you have earned by what you do, by who you are. He wants to be you!

ROBESPIERRE Oh I doubt if Georges would change places.

ST. JUST He wants to sit where you sit. He'll kill for it.

ROBESPIERRE That – is a very dangerous accusation to make of a colleague and a brave man.

He rises, frigid, frightening.

ST. JUST I'm sorry.

ROBESPIERRE You are destructive.

ST. JUST I'm sorry, I'm sorry. It's the truth, should I keep it to myself? I smell it, I honestly believe you're in danger – physical danger. Maxime, these are not normal days.

ROBESPIERRE And you think Georges wants to put a knife in my back? That he's capable of murder? Well, do you?

ST. JUST All I know is that I'd die for you.

ROBESPIERRE Rubbish – stop it. I will not be an icon to replace the pietas you're ripping from the altars of France. We'll have less talk of violence – violence is for despots and criminals. If there is one achievement we may hope for in this unprecedented...

ST. JUST Struggle?

ROBESPIERRE ...Enterprise ...endeavour ...it is to emerge from brutish medievalism. You must learn to stop fighting. I've seen how bored you are in the endless meetings, but let me tell you – meetings are my rapier! Learn to persuade. You want me to muzzle Georges – what are you talking about, he's our man of the people!

ST. JUST No he isn't. Any more than we are.

ROBESPIERRE We are educated men who have responded to the need for human justice.

ST. JUST From – nonetheless – positions of privilege.

ROBESPIERRE And Georges Danton is abusing that privilege? That's what you're saying?

ST. JUST The whole of Paris knows it. The man's corrupt – it's common knowledge. *(ROBESPIERRE shakes his head)* The more you indulge him, the more he swells. He misunderstands you – he thinks you connive! What do you want – proof? I'll get it for you!

ROBESPIERRE sweeps up his papers from his desk, leaves. ST. JUST, angry, hurries out after him. STANISLAWA utters a shuddering groan.

STANISLAWA Ohhh!

The pencil falls from her frozen hand. She staggers, and reels, lurches to her feet unsteadily. She stamps her stiff legs, and walks up and down to get back feeling. She crosses to the window.

STANISLAWA Snow, damn you!

She finds a sack and drapes it over her shoulders, clutching it to her. She puts more wood on the stove, squats on the floor, hunched as close to the fire as she can and goes into a stupor.

STANISLAWA Mamushu... Mamoo... *(murmurs)* I'm cold.......

Her MOTHER enters, a tall, handsome woman with a scarf wrapped about her head, pinned with a large jet brooch. STANISLAWA jumps up as her MOTHER, searching, finds a bottle of vodka hidden in a bundle of clothes. She looks about for a glass, STANISLAWA silently hands her a cup.

STANISLAWA *(matter of fact)* You told me my father was the big Swede.

MOTHER *(absently, busying herself with the bottle)* No-o, I just said that.

STANISLAWA What for?

MOTHER *(irritable, unable to open the bottle)* I don't know!

She gets the top off, pours herself a drink and savours the first mouthful.

STANISLAWA Why him?

Her MOTHER shrugs, pulling a face, just like her daughter.

STANISLAWA *(grumpy)* I looked him up in the Almanac in the Library. I've been reading Swedish history!

Her MOTHER, after another swallow, sits, placated, undoing her jacket. She belches discreetly.

STANISLAWA I thought I might be descended from Queen Christina of Sweden... royal!

She pulls a silly face.

MOTHER You could have been! – well, if he *had* been your father... the Swede.

STANISLAWA Don't be silly. If it wasn't him who was it? Or were there so many you can't remember? *(Refusing to give her MOTHER more vodka)* Tell me about him.

MOTHER Who?

STANISLAWA My father!

MOTHER That lecher.

STANISLAWA Who is he, what's he like?

MOTHER You'll get nothing there.

STANISLAWA What's he like... is he handsome?

MOTHER No... ugly. *(STANISLAWA groans.)* I should stay clear if I were you – he's killed more than once.

STANISLAWA You chose well.

MOTHER I know! Sorry. *(apologetically)* I did try to get rid of you.

STANISLAWA gives her a dry look.

STANISLAWA Is he Polish?

MOTHER Yes.

PRZYBYSZEWSKY enters, stands behind her. From now on, he fondles her breasts, but STANISLAWA does not see him – he is not visible to her.

STANISLAWA So a madman. What's his name?

MOTHER Przybyszewsky. The bastard.

STANISLAWA No. I'm the bastard.

(joking) Not Stanislaw Przybyszewsky?

MOTHER Yes that's him.

STANISLAWA You don't mean Przybyszewsky the dramatist, the novelist, the friend of Edvard Munck – all those avant-garde artists – ?

MOTHER Yes.

STANISLAWA You mean I'm his daughter?

MOTHER Yes!

STANISLAWA I'm the daughter of Stanislaw Przybyszewsky?

MOTHER *(shrieks)* Yes!!

STANISLAWA I don't believe it. *(She stands, dumbfounded.)* Are you sure?

MOTHER *(groans, then)* Yes.

STANISLAWA I'm the daughter of a famous man. I'm Przybyszewsky's daughter.

The significance of her Christian name penetrates.

STANISLAWA Stanislaw... Stanislawa!

She stands before her mother, beaming idiotically with pure happiness.

MOTHER I shouldn't get too ecstatic if I were you. You're not his only fly-by-night.

STANISLAWA I've got a father.

Her MOTHER looks ironically up at her FATHER, but he is otherwise engaged with her bosom.

STANISLAWA I've got a famous, brilliant man for my father!

She wheels on her MOTHER.

STANISLAWA *(with a hoarse shout)* Hey!!

This makes her MOTHER jump so that her FATHER has to steady her MOTHER's chair.

STANISLAWA You never said! Why didn't you say he was my father!

They ignore her. STANISLAWA raps her knuckles on the table to attract their attention. But they are otherwise and increasingly engaged. STANISLAWA, perplexed, turns away discreetly. But cannot contain her need for more information. She crosses and frowns over her MOTHER who is being slobbered over by her FATHER, and who lifts her MOTHER's leg over him, exposing her thigh at the top of her stocking.

STANISLAWA What happened? *(They ignore her.)* Did he leave you or did you leave him?

Her MOTHER cannot remember, shrugs, adjusts her suspenders and renews her lipstick.

STANISLAWA Was it because of me?

Her FATHER sneers, does up his flies and goes.

MOTHER Can't remember *(sitting with legs apart).* We had some good times.

She rises and prinks, then goes with a casual wave. STANISLAWA begins to prowl, clutching herself against the cold, then sits abruptly to write.

STANISLAWA Cold. Wet. A third bad harvest. Paris runs out of bread. The Queen, Marie Antoinette, asks for fine flour, brioche flour, to be released for sale to the poor to ease their suffering, is damned illogically by history for reputedly saying: `Let them eat cake.'

1789. The people have had enough... they storm the Bastille, let out a few surprised old prisoners and, for the first time in history, the Rights of Man... and Woman... are agreed, listed and declared.

1790. The first government by the people, set up, swept forward by Maximilian Robespierre, "the Sea-Green Incorruptible" – and smiling Georges Danton, lawyer, lecher, and people's friend.

1791. King Louis makes a run for it, is recognised from his coins and hauled back to Paris with the Queen.

1792. The whole world... except America... hostile. France stands alone.

The door is flung open. Her MOTHER, looking ill, stands there. STANISLAWA helps her to lie down. Her MOTHER is very noisily sick. STANISLAWA, who looks as though she is used to this, shoves an enamel bowl at her. She fetches newspaper and a cloth and cleans up the mess. She pulls a piece of old carpet over her MOTHER to keep her warm, and dashes off in her coat. Her MOTHER groans quietly. STANISLAWA returns with medicine, gives her MOTHER two spoonfuls, sits down by her side.

MOTHER You'll miss school.

STANISLAWA Doesn't matter.

Her MOTHER moans quietly.

MOTHER God, I feel bad.

STANISLAWA sits by her, motionless. The light goes.

MOTHER *(murmurs, in her sleep)* Oh dear...

STANISLAWA bends over her, fetches her a drink of water, helps her to sit up and drink.

MOTHER I haven't been much of a parent.

STANISLAWA Doesn't matter.

MOTHER I used to leave you in the car...

STANISLAWA With a bag of liquorice.

MOTHER Somebody said it was good for kids. *(She drifts off.)* They don't think you need to enjoy yourself. What's wrong with it? He used to say...'there's nobody up there, do as you want'... *(she shudders).*

STANISLAWA What?

MOTHER Look, promise me. Don't go near him.

STANISLAWA My father? Why not?

MOTHER Keep away.

STANISLAWA Why?

MOTHER *(indistinctly)* He won't see you. If he does – if he's charming – watch out. Mischief.

STANISLAWA Mischief... what do you mean?

MOTHER Horrible... you can't do that to people...

STANISLAWA Do what?

MOTHER You're lovely. *(becoming indistinct)* Don't let him... promise me. Go to your aunt in Cracow – she'll look after...

STANISLAWA I want to meet my father.

MOTHER No. Ask Helena – oh Christ!

She heaves, as if to be sick, but the spasm subsides. STANISLAWA rises, with the bowl.

MOTHER *(weakly)* Don't move the bowl, Stashoo.

So STANISLAWA sits by her MOTHER. Who slowly becomes quiet. Lights down until STANISLAWA is alone in a wan light. Slowly she rises and stands, centre, as if lost. But shakes herself free of painful memory and returns to her writing.

STANISLAWA Spring, 1794. Robespierre recovering from malaria, Danton back in Paris after enjoying his new country estates and the young body of his sixteen-year-old bride. Saint-Just tables a motion for the necessity of a rule of terror – temporary, of course.

The imposition of Terror.

(looks up) The imposition of Terror...

ST. JUST *(V.O.)* The Imposition of Terror...

STANISLAWA ...is an act...

ST. JUST enters with papers.

ST. JUST ...is an act...

STANISLAWA ...of cauterization.

ST. JUST *(his voice overlapping)* ...is an act of cauterization.

ROBESPIERRE enters.

ROBESPIERRE You can't at least, accuse *Danton* of extremism.

But he goes silent as ST. JUST puts papers before him.

ST. JUST He's growing like a fungus. With foreign support non-existent, bread running out again and people dropping in the gutters, our brother revolutionary, seeing the pickings dwindle, not only sucks every tit his fat hands can squeeze, but begins to spread reaction!

ROBESPIERRE Are these accurate?

ST. JUST Yes.

ROBESPIERRE Reliable sources?

ST. JUST Your own people.

Silence. ROBESPIERRE rises slowly.

ST. JUST They must be arrested. *All* of them. Including Danton.

ROBESPIERRE Arrest Georges? *(He rises, speaks dreamily, looking out of the window.)* I'm fond of Georges. Doesn't do to let him know - he takes advantage.

ST. JUST stabs at the papers on the table.

ST. JUST Proof of fraud. Proof of embezzlement. Proof, written and witnessed, of treason to the state.

ROBESPIERRE *(looking up into ST. JUST's face)* You want me to put the people's champion on trial?

ST. JUST Are you saying he's above the law? A special case? A woman out there who hoards a loaf of bread has her head chopped off!

ROBESPIERRE Not if she has the popular support enjoyed by your adored fellow revolutionary, Danton. In an open fight –

ST. JUST In an open fight you'd carry the Convention *nem con*!

ROBESPIERRE My dear Antoine... how young you are.

ST. JUST It is not a matter of experience but of fact – and conviction.

ROBESPIERRE *(sharp)* Then I must tell you that at this time my conviction is for a delayed decision on the matter of Danton.

ST. JUST Have you got a temperature?

ROBESPIERRE No.

He rises and walks to the door.

ST. JUST *(pursuing him)* Then you're afraid of him.

ROBESPIERRE *(turns on him)* No! I am afraid of the horror we shall release if we split into faction. Do you think we can waste energy in internal wrangling? You think that's the way forward for France?

ST. JUST Maxime... in the name of justice...

ROBESPIERRE Justice? My dear Antoine, I hardly think that is a luxury in which we may indulge ourselves. For the present. *(As ST. JUST tries to argue)* Nor shall we permit ourselves the fatally easy course of a sustained reign of Terror. That is for thugs.

ST. JUST throws himself down, sulky.

ST. JUST What then?

ROBESPIERRE For the sake of our souls, we shall compromise.

ST. JUST Compromise? With that lecher?

STANISLAWA *(murmurs, frowning)* Lecher?

ROBESPIERRE With our revolutionary co-patriot, Danton. I shall arrange a meeting

ST. JUST The whole of Paris will gloat, they'll assume he's suborned you... you'll be seen as complicit, weak, if nothing worse...

ROBESPIERRE Oh my dear, what are humiliations when the future of the republic is at stake? I doubt the necessity to kiss Danton's shoe but... should France demand it of me...

They go.

During the above a trio plays Mozart. A low buzz of voices, and clatter of cutlery. DANTON enters, cutting off sound as he shuts the door. Dressed floridly for the evening, he inspects the laid dining table. He makes a few changes, puts the chairs closer, sniffs the wine.

ROBESPIERRE enters soundlessly. DANTON, caught on the wrong foot, sits as ROBESPIERRE, equally carefully dressed, seats himself with a small smile.

DANTON offers food, ROBESPIERRE shakes his head.

DANTON *(helping himself liberally)* Maxime!... good to see you! I heard you'd been ill – how are you feeling?

ROBESPIERRE I hear you've been having me followed.

DANTON For your own protection! *(He leans over the table fondly.)* We all know who's the heart and engine of this great endeavour of ours. The mind, the intellect of France! – Always were, never knew a case brought to court you didn't read clear.

ROBESPIERRE And sometimes lose against you.

DANTON Only because I made them feel sorry for me. 'Here comes old Georges with his big ugly mug, making a mess of it again.'

ROBESPIERRE A most inaccurate appraisal. As you know.

DANTON I used to find it helped to smile a lot.

ROBESPIERRE You recommend false demeanour in court.

DANTON We're talking about the law, not justice!

ROBESPIERRE Touché.

DANTON Not that your face is your best friend.

ROBESPIERRE I've never pretended to beauty!

DANTON Only one of the best-looking men in Paris. That profile!

(Despite himself, ROBESPIERRE preens.)

But so open! Not always in the client's interest, d'you see? Honest aspect, yes. But not necessarily conveying dictionary, thesaurus and almanack at a glance. Those eyes! Like an ocean, signalling every hour of the tide... slack, full, dangerous ebb. A handicap for a lawyer. In a politician, downright frightening...

DANTON shudders.

ROBESPIERRE I frighten you?

DANTON Maxime – I'm frightened *for* you.

ROBESPIERRE I see. What do you suggest I do to protect myself?

DANTON *(laughs)* Come on! You won't catch me there! No lawyer asks a question to which he don't know the answer. We ain't in court now.

ROBESPIERRE suddenly seems tired, ill.

ROBESPIERRE What do you want?

DANTON You know what I want – your friendship! Trust! *(He leans forward, tucks a rug around ROBESPIERRE's knees with loving skill.)* That's better. You shouldn't be out – she's not looking after you properly. They're all the same, these women, they like us on our backs, oh, we'll take care of you, what they want is to colonize us, story of Samson eh... only it isn't our hair they want to cut off... sit still... *(He picks up a spoon, feeds ROBESPIERRE soup.)* It's just a little fortified meat soup, it won't harass the digestion – you must recover your strength – for the sake of France! *(So ROBESPIERRE takes the soup.)* I should have been here, seeing to you, instead of... *(He sighs)*... tell you the truth I'm exhausted. We've been through too much. Responsibility for life, death – the sights we've seen!... it binds you together. Those who haven't been where we have... God knows I never sought high place... no, takes it out of you... *(He spoons the soup).*

ROBESPIERRE Your courage has been a lamp to us all.

He lifts his hand, DANTON puts down the spoon, pours a glass of wine. ROBESPIERRE watches him, deft with bottle, glass and snowy napkin.

ROBESPIERRE I have always admired you. Your voice, booming through chambers, across courtyards... that enormous laugh like the thunder of gods... your capacity for... camaraderie...

He accepts the glass of wine, drinks at DANTON's smiling encouragement. Puts down the glass.

ROBESPIERRE I have never acquired a facility for living.

DANTON You should try it. Nothing wrong with enjoyment.

ROBESPIERRE In its proper place.

DANTON I agree. Question of balance. Like the law... based on what's reasonable. Too much this way, no good... too much that way – disaster. If you get my meaning.

ROBESPIERRE Your point?

DANTON Retrenchment. For the sake of us all... your head as well as mine. We're offering devoted loyalty, total support.

ROBESPIERRE I have reports of your group. In all the years that we have shared acquaintance it never occurred to me that Georges Danton, professional colleague, fellow-revolutionary, and brother-in-arms, was as rotten as a dead stick on the forest floor.

DANTON *(rises, grim-faced)* What? What?

ROBESPIERRE throws a piece of paper to him.

ROBESPIERRE I also have my spies.

This revolution – if it survives – will survive through, and only through the most stringent sacrifice and devoted service. And by example.

DANTON They love me!

ROBESPIERRE You think the bourgeoisie, our new backbone... you think the farmers, journeymen, labourers... d'you think the Sans-Culottes will follow you to the barricades for *collusion*? That they have such a low opinion of themselves? You think people live by the Deal? By mere transaction? By the banality of trade?

DANTON By God, there are worse ways to live.

ROBESPIERRE *(his voice shrill)* Insufficient! It ends in criminality. In the withering of the soul. In bestiality. In the rape of children.

Silence.

DANTON *(low and murderous)* My marriage is a love match.

ROBESPIERRE Would you have got her without your money and position?

I'm sorry. But you must see. Without the backbone of morality, society cannot hold any more than this. *(He smashes his hand down on a jelly, lifts it, shining red like blood.)* Where's the resistance? Every man for himself? Can that create a nation with heart, pride, identity – self-respect?

Silence. DANTON scans the piece of paper with the charges.

DANTON *(looks up at last)* These areas of finance – I should never have been left to my own devices, I needed assistance... and with the war councils and the edicts and instructions from the Committees and your office... you've overloaded us! Change everything? In a year?! Impose democracy... fight a foreign war, de-Christianise – all right, we pulled back there on your advice... yes – I agree! 'Fairness for all'... but when the harvests fail, how are we to achieve even one crust a day apiece, tell me that.

You want redistribution to provide poor relief, money for widows, free medical treatment for all... Maxime! On paper – divine! The most inspired humanity the world has ever seen. But within a year?

Is it surprising that we fail you?

All right, I've slipped. I do my best – yes, there has been error. But no malice, I've always been your man... Dammit, we stand for the same thing, how can we be enemies?

Maxime...

Please... make me the Mayor of Boulogne – I'll leave tonight, with my little woman. To tell the truth I'd be happier – I'll take my girl and go, with your blessing – serve France in whatever –

ROBESPIERRE Impossible! You know that. Leave now, you leave chaos and a total loss of morale behind you.

DANTON We'll make arrangement, my people and yours. A new *entente.*

ROBESPIERRE finds a document.

ROBESPIERRE I have drawn up a list of requirements. In times of crisis the Committee of Security must have support from every faction. There must be discipline.

DANTON *(scanning the list of charges)* I'll account for every penny of this.

ROBESPIERRE Perhaps you would be good enough to sign to that. There... there... and there.

DANTON signs.

DANTON Maxime! Come here! You never needed to worry about old Georges! My dick's in your back pocket, surely you know that? Mind you... you're asking us to sign our death warrants.

ROBESPIERRE What did you say?

DANTON Anything that's possible – I'm your man, but... change human nature? Abolish crime? You might as well try and stop us all pissing!

People work for one thing – themselves! *(He crashes a fist on the table, making ROBESPIERRE jump.)* You think they'll do it for virtue – where's the profit in that now we've abolished God and the Hereafter? *(He laughs.)*

ROBESPIERRE The soul of man is -

DANTON The soul of man? Testicles! Why are they with us, that rabble out there, I'll tell you... because we promise a better share-out...

and what's wrong with that? The freedom to be a self-supporting unit – that's democracy. Every man for himself... human nature, Maxime... human nature! *(He leans forward, grasps ROBESPIERRE by the lapel.)* Pull back. We've gone far enough. *(He flops back in his chair. Drunk, his attention begins to go.)* Too much blood... it's devaluing property. *(He leans forward, benign with wine.)* Maxime! You and I, Maxime, between us, we could rule the world together. It's our destiny. Men aren't created equal, never will be.

ROBESPIERRE Ability... may not equate virtue.

DANTON Virtue? *(He laughs)* The only virtue I know is what I put into my wife's little hole three times a night.

ROBESPIERRE *(mutters)* Sickening.

DANTON And vice versa, my friend. Nothing more sickening on this earth than an honest man. Not an ounce of understanding for the rest of us – who do you think you are – God? Roast in hell for your arrogance. Anyway, it won't work. Impose virtue by force and your vice will ooze out sideways.

ROBESPIERRE You doom us all to criminality then?

DANTON Didn't say that. Must have a system... reward ingenuity, punish the idle.

ROBESPIERRE Carrot and stick? Conditional love?

DANTON What's love got to do with it?

ROBESPIERRE gets up, moves carefully to exit.

DANTON What's the matter? What's up?

ROBESPIERRE Nothing. You make me sick.

He goes. DANTON, furious, lurches to his feet, blunders about, goes.

STANISLAWA *(thoughtfully)* You make me sick.

She prowls, pokes the fire with the broken piece of a chair back.

A rat-a-tat-tat on the door. STANISLAWA is startled. Another knock. She watches in alarm as the latch is gently lifted. The door opens and ANNA looks in. She is young, well-dressed in a crimson coat with a fur neckpiece and a fetching fur hat. She carries a basket and an enamel milk pail. STANISLAWA tries to block the way but ANNA slides past her with a warm smile which fades as she takes in the room.

STANISLAWA What can I do for you?

ANNA But... *(She looks round, her manners forgotten.)* How do you live? Where do you sleep?

STANISLAWA Was there something you wanted?

ANNA I... my husband thought... *(She still looks round compulsively, her head craning this way and that, her eyes wide.)*... we – dinner. We thought if you would come to dinner. There's no need to walk – my husband has a car now, it's outside... we have a chauffeur! *(Excited, she takes STANISLAWA by the arm and forces her to the door, impelling her outside.)*

(Outside) Do you like the colour? I chose it, we were going to have red but blue is my favourite.

(As they come in again) Do you like the wine upholstery?

STANISLAWA nods abruptly. Silence. The sight of the room makes ANNA falter again. But she braces herself.

ANNA You can't stay here – you can't!

But STANISLAWA crosses and stands by the door to see her out.

ANNA Please, won't you come?

She approaches, smiling, and puts a grey-gloved hand on STANISLAWA's arm. STANISLAWA is slightly mesmerised by her warmth, her scent, her clothes.

ANNA My father-in-law sent us a brace of pheasant – nothing formal... no need to... *(again she trails off with a covert glance at STANISLAWA's appearance.)* Please... we know so few people in Gdansk and you were so kind about the dog. Jaroslav's found some books that might interest you. About the French Revolution.

STANISLAWA Who by? The new stuff? Re-instating Robespierre?

ANNA Oh heaven knows... I'm afraid I don't have time for reading. *(She puts her hand on STANISLAWA's arm again.)* Please. Just a nice warm supper, and we'll drive you back, in the car...

STANISLAWA wavers, mainly because ANNA's smile is genuinely warm and infectious. She nods briefly, removes the sack from her shoulders. ANNA watches, fascinated, smiles encouragingly and turns for a last glance at the room, to take everything in, for her friends.

ANNA There'll just be my sister-in-law and our colleagues the Krassowskis – and... *(triumphant)*... the Deputy Headmaster and his godson are looking in to listen to our gramophone.

STANISLAWA, aghast, stops in her tracks.

ANNA No?

STANISLAWA shakes her head briefly.

ANNA Can't I tempt you? There's a nice warm fire – huge logs, we could bring back some wood in the car –

STANISLAWA Thank you, no. Good night.

ANNA sulks.

ANNA My husband said you wouldn't. *(She pouts, having lost her bet.)* Well, anyway... *(She proffers the basket.)* There's a meat pie and some sausage, and a winter pudding.

STANISLAWA Thank you, I have provisions.

ANNA stands, embarrassed, holding out the basket and the little pail of milk.

STANISLAWA You mustn't keep your car waiting. It'll get cold.

ANNA Oh, yes!

She looks outside, puts the basket and the milk on the table hurriedly and goes, with a wave of her gloved hand.

STANISLAWA You've forgotten your groceries!

She lobs the basket out of the door. Energised, she wheels back and walks about muttering, her arms wrapped about her for warmth.

STANISLAWA Winter pudding!

"Poor thing!... and here am I, a warm, cosy bunny with my man and my little bunnies and my things to define me, all my muffs and ruffles and aren't I the bees knees. Who can take his eyes off me I'm the crystallised violet of Gdansk, perhaps I'll even let him tonight, ooh he's given me a rash, would you like to see my portrait?" *(She sits, exhausted.)* God murder every coquette in this world. *(She sits, gazing into the fire.)*

(dreamily) He bought me pheasant. Not the first time. The first time we had lamb. Smoked herring in a sour sauce and then lamb, with spring cabbage. And he didn't like sweet things. *(to her FATHER)* Don't you like sweet things?

Her FATHER is sitting at the table. She sits across from him, leans over and inspects his dinner plate.

STANISLAWA It doesn't look as though you like any of it. Do you mind? *(She takes his plate, scrapes his food on to her own and eats, her head down with pleasure. After a few mouthfuls she looks up.)* First thing I've eaten since Cracow! *(She takes another forkful, chews in* *ecstasy, then drains her glass. He refills it.)* I haven't got a single zloty – not a pfennig, not a rouble!

She said you wouldn't either. (*Her FATHER regards her through cigar smoke.)* Helena. Mum's sister. *(with her mouth full)* I've lived with her since I was eleven. She's lovely. *(leans across the table confidentially)* Married to a bastard. *(She finishes, wiping the plate clean with a piece of bread.)*

The WAITER refills their glasses. STANISLAWA blows out her cheeks, enjoying being full, and warm, and with her FATHER. She glances at him covertly, with avid appreciation.

STANISLAWA Do you remember my mother? *(He looks at her through the smoke, drawing on his cigar.)* She was a painter.

Name of Pajak. Aniela.

It doesn't matter. *(She helps herself to an elaborate chocolate confection, takes a mouthful, then puts down her fork and bursts out laughing, spraying him with food.)*

Sorry.

It's the hair.

You look like a potato with a sprout on top! (*She laughs, giggling at him.) (leans over to him)* And I was afraid you'd be ashamed of me – this is the only dress I've got.

He inspects her appearance, sucks his teeth.

STANISLAWA What I'd really like is a new hat. Red – offensive! (*She finishes the pudding swiftly and avidly, sits back and looks around the restaurant, amazed.)* Sensational. Everybody here looks famous... beautiful... utterly unique! *(She empties her glass. He refills it at once and she lifts it high.)* To Warsaw... the queen of cities! *(He lifts his glass. STANISLAWA licks the wine from her lips, looks around again and then leans towards him.)* Is my neck as long as my mother's? *(He thinks, lifting his head. She looks at the other diners.)* I'd like a choker of rubies, no, fire opals, foiled with silver to make them glow. *(getting drunk)* I want to look Mexican, sensational! *(He gives her a sneering look. She jumps, startled, then laughs, delighted as the restaurant band breaks into a noisy Polish dance.)*

Oh!! *(She jumps up.)* I'm going to dance, dance, dance till my ankles crack and my feet fall off then I'll hop, hop, hop on my bones till they're polished ivory stumps and I'll earn my living making holes for fences and buy my own clothes and sail to Madagascar!

She dances to the music. Her FATHER rises and dances, circling her, his arms high. When the music stops he lifts her high in his arms, part of the dance. She laughs, triumphant. But as he lets her down he holds her, close. She releases herself, embarrassed and he falls flat on his back.

Papa? Father?

(Her FATHER is out cold. She tries to lift him, looks round for assistance.)

Can you help me?

The WAITER comes forward indolently. Cigarette in mouth. He looks down, kicks the FATHER lightly.

WAITER He's finished for tonight. Do you want to go through his pockets?

STANISLAWA You fool, he's my father.

WAITER Oh.

She glares ferociously and then they both burst out laughing. They drag her FATHER out between them.

ST JUST *(crosses)* Kill Danton.

(V.O.) Kill Danton. Kill Danton.

ANNA, in another elegant ensemble, knocks, then slips in circumspectly, and leaves a basket of food, tops up the enamel pail of milk. She looks round at the room, is glad to leave.

STANISLAWA returns. She notices the food, inspects it laconically.

STANISLAWA He gave me pheasant. And carp. And wild boar.

And green lizard shoes with extremely high heels.

She looks into the enamel pail, adds pieces of chair to the fire, puts milk in the pan and warms it, standing over the stove and humming to herself.

STANISLAWA At least I don't come on now. Indians drink their own piss. *(She stands over the milk.)* I wonder how that started – ah, a glass of lemonade, thanks, I'm feeling thirsty... mmm, ye-es – smells familiar, can't quite place the taste.

(Forgetting the milk on the hob, she paces.)

Maxime... the virtuous man.

Is virtue truth – truth virtue?

Truth as reality.

And how is that, pray, related to love? (*She grimaces to heaven.)* Loving mercy? No, no, no – that's the old God... Christ, I know nothing!... I don't know anything. *(She calls heavenwards)* Some of us don't know very much! We're dense! Why don't you do something?!

Huh.

Demoted.

(She prowls, recapitulating her thoughts on her fingers.)

Robespierre, respecting Danton for his animal courage, his generosity of spirit, his revolutionary achievements... detesting his greed, his smiling, calculating deviousness – ahh!

A cry of anguish as she remembers the milk. She dashes to the stove, but the milk is by no means hot. She crouches, opens the fire at the front, pokes at it through the bars, rising as her FATHER enters, dashing the snow from his hat and taking off his gloves.

STANISLAWA Do you love me?

FATHER *(frightening face)* What?

He looks at her in surprise.

STANISLAWA No, why should you, there's no reason why you should.

She watches him hungrily as he takes off his heavy coat. He sits, somnolent. She crouches on the floor beside him, gazing at the open fire.

STANISLAWA I always knew.

That I was somebody.

Mother was talented, but never to the hilt. Whenever she got somewhere, she stopped! Put her foot through the canvas and started again.

FATHER Frightened of her own shit.

Silence. She looks up at him, watches him.

STANISLAWA But not us. We're alike, aren't we? *(He seems half asleep.)* Everything to the utmost. True Poles.

She laughs, scrambles to her feet, looks into the saucepan and takes it off the stove.

STANISLAWA Coffee? *(She pours coffee into glasses in silver holders, adds cream from a fine jug, with a liberal dash of cognac for him. They sip in silence.)* Same at school. *(He looks at her briefly.)* The nuns. *(His eyes flicker with interest at 'nuns'.)* Coming at you with eyes like a furnace – 'God is Love, God is Love!' 'Listen' I said. 'I don't want love – I want justice.'

His chair scrapes as he turns to her. But she pulls a face as she realises it is not in response... he needs another drink. She pours more cognac into his glass till he gives a short nod. She watches him knock back the cognac and settle back, legs stretched.

She finishes her drink, begins to undress unselfconsciously for bed, unaware that he is watching her like a predator. In her nightie she does a stance, grinning.

STANISLAWA Nuns!

FATHER Turn round.

He looks at her and she shudders slightly. He gazes at her, unblinking. She is held, then turns away.

STANISLAWA I've been trying to read your books. Hopeless, I'm useless at the avant-garde, I must have a literal mind. *(Unnerved by his gaze, she giggles. She rolls over at his feet.)* You know what you are. *(She sits up, cross-legged like a child, gazing up at him. He prods her with his foot.)* An explorer! You don't map jungles, you *create* them! Chaotic new worlds. *(Still no response. He exhales smoke.)* You could give me some help! Say something? Speak to me!

Her FATHER looks at her appraisingly.

FATHER You're filling out.

STANISLAWA resumes writing. A door bangs. He is alert. And relieved at voices, off, and DESMOULINS, calling to him.

DESMOULINS Danton... come *on*! Make up your mind!

DANTON About what?

DESMOULINS enters.

DESMOULINS My God, man, you must know the danger we're in!

DANTON Danger, what danger... what are you talking about?

DESMOULINS Georges!... He's out to destroy you!

DANTON *(laughs loudly)* Robespierre? That little puke?

DESMOULINS We're leaving Paris – are you coming?

DANTON Running down your legs, is it?

DESMOULINS *(as he exits)* Yes!!

DESMOULINS exits.

DANTON Bloody fools! You'll miss the best of it!
I can read it now, in the history books. *(He takes a stance.)*

In the glorious spring of 1794, Danton's heart, despite affairs of state, because Danton was a man, turned to thoughts of love – to dreams of lovers walking, talking, speaking the soft, tender filth between a man and a woman..."

His voice dies to a caressive murmur.

PRZYBYSZEWSKY reads, making notes in the margin of the book dismissively. STANISLAWA, opposite him at the table, writes rapidly, nose down. She pauses - looks up and across at him.

STANISLAWA You know what you are. (*He looks at her.*) A devil. You despise everything. *(She leans over the table, close, and grinning at him, but he merely turns away from her.)* It's not even contempt... no! – nothing so warm. Phenomena – that's all we are to you. Objects.

The idea disturbs her. Pencil in hand she watches him covertly. He looks at her work.

FATHER *(sneers)* French Revolution?

STANISLAWA It's when everything started – it's where we began – the people!

Her FATHER throws back his head in a scoffing gesture.

STANISLAWA Oh I don't count you. You're from the carboniferous layer. This book is going to make me famous, like you. And rich. So rich I'll be able to buy you some new trousers, those are green with piddle stains, people can't take their eyes from your crotch.

He gives her an evil grin.

She crosses, sits on the arm of his chair and inspects him, peering into his face and examining it minutely.

STANISLAWA God, map of Waterloo! Where did you get that scar, it's down to the bone... you're all pock marks and purple veins. Keep still. *(She leans over him and squeezes a blackhead on his cheek.)* Hold still, it's huge.

He puts his hand up to the spot, rubbing it. She takes his hand, peruses it.

STANISLAWA Another lab specimen. *(She strokes his hand.)*

He watches, then takes her hand and kisses it with mock gallantry.

STANISLAWA *(laughing)* My ugly angel. *(He lifts both her hands, kisses the inkstains and then begins to lick them.)* Don't.

She gets up and moves away. Shivers. Moves to the stove, touches the pipe. The light fades. And up immediately. She is sitting on the low hearth, scribbling quickly. Her FATHER watches, drink in hand. She throws down the writing block, exhausted. He bends, picks it up, reads.

FATHER Robespierre? Want a revolution, you want a Danton.

STANISLAWA No you don't.

FATHER Why not?

STANISLAWA Because they're the same. Robespierre and Danton. Men. Wanting blood. And then sick of it. Men like to kill. Experience killing. Until they do it. Then it's too late. The damage is done.

FATHER *(jeers)* And women?

STANISLAWA Women bleed anyway.

He mutters under his breath.

STANISLAWA What?

FATHER Danton's a man! You know what a man is, don't you?

STANISLAWA *(bleak)* Yes. I've just had him arrested.

He rises, glares, and steps forward, as though to clout her. She stands her ground, and he shoves her heavily, so that she falls. He exits. The sound of a heavy door slamming, offstage. STANISLAWA scrambles clumsily to her feet and moves to the stove, waiting for her pan of milk to warm.

STANISLAWA *(V.O.)* Now it's a stalking match. Paris is anarchy. Factions form by the day. One thing is clear... to the Convention... to the Committees... to Paris itself. Control must be established. By one man. It must be Robespierre – or Danton. Revolution – or reaction.

She crosses to the table, sits and writes with increasing rapidity for a long moment. Silence but for the rustle of paper as she covers swift pages. An atmosphere of rapt serenity. A letter drops through the door. She reads it aloud.

HELENA ...My dear, again no word from you. Even the-man-without-imagination,your in-love-with-his-own-importance Uncle looked in the letterbox this morning... probably to see if his elevation to the nobility had arrived... anyway, anyway, dear heart, here's a little money for food and fuel... *(STANISLAWA is grasping the letter in her left hand as she writes, now puts down her pen, opens the letter to enjoy the sight of the money... re-reads the letter as we hear HELENA's voice.)* ...Pani Nowicka did a pattern for my dress with the new neckline – what do you think? *(STANISLAWA looks at the sketch, laughs.)* ...will it excite the choir too much, I don't want to cause seizures. *(STANISLAWA laughs.)* How is your dreadful Pere – demonic as ever? Be careful, dearest. He is not a good person. I must stop now, I have a sheep's head to pickle – no, FOR your Uncle – the only man in Cracow who thought a lemon had legs and squeezed a canary into his schnapps.

STANISLAWA puts down the letter, smiling. She laughs quietly, looks up at the noise of her FATHER's entrance. She rises and backs away as he lurches towards her, drunk and dangerous.

FATHER Get out.

STANISLAWA What's the matter?

FATHER Get out!

Silence. STANISLAWA is shocked.

STANISLAWA I haven't anywhere to go.

He crosses to the door, re-enters with a WOMAN.

STANISLAWA Oh. I'm sorry. I -

But she stands, shocked, unable to move. The WOMAN whispers to her FATHER, who begins to grope at her. Ignoring STANISLAWA, they embrace noisily. Then the WOMAN pulls away.

WOMAN What about the money, where's the money?

He cracks her across the face, begins to rip her clothes off. But the WOMAN fights back. She lifts the piece of chairback, clouts him over the head. He reels. The WOMAN sees HELENA's money, takes it, makes her escape, but he follows her. Sounds of the fight outside the door... screams and shouts... her FATHER's hoarse swearing. Then the sounds die away to silence.

STANISLAWA stands. Her FATHER enters. His head is bleeding from a head wound, and the blood is running down his face. STANISLAWA bursts out laughing.

STANISLAWA Hah... borscht soup!

He slumps into a chair, she runs for the enamel bowl, and washes his face with a flannel.

STANISLAWA Serves you right. (*She takes a prudent step back as his head rears up, one eye closing. But he looks up, with a gap-toothed smile.*) Oh, you devil... you love it, don't you? *(She cleans his face.)* You're a devil, d'you know that? *(She clasps him to her protectively. He lifts her onto his lap, covers her with tender kisses.) (laughing)* No... no! Wrong woman! *(But he kisses her on the mouth. She slides down, backs away from him.)* It's me, Stanislawa... what are you kissing ME for?

He begins to stalk her.

She laughs, hides, jumps out at him. He grabs at her and she wrestles herself free. He catches her, she escapes again. And then he grabs her, tearing her clothes. This startles her, and she stops playing. But he continues to stalk her. And now it is certainly not a game.

There is a prolonged, silent tussle. Then he traps her and throws her down, lifting her clothes and forcing her legs open. She makes a last, despairing effort to escape. He puts a hand on her neck, half-throttling her. And then reaches out, taking up an empty wine bottle.

She shrieks, one awful howling shriek.

ACT TWO

AUNT HELENA has come to collect STANISLAWA and her belongings. She moves about quietly, packing with efficient precision. STANISLAWA sits, white-faced. HELENA folds clothes into a wicker basket, packs books into straps, holds up an old garment to her niece, gets no response, packs the garment. STANISLAWA rises, moves away, deep within herself. She moves, then stands by the table. Her manner is odd. HELENA exits with books and returns, observes STANISLAWA.

HELENA Are you on morphine? *(STANISLAWA looks across at her with a level stare.)* When did you start? Never mind. We'll wait until you feel more like yourself. *(STANISLAWA shakes her head violently, turns away.)* You will. Trust me.

STANISLAWA No.

She turns with a sudden, frightening violence, reaches out as HELENA steps back, lifts a plate high and drops it. It smashes.

STANISLAWA Finished.

HELENA No.

That's not true, by God, if that were true would Poland ever survive, crushed between the Hun and the Russki? Trample a plant, it springs up again... sun, water, the right soil... *(as STANISLAWA shakes her head)*... ohh, you are a Pole! Swords against guns, horses against tanks... learn to bend!... you won't be the first woman to... *(as she gets hot milk)* ...where is he, by the way? Your father.

STANISLAWA Gone to Posnan.

HELENA What for?

STANISLAWA I don't know! To frighten the women and children I suppose.

HELENA smiles. She gives STANISLAWA a drink of hot milk. STANISLAWA sips.

HELENA You're as mad as he is.

STANISLAWA Well, I'm his daughter! *(But the milk makes her feel better.)* You don't understand.

All my life, until I found him, I was in the wrong place. The wrong planet. I kept waiting – waiting for it all to stop – for my own life... MY life, to begin.

HELENA Oh my dear.

STANISLAWA What?

HELENA Don't you know? I thought you knew.

STANISLAWA What?

HELENA All women feel that. In the centre of things, but exiled.

STANISLAWA looks at HELENA. They sip hot milk.

STANISLAWA I used to dream about him. My father. This big handsome Swede... not a slight, fine-boned... at least, not until one day at school in Paris, we started on the French Revolution.

ROBESPIERRE enters silently during the above and works with rapid intensity at his desk. Now and then he rings a small bell which the women half-hear. ST. JUST enters, takes away signed papers.

STANISLAWA I couldn't take it in. All these people – a whole country – believing that it was possible to start again, make an entirely new society – *(HELENA smiles.)* – think of it – to rule not by power but by decency! *(HELENA laughs wryly.)* Oh, I know it only lasted a couple of years – that came as a shock –

HELENA Too fast. Gardens take time to grow.

STANISLAWA I'm not an onion! *(HELENA ruffles her hair affectionately.)* Perhaps you're right.

HELENA Poor husbandry, I call it.

STANISLAWA Yes, but what they achieved!

HELENA While they had their heads.

STANISLAWA New criminal codes, equality before the law, trial by jury! Nepotism abolished, freedom for Jews and Protestants, education out of the hands of the Church... Robespierre even wanted the right to fair employment legalised! I couldn't stop talking, I tried to tell people how phenomenal it all was – of course nobody listened. At school they thought I was cracked and who else was there to tell?

HELENA Your mother?

STANISLAWA When I wasn't hiding the bottles. It didn't matter. None of it mattered. I wasn't alone any more. HE was there.

HELENA Your hero?

STANISLAWA Maximilien Robespierre. I couldn't believe it. Everything I thought, felt... his thoughts... his feelings...

She shivers in ecstasy. HELENA unwraps waxed paper, offers STANISLAWA an iced cake. She takes it and bites, murmuring with pleasure.

ROBESPIERRE sits back, closes his eyes, exhausted. ST. JUST enters with a tray of food but ROBESPIERRE is too tired to eat. ST. JUST pauses but ROBESPIERRE continues to work. Looks up as ST. JUST hovers, worried that ROBESPIERRE is ill.

ROBESPIERRE How can I stop when so much is unbearable?

ST. JUST goes.

STANISLAWA Sometimes... when we were in the money... my mother would splash out. Once in Venice new clothes from the skin out – hats, shoes, handbags, we spent a fortune on costumes for Carnival, she was with this Armenian, in tungsten. The Lido, the Opera, gondolas... it was as if we were in a spell.

Only there was this beggar. With no nose. You kept seeing him – Venice is a small place.

Another time, on the Riviera, one of her lovers had built a hotel – all glass and marble, you would have hated it. There was this dog, under my window at the back where the garden hadn't been made up. He howled, all the time. Nobody took a blind bit of notice and in the end I couldn't stand it and said couldn't something be done, so one of the waiters hit him on the head with a spade. In front of me. And waited for a tip.

HELENA Oh! Killed it?

STANISLAWA *(shaking her head)* It crawled off into the pines. I could hear the noises for two days but I couldn't find him. Then they stopped. How can you enjoy yourself?

ROBESPIERRE pauses, tired. ST. JUST enters with more paper for him. ROBESPIERRE grimaces.

ST. JUST At least you're safe now.

ROBESPIERRE Safe!

ST. JUST Danton will be where he belongs, where all dangerous animals belong. In a cage!

STANISLAWA is suddenly overcome with laughter. She cannot stop, stuffs her skirt into her mouth. HELENA watches patiently.

STANISLAWA My Hero! *(She cackles with laughter.)* When I saw him! The clothes... his smell... perfect ugliness!

HELENA His books! Did you read them?

STANISLAWA Terrible!... each one worse than the last!

HELENA A long way from Robespierre.

STANISLAWA *(her mood darkening)* At least they both want change.

HELENA He's a destroyer. Out.

STANISLAWA So's Robespierre.

HELENA Now you're being – *(picks up FATHER'S coat)* Ugh! He's left his stink behind!

STANISLAWA What's wrong with that?

HELENA There's no virtue in filth. It gives you disease.

STANISLAWA Perhaps disease is more interesting.

HELENA Don't be silly.

STANISLAWA *(slight pause)* Anyway, it was my own fault.

HELENA The fact that he did his best to murder you.

STANISLAWA He was drunk.

HELENA Stashinka, face the truth.

STANISLAWA You don't understand.

HELENA Understand what? Mystical rubbish about being an artist? Normal rules please ignore? He's flawed! A monster! He thinks there's no God, that he's on his own, that he can do as he likes... and survive. All right. He is your father. You found him. Now let go. We have to survive our parents.

STANISLAWA rises, stands before HELENA.

STANISLAWA You have such a clear mind.

HELENA Survive. For me.

STANISLAWA For the work.

She gets out the morphine.

HELENA My dear, do you need that?

STANISLAWA Oh yes. It releases the mind wonderfully.

HELENA Isn't it risky?

STANISLAWA It keeps me going.

She sits, reaches for paper, ignoring HELENA. HELENA watches her for a moment, then puts on her hat and coat and goes.

ST. JUST It was necessary! You saw them on the streets, inciting the Sans-Culottes, every peasant and journeyman to rage and outrage! It had to be stopped.

ROBESPIERRE We have lost colleagues.

ST. JUST Enemies of France.

ROBESPIERRE Men of ability.

ST. JUST The more culpable then.

ROBESPIERRE Give them their due –

ST. JUST The misuse of influence!

ROBESPIERRE They believed –

ST. JUST Believed what – what? To identify with the unwashed, the uneducated, the helpless – sanctimonious sentimentality! Democracy *must* be directed from above... you can't rely on spontaneous ardour, the roar from the boulevards. You've said it yourself – we have eradicated extremists. They were dangerous – destructive and divisive.

ROBESPIERRE Mostly misguided. Yes! – I signed their death warrants. For the safety of... nonetheless, we have lost men of fine feelings.

ST. JUST All men have their price – for some it's martyrdom.

ROBESPIERRE Cynicism? From you? Antoine!

ST. JUST turns away, looks out of the window.

ROBESPIERRE Why will a mother die to defend her child?

ST. JUST Animal instinct.

ROBESPIERRE A man will lay down his life for a friend... for his dog... his horse! If there were no feelings beyond the mundane, the self-concerned, society would never have emerged to its present complexity and mutual dependence. Man would still forage as predator, in the chaos of jungle. Or be as extinct as the dinosaur. By asking less of man, you will diminish him to the mean creature you despise. *(He looks up at ST. JUST.)* Having nullified the danger from the Left, you now want me to excise Danton. Who's next? Me?

ST. JUST *(genuinely shocked)* Maxime!

ROBESPIERRE I'm sorry. You must see the dangers within, as well as –

ST. JUST And you must see that he's after your blood... all the more since you – we cut down his friends... you know he courts men in every quarter. Maxime, we cannot lose France... this revolution... after the sacrifices that have been made... because you find a man charming.

He is not charming. He is a thug. Growing meaner and more dangerous with fear by the day. You believe in human virtue. Do me the courtesy of conceding human vice. It is all around you.

The Terror has been established, not for revenge, but for control. Without control, we are open to the most savage exploitation by the most criminal. Better the Ancien Régime than that. The use of Terror has been sanctioned by the Convention. Please have the statesmanship to use it.

A pause.

ROBESPIERRE I am seeking to preserve. For France. Yes, he is a venal man – but he knows it. He respects me. He will do my bidding. We need his voice. I can't afford the luxury of more heads in the gutter.

ST. JUST rises in fury. He sweeps up his papers and his jacket.

ST. JUST Paris will never forgive you.

He goes.

Lightning, thunder, a loud clap which frightens ROBESPIERRE. STANISLAWA turns, looking dazed. ROBESPIERRE finds it hard to breathe. He holds onto the table to steady himself, breathes deeply and goes as the thunder rumbles. STANISLAWA sits, as if exhausted.

DANTON enters, vigorous and alive in a greatcoat. He dashes the rain from his hat, takes off his coat, throws it down.

DANTON My God... *(He laughs, excited, looks out of the window, breathes deeply.)* ...the air! Ohh! The first night of spring... I could pleasure the world!

He strides back and forth, unable to keep still, smirks briefly at STANISLAWA, then returns to the window, surveying the scene below him.

DANTON *(softly)* Well, Paris... are you mine?

But as he turns away from the window, his mood darkens. He stands, his head between his shoulders like a bull at bay. He mutters incoherently to himself, moving about restlessly. Then, with an effort, he pulls himself together.

DANTON Danton...! You're not finished yet!

STANISLAWA drops something. DANTON turns wildly, his eyes wide with alertness. He staggers back at what seems to be a spectre. STANISLAWA sits to write.

He sighs with relief. The spectre is his young wife LOUISE, standing, like a ghost in her white nightclothes. She holds a candelabrum high and waves it slightly, to see who is there. When she recognises DANTON she turns at once to go out again.

DANTON No, don't go.

She turns at the door, then, unwillingly, approaches him like a sullen schoolgirl. He looks at her. And cannot resist her. He takes the candelabrum from her and puts it on the table. She backs away but he grabs her fiercely and begins to cover her face and neck with fierce kisses. He groans and starts to shiver unrestrainedly with desire.

LOUISE Don't...

She manages to shake him off and moves away. As he approaches her the cold passivity of her face stops him. He turns his head away, grimacing horribly.

LOUISE What is it? *(She touches his arm and he turns and his expression frightens her. She shudders, stammers)* What's the matter, are you ill?

He shakes his head, comes close, standing before her, head bent, like a submissive animal.

DANTON *(mutters)* Please...

LOUISE *(jerks back at his smell)* Don't, I don't want to!

He grabs her arm and she shrieks as though scalded, making him jump. There is a tussle.

LOUISE *(breaking away)* I'm pregnant!

He looks at her open-mouthed, then a slow smile suffuses his face. He comes forward.

LOUISE How can I carry a child, I'm not even fully developed!

DANTON I'll be very gentle, I'll hardly go inside – *(grabbing at her).*

She spits in his face. Shocked, he lets her go. She hisses, from a safe distance.

LOUISE You really think a woman goes with an old man for pleasure?!

DANTON I've been very patient with –

LOUISE You bought me like a dog on a string!

He steps back, mesmerised by the hate in her face.

LOUISE When was I asked? Who consulted me? I can wait.

DANTON Wait? For what?

LOUISE Every time you slander him I know he's won... taken one more day away from you. And I thank God for it.

Silence. He crosses, gazes out of the window, his back to her. She waits, trembling. He turns at last.

DANTON *(growls)* You should have kept your mouth shut. I was going to let them butcher me.

She backs away from him but he laughs suddenly, very loud. He seems all at once suffused with life, he looks bigger, younger, more handsome.

DANTON A Robespierre? Demolish a Danton? *(He laughs.)* What do you know of the world? You think I can't turn Paris? In a night? *(He closes on her, his eyes glittering.)* I'll make you a present. Crush the little reptile and give you his bones for an eggtimer.

He smiles at her triumphantly.

The sound of marching. It ceases, close. A heavy pounding on the door. They both freeze.

ST. JUST enters. He hands a paper to DANTON, who scans it briefly, screws it, and throws it down. He moves towards LOUISE, who moves away from him. DANTON, horribly embarrassed by her show of disloyalty, embraces her, grabbing her and kissing her passionately. He waves a contemptuous hand to ST. JUST... he is ready to leave. But LOUISE has drawn ST. JUST aside in whispered conversation. They both look at him. DANTON smiles gaily. She points to his coat, but he waves a dismissive hand, he will not need it. She rolls it into a bundle and thrusts it towards him. He will not take it. ST. JUST takes the coat brusquely, indicates for DANTON to leave. It looks as though DANTON will strike him, but then he smiles again, a wide, sickening smile, and sweeps out. ST. JUST looks keenly at LOUISE, who stands like a statue, then moves to the window, to see them leave below. She goes out with the candelabrum held high.

STANISLAWA, from her table, observes ST. JUST.

STANISLAWA *(to ST. JUST)* You've been down to the Convention?

ST. JUST I've just come from the floor.

STANISLAWA And?

ST. JUST Hostility and confusion. But once the air is cleared, oh!... everything possible!

STANISLAWA smiles at him disbelievingly. He jumps onto the table.

ST. JUST Maxime! The air's suffused – can't you feel it, smell it... the new century, so close! Think of it – a new age. An age of science... reason. Imperialism as dead as Attila the Hun.

STANISLAWA Gone? That easily?

ST. JUST By the stroke of the pen. Aristocracy... privilege of random birth... nepotism... domination of the church... all removed – by edict.

STANISLAWA You believe it, that the lawyers will rule the world?

ST. JUST Justice –

STANISLAWA Ah, well, justice. And who will enforce it, your justice? The warriors? Whose tents you've burned, whose honour you deride?

ST. JUST Honour? Medieval superstition. An impulse to suicide. There must be force... yes... to protect us... a properly organised body of men devoted to just aims and –

STANISLAWA They'll be needed.

She sits, as if defeated.

ST. JUST Maxime! *(softly)* Courage! *(fierce)* You cannot turn back now.

STANISLAWA *(looks up at him)* Oh I don't intend to.

ST. JUST He must be eliminated.

STANISLAWA I agree.

ST. JUST I'm glad to hear it. Every stone in the path of –

STANISLAWA *(waves a hand)* Please. I shall kill Georges because if I do not, he will kill me.

ST. JUST Thank God. His ambition –

STANISLAWA Not even ambition. Georges believes himself to be the better choice.

ST. JUST Hah! The degree of self-delusion alone denotes a lesser –

ROBESPIERRE enters.

ROBESPIERRE Antoine... how can Georges Danton... idol of the people... lover of women... allow himself to be dominated by a man with a smaller member than himself?

ST. JUST Primitive!

STANISLAWA He would say human.

ST. JUST At all events behind bars.

ROBESPIERRE If we can keep him there. Hah! 'You have one bad card Georges.' *(ST. JUST frowns in enquiry.)* He is a romantic.

ST. JUST Good, he can go down as the main martyr of the Revolution if it makes him feel better.

STANISLAWA He won't see that as his role.

ST. JUST Because he thinks he's going to win?

ROBESPIERRE Are we so sure that he won't?

He goes to the door. Sounds of pandemonium.

LEGENDRE *(V.O., dominating)* Friends... members of the Convention! Permission to speak... permission to speak!

We have just been shocked and outraged to learn that members of this government have, this night, been arrested...

STANISLAWA writes swiftly.

LEGENDRE ...we hear, to our amazement and disbelief, that one of the accused is Citizen Danton! *(Reaction.)* Comrades... brothers... I move that those who have been arrested are permitted to answer charges against them on the floor of this Chamber. They deserve, they have earned... the right of reply. *(Reaction.)* Only then will we discover whether envy and spite are at the root of these shocking arrests.

Noise. ROBESPIERRE AND ST. JUST look at each other.

ROBESPIERRE *(addressing the audience, shrill, against the noise)* I request the right to speak... I request the right to speak! *(He stands, immobile, waits a long time for the noise on the P/A to die down.)*

(mildly) It's a long time, gentlemen, since we began our sitting with such a display of temper. *(He pauses, looks around.)* Today... today we shall see what we value more – the Republic – or the individual.

STANISLAWA We'll see if you deserve to rule, tyrant!

ROBESPIERRE *(looks across at her coolly)* I will raise that point too. *(He waits for silence on the P/A.)* Citizen Legendre demands that the accused be allowed to answer charges from this floor. *(Shouts of agreement. He raises his voice.)* Are you saying – are you saying that you wish to accord to those now under arrest privileges that have been denied those preceding them? If Citizen Legendre believes in special consideration then that is a mistake which we must correct for him. It is not the function of a revolutionary Convention to grant privilege. That is what we are here to abolish.

Silence.

LEGENDRE *(V.O.)* To hear the accused from this floor is not privilege, it's simple justice!

COURTIS *(V.O.)* And you watch out – the fall of Danton will crush you to pieces!

Noise.

STANISLAWA Robespierre?

He nods at her briefly, again waits for silence.

ROBESPIERRE If... if by some mystic law the destruction of criminality should bring about my ruin, well... what of it?

What is so devastating about that?

Are we... are we to allow private danger to inhibit public decision?

Of course not.

He pauses, and looks about him keenly, as if to note every man present.

ROBESPIERRE I move that the order for the arrest of Danton and his confederates be confirmed.

Loud cheering on the P/A. He allows himself a small smile towards STANISLAWA, picks up his papers and goes.

STANISLAWA, frozen and exhausted, puts down her pencil and tries to rise. She cannot. She crawls over to the fire, hauls herself onto her knees, collapses, then manages to get to her feet. She picks up a painting, feebly tries to wrench off the stretcher for firewood. She is too weak and begins to cry silently with frustration.

She reaches for two letters, rips them open, searches feverishly, tearing the envelopes apart.

STANISLAWA No – money!

She screws the letters violently in her fists, throws them down unread. She sits, exhausted.

HELENA *(V.O.)* ...I'm sorry, my dear, but all my jewellery is gone, I've tried everything... *(voice fades and up again)* ...I hope you used the zloties from my little table to buy a warm coat... *(voice down and up)* WHY can't I come and see you...? You say you're well but... *(voice down and up)* ... still nothing from you *(cross fade)* What do you mean, how can you ask me not to write, I'm your Aunt! *(voice down and up)* ...My dear, if that is what you wish... *(voice down and up)* ...there was no need for you to... *(voice down and up)* ...My dear Stanislawa, I am in receipt of your brief note and regret to tell you that the university will not renew your grant.

They say that you must attend a sanatorium for the withdrawal of drugs. Sincerely, Your Aunt Helena.

STANISLAWA rises, knocking over the chair in fury.

STANISLAWA What is the matter with them! Do they think I'm mad!! It is my right to have the money, I have a right to it, I am an artist, that is what the money is for, do they want proof, what proof do they want? I work! Till four in the morning! Is it because I see no-one? What do they want me to do, lead the literary life, inhabit the anal orifices of publishers, literary hostesses?

No, I am not depressed! Nor am I lonely. I am alone in order to work and I cope with loneliness by working. If you inhabited the world that I inhabit, a world of the most potent, the most thrilling thought, then you would not be in the least concerned for my welfare.

I am in a fever, yes. But of excitement, for the work! There is not a character whose nerves are not stretched into red hot wires across chasms of fright – I can hardly stop them disintegrating! *(Slight fade on voice.)*

Noise, the sound of voices approaching. The name of Danton is heard. DANTON enters.

DANTON Gentlemen – *(Shouts of 'quiet'.)* Gentlemen, to business *(He waits for quiet.)* Friends... I, Danton, I alone can save you. So, if you don't want to end up as dog's meat... *(He laughs loudly. Some other laughter, subdued.)* My friends... a political trial is not a trial. It is a duel. The government accuses us? Then we accuse the government... believe me, the game's not over yet!

DESMOULINS *(by the door)* I don't want to die - I want to live! Georges!

He laughs, loud and long on the P/A. He sees STANISLAWA and sobers somewhat.

STANISLAWA Robespierre came to see Desmoulins this morning. *(DANTON shrugs.)* You persuaded Desmoulins not to see him. By that you have sent your friend to his death.

DANTON What do any of them matter? You think their lives are worth one hour of Danton's existence?

STANISLAWA, repelled, draws back but he does not notice.

DANTON Cut me down like a common conscript? I'll see him choke on his own vomit first. *(to STANISLAWA)* Watch me face the Tribunal... *(laughs)*... once I let out the roar, bathe them in my loving eyes... carried by acclamation! As I sweep past in triumph shoulder high he'll be stumbling down the steps to perdition – ohh, we'll see his little toes twitch!

STANISLAWA And then?

DANTON And then... ohh... and then...

(He laughs in ecstasy.)

And then...

Why, Life! Pleasure!

Pourquoi pas?

Why not splendour... processions, music... fine food, fine houses in the most beautiful country in the world, ohh, La Belle France! – I could eat you, every morsel, from the Manche to the Mare Nostrum – oh, my beloved country! And to think I believed myself finished with it all!

(He turns to her, his eyes shining) Danton, finished – with Living?

I want it – now! My Life! All of it, stretching ahead of me till I'm old and tired and quiet... till I'm ready, made my peace, paid my dues, kissed my grandchildren farewell... I *must have* my Life! Christ, I can't wait to get my boots on... I can't wait for the light!

He wraps himself in his cloak and lies down, out of sight as STANISLAWA groans, and collapses in a heap on the floor.

The light goes.

A pause. Lights up on the empty room. The sound of the cat mewing. STANISLAWA is aroused. She finds her morphine and takes it. A tap at the door.

STANISLAWA *(abrupt)* What?

ANNA sticks a head round the door. She has a basket of food. STANISLAWA looks at her, then at the basket.

STANISLAWA Put it on the table.

ANNA does so, waits. STANISLAWA, unpacking her basket, ignores her. She hems.

STANISLAWA That's all. You can go.

ANNA gapes, and then smiles, as at a lunatic and goes, clipping the door sharply. This rings round STANISLAWA's head, making her wince. But she goes to the basket and eats, not even looking at what she is eating. She clears the table in one swoop, gets out her work, sits. The unaccustomed food makes her feel slightly ill. She half collapses in her chair.

ROBESPIERRE enters, is helped into a chair by ST. JUST. ST. JUST puts drops from a phial into a glass, gives the medicine to ROBESPIERRE who drinks it, wincing at the taste. He sets the glass down shakily. A knock at the door. ST. JUST goes out, we hear him talking urgently. He re-enters.

ST. JUST They're waiting for you.

At once ROBESPIERRE is on his feet, smiling and in apparent good health. He sweeps out followed by ST. JUST. STANISLAWA gasps, trying to pull herself together for work... But her head goes back on the chair.

STANISLAWA Either you can get me money, get my manuscript typed... or you're of no use to me!!

You're not my mother! What do you want – gratitude?

You can see how grateful I am! – I'm *working*!!

I'm doing what I'm *for*!

All I want is money for drugs, and a little food.

Don't keep sending letters!

She picks up her pen, writes a letter to her Aunt.

STANISLAWA *(live, writing)* Helena – I don't want to call you Aunt any more, it's too cloying... please know that I reserve the ownership of my life exclusively for myself. At the cost of comfort, companionship and dignity. None of it is important. *(She stops writing.)* It's amazing what you can do without. Were you aware that one can live indefinitely on snow? *(She looks around.)* My beautiful... beautiful Snow Palace! If you could see the frosting on the windows! I'm surrounded by jewels! My breath on the air keeps me company, the icicles on the window are my guardians. This is all there is. This and *work*. If you have no money to send, forget me. If necessary I shall beg on the streets. So please... no more interruption. I have Danton's trial to deal with.

ROBESPIERRE enters quickly, throws himself down at the table as the sound, from several separate sources, rises on the P/A. STANISLAWA crosses to him urgently and speaks, out of breath, her voice raised against the hubbub on the P/A.

STANISLAWA Danton's star... is rising by the minute... keep away from the Tribunal, the galleries have gone mad, they're screaming for your blood... you... *(gasping for breath)*... all the Committee, they want to guillotine the lot of us!

She exits. Noise on the P/A.

Silence. ROBESPIERRE plays with a knife on the table.

ROBESPIERRE *(looks up)* I don't know. For the moment I cannot see a way out.

The following are all in STANISLAWA'S voice:

BARERE *(V.O.)* But our lives are threatened!

COLLOT *(V.O.)* We could be dead tomorrow!

CARNOT *(V.O.)* We shall have to give in.

BARERE *(V.O.)* Yes... we must release Danton at once!

COLLOT *(V.O.)* Yes, you must sign the order now!

CARNOT *(V.O.)* You said yourself, what is humiliation where the good of the state is concerned?

BARERE *(V.O.)* At least we might survive –

COLLOT *(V.O.)* For the greater good, Maxime –

BARERE *(V.O.)* Do it, do it for all of us –

ROBESPIERRE *(to STANISLAWA, as he rises, jams the knife into the table)* No!!! *(Silence.)* That's enough. *(He pauses, then continues in a trembling voice.)* You think this country can be governed by cringing weakness?

Enter ST. JUST.

STANISLAWA *(to ROBESPIERRE)* The Tribunal's completely surrounded. Counter-Revolutionaries in all the galleries... they've smuggled arms into the chambers... *(She gasps for breath.)* they're ready to slaughter every deputy in the Chamber...

ST. JUST What are you going to do now?

STANISLAWA Robespierre?

ROBESPIERRE *(looks up in cold fury)* I will tell you what now. Your miserable and unimportant lives have been saved for you. *(raises his voice, calls)* Saint-Just! Take an armed force and surround the building! All citizens found to be carrying arms to be arrested on the spot!

STANISLAWA It's all right then?

ROBESPIERRE No, it is not all right. Now we rule by Terror and Terror alone. *(He groans loudly.)* God knows I never foresaw this.

STANISLAWA But are we safe?

ROBESPIERRE *(looks up, tired)* For the moment.

ROBESPIERRE rises, then falls back onto his chair.

ROBESPIERRE I'm sorry. I'm deadly tired. Go down to the floor for me. Tell them – let Danton talk for as long as he wants. But arrest his defence witnesses. Let's see what he is on his own.

STANISLAWA waits restlessly by the window. She goes outside, clears a hole in the frost and snow on the window panes, returns.

STANISLAWA Come on... come on...

A sound of steps. A knock. She throws open the door, returns with a letter, rips it open, looks for money. There is none.

STANISLAWA Nothing.

Nothing.

Nothing.

Nothing.

Nothing.

(Pause.)

I must keep the margins straight.

She looks for something to use as a straight edge, goes outside, comes back with a piece of piping. She looks at the pencil stubs on her table.

STANISLAWA Three left.

I could ask.

I could go to the school.

Go out.

Am I dissolving?

If no-one sees me, do I exist?

Perhaps I am just beginning.

I must...

Dear –

She sits, half collapses onto the chair with difficulty. All her movements are stiff, slow, erratic, strange.

STANISLAWA *(V.O.)* ...20, Frimaire...

which to you is the tenth of December, 1928.

Zero centigrade. I can no longer afford a fire.

Odd reactions of the body to the cold.

The atmosphere penetrates. All the tissues contract.

Everything grows stiff, like hardening wax.

You can't think. You can't eat, at any rate, not stone cold bread and butter. Your tongue, your throat, your palate isn't warm enough. You can't swallow. If you do, your stomach rejects.

You can't think.

But she starts to write. Her chair is at an angle to the table and she cannot straighten it. It takes her a long time even to pick up her pen. But, slowly, she begins to write.

DANTON appears in the dock. His face is savage, his eyes wild. He looks about him, and his look is fearsome.

DANTON *(to audience)* You vile, stinking rubbish. You mindless weak-willed ordure... what are you, you braying flock of offal? Oh you'll roar, when some whimpering wretch is being crushed underfoot, that gets your blood going – but *loyalty*?! I know you, you rabble. *(Sounds of laughter.)*

Laugh, would you? When you should be pissing your own blood away for shame? You're spit in the wind... anybody's.

And for what? You? The people? Take over the world? Allow me to make room for you. Felicitations, brothers. You'll be in blood up to your eyeballs.

It's waiting for you – the cart. Can't you hear its wheels creaking – it's waiting for you – yes – you – and you – and you –

And Him! He'll rot! Smell him – that's him... Maxime Robespierre... rotting... dissolving... beside the bones of Georges Danton!!!!!!!!

He stumbles out noisily. ROBESPIERRE moves out of the shadows, watches discreetly from the window.

The sound of a crowd approaching. The sound of the wheels of the tumbril on cobblestones. ROBESPIERRE watches, immobile. DANTON can be heard, bellowing.

DANTON *(as the tumbril passes the window)* I bequeath you my balls, Robespierre. You'll need them!

The sounds die away slowly. ROBESPIERRE stays by the window.

ROBESPIERRE *(murmurs)* Requiescat in pace.

He staggers as he moves away from the support of the wall by the window.

ROBESPIERRE Danton...!

It seems that he will faint. He sways.

With an enormous effort of will he crosses, sits in STANISLAWA's chair and begins to deal with state papers. He works for a prolonged moment, his movements rigid, orderly and precise. She sits at his side, writing.

At last the pile of papers is finished. He puts them in neat files and into folders, ties the folders, straightens his pens, the things on the table, sits up for a still moment, breathes deeply.

ROBESPIERRE Finished.

STANISLAWA puts down her pencil and looks at him. He rises, tucks the folders under one arm and walks out with a rigid gait.

Silence.

The door is open and there is snow in the room. Snow is banked against the window, covering the panes entirely. STANISLAWA sits. She is frozen to her chair, her arm frozen in the act of writing, seemingly turned towards ROBESPIERRE'S chair in a permanent gaze.

Lights down.

The end.

PREFACE TO SWEET DREAMS

In his short-lived treatment of eighteen-year-old Ida Bauer, to whom he gave the pseudonym *Dora*, Sigmund Freud, the father of psychoanalysis, makes ill-founded, subjective assumptions about female sexuality and desire, subsequently tarnishing, in the eyes of many, his eminent legacy. He wrote the case study from memory in January 1901, shortly after Ida's treatment ended, and eventually published it in 1905. I welcomed the opportunity to grapple with *Fragment of an Analysis of a Case of Hysteria* – one of Freud's most contentious case studies – in the stage play *Sweet Dreams,* commissioned by Sphinx Theatre Company.

In the play, Ida isn't simply portrayed as an innocent victim, dissected on the slab of patriarchal Viennese *fin de siècle* psychoanalysis but as an intelligent, precocious young woman unafraid to speak her mind, who refuses to go along with Freud's interpretations of what he perceives to be her manifold sexual cravings. She is, however, trapped in a web of subterfuge, delusion and lies perpetrated by her father, his mistress and the mistress's husband who has clumsily attempted to seduce Ida. Their dark deceptions and hypocritical behaviours inform much of Ida's so-called 'hysteria'. Another contributing factor is Ida's compulsive-house-cleaning mother. Although she never graced his couch, Freud concluded that her mother was suffering from 'housewife psychosis'.

As for Freud himself, his blind spots and vulnerabilities are on display, along with – in my opinion at least – his abiding genius. While Ida was certainly one of his most frustrating patients, her brief, self-terminated, eleven-week analysis gave birth to a core pillar of psychoanalytic theory: the concept of transference – whereby a patient will unconsciously project onto their analyst emotions they have towards a significant figure in their life. In later years Freud became less certain that he understood a woman's psyche or her sexuality. His alleged *cri de cœur* in 1925 'What does a woman want?' was followed a year later with the acknowledgement that the sexual life of adult women was a 'dark continent' for psychology.

The episodic structure of *Sweet Dreams* reflects the fragmented nature of the case study itself which largely consists of Freud's memories, reveries and reflections. The play's dream-like ambience is mirrored in its non-naturalistic, dimly-lit set, which is, at times, almost obscured by the smoke emanating from Freud's chain-smoked cigars. The actors, too, are fluid, switching roles to embody different characters and projections. From time to time they become a chorus chivvying, haunting or taunting the main protagonists.

Sue Parrish's inspired, thought-provoking direction helped to make the play accessible and relevant to a modern-day audience. To accompany the play, Sphinx organised stimulating and at times heated pre-performance and post-performance talks and debates, on issues relating to Freud, feminism and sexuality. These lively discussions involved academics, psychoanalysts, feminists and theatregoers who had little or no previous knowledge of Freud or *Fragment of an Analysis of a Case of Hysteria*.

Diane Esguerra

Sweet Dreams by Diane Esguerra
Photo © Dee Conway 1999

SWEET DREAMS

DIANE ESGUERRA

Sweet Dreams was commissioned by Sphinx Theatre Company, and first performed at the Chelsea Centre Theatre in London in October 1999. It was subsequently performed on a National Tour in 2000 – a hundred years after Freud began Ida's analysis. Educational tours followed between 2001 and 2004, and in 2006, the play was performed at the Charleston Festival.

Director	Sue Parrish
Designer	Annabel Lee
Lighting	Natasha Chivers
Sound	Alistair Viles
Choreographer	Claire Russ
Cast	Sam Cox, Jonathan Oliver, Jane Robbins, Sophie Walker and Anne White.

CHARACTERS

IDA BAUER	Attractive, intelligent, hysterical 18-year-old.
PHILIPP BAUER	Ida's father, a middle-aged, self-deluding manufacturer.
KÄTHE BAUER	Ida's distracted, obsessive mother. Mute throughout.
HANS ZELLENKA	A handsome, shadowy, sexual predator.
MARIE ZELLENKA	His beautiful, sensuous, manipulative young wife.
SIGMUND FREUD	Bearded, depressed 44-year-old.
MARTHA FREUD	His matronly wife, concerned with domestic issues.
CHORUS 1	Actor playing Marie Zellenka.
CHORUS 2	Actor playing Käthe Bauer/Martha Freud.
CHORUS 3	Actor playing Philipp Bauer.

The following parts are played by the same actor:

Sigmund Freud and Hans Zellenka

Martha Freud and Käthe Bauer.

BACKGROUND

In 1905, four years after Dora (Ida Bauer) ended her analysis, Sigmund Freud published *Dora: Fragment of an Analysis of a Case of Hysteria.* In time, this case study, based on his memory of her dreams and his post-analysis reflections and observations, came to tarnish his reputation as a twentieth century genius and sexual liberator. In the words of Peter Gay, a leading Freudian scholar, "What is astonishing about 'Dora' is not that Freud delayed publishing it for four years, but that he published it at all."

SET, ATMOSPHERE AND STRUCTURE

The set consists of a couch, a high-backed, analytic swivel chair, a desk with an ashtray, and an ornamental, sloping desk with lock-up drawers. On the wall is a bookshelf which contains an Encyclopaedia, Mantegazza's *Physiology of Love*, and Freud's own, recently published, *The Interpretation of Dreams.* Morally ambivalent images by contemporary artists such as Klimt, Schiele, and Kokoschka, and the music of Strauss, Mahler and Schoenberg can be drawn upon to evoke the atmosphere of *fin de siècle* Vienna.

The play is set in the 'real time' of Freud's consulting room in Vienna, New Years Eve/Day 1900-1901, and April 1st, 1902, and in the 'unreal' time of his memory and imagination. As Freud's memories of Ida's history, dreams and analysis start to emerge, the set becomes fluid, and with the imaginative use of costume, mirrors and lighting, metamorphoses into a landscape of fragmented recollections, dreams, reflections and aberrations.

A 'chorus' weaves in and around the drama. Animated and static, visible and invisible, at times it reflects the primitive, unconscious, inarticulate drives of the characters, and echoes their internal voices, or 'furies'; at other times it assumes the shape of a collective, clinical super-ego, and passes judgement on the main protagonists from a contemporary perspective.

ACT ONE, SCENE ONE

Smoke. Darkness. Breathing. Gentle inhalations and exhalations give way to sharp, hysterical intakes of breath.

Mirrors are subtly illuminated. We see the faces of the CHORUS reflected in the mirrors.

CHORUS 2 A myriad of selves.

CHORUS 3 Recollections.

CHORUS 1 Dreams.

CHORUS 2 Reflections.

CHORUS 3 Projections of others.

CHORUS 1 Doomed to be suspended in time.

CHORUS 3 Fragmented.

CHORUS 2 Fragmented by time and the unconscious.

IDA enters.

CHORUS 1 'A Fragment of a Case of Analysis.'

CHORUS 3 "The distinction between past present and future is no more than an illusion"...

CHORUS 2 Said Einstein –

CHORUS 3 "... even if a stubborn one."

CHORUS 1 Little did you know,

CHORUS 2 A century ago,

CHORUS 1 When you ended up on his comfortless couch in the Berggasse,

CHORUS 2 Barely able to breathe,

CHORUS 1 That you, Ida Bauer, were destined to become one of the most famous hysterics of all times.

CHORUS 3 Anatomy is destiny – or so he claimed.

CHORUS 2 You thought it would be your brother, the brilliant socialist leader Otto Bauer, who everyone remembered.

CHORUS 3 But it is *your* name – or rather the pseudonym he gave you –

CHORUS 1, 2 & 3 Dora –

CHORUS 2 The name of his sister's servant –

CHORUS 1,2 & 3 Dora –

CHORUS 3 Which is on the syllabuses of all the best universities,

CHORUS 2 And continues to claw away at his reputation.

CHORUS 1 Oh Ida Bauer. Ida Bauer. Bauer means cage.

CHORUS 3 And you're still in one.

CHORUS 1 A woman trapped in a cage of analysis.

CHORUS 2 Destined to dance for eternity.

CHORUS 1 To dance with your shadows,

CHORUS 3 Your lovers and your persecutors,

CHORUS 1 A bizarre quadrille,

CHORUS 3 Of contraction, volition, submission, control.

CHORUS 2 The dance of death.

CHORUS 3 The dance of LIFE!

Bright lights. Music: Strauss.

PHILIPP, KÄTHE and IDA BAUER, HANS and MARIE ZELLENKA, are waltzing together.

IDA dances aggessively with her father. KÄTHE BAUER dances in a world of her own. The ZELLENKAs dance with each other in a cold, detached manner.

IDA dances with MARIE and gazes at her in adoration.

MARIE and BAUER dance together slowly and sensuously. ZELLENKA and IDA look on unhappily.

ZELLENKA smiles at IDA. She looks at him shyly. They dance together. ZELLENKA holds her closer to him and starts to dance faster. IDA looks nervous and starts gasping, asthmatically, for breath. ZELLENKA steers IDA onto the couch. She remains there. The other characters exit.

SCENE TWO

FREUD'S CONSULTING ROOM. IDA is lying on the couch, gasping for breath. FREUD strolls in, lights a cigar and sits down in the analyst's chair. We see his profile.

FREUD Everything that we discussed yesterday, and indeed, everything that we've talked about for the last eleven weeks, still points to the fact that you took all the business with Hans Zellenka far more to heart than you're prepared to admit.

IDA Does it?

FREUD It does indeed. And once again, I would venture to suggest that you desperately hoped Zellenka would marry you.

IDA Really.

FREUD The Zellenkas had talked about getting a divorce...

IDA She's agreed to it finally, but he's no longer interested.

FREUD Because he knows he has no hope of marrying you now. But before – in view of his wife's affair with your father – it could have been quite feasible. In fact in many ways, such a scheme would have been the most practical course of action for all the parties involved.

IDA I was too young to marry him.

FREUD You told me your mother was engaged at seventeen. A daughter usually takes her mother's love story as her model.

IDA If you say so.

FREUD You no longer remonstrate Ida.

IDA I no longer remonstrate.

FREUD No. So you are finally prepared to admit that you are, and always have been, passionately in love with Hans Zellenka.

She yawns.

IDA *(bored)* Yes, yes, yes... Can I go now?

FREUD It isn't time.

IDA It's New Year's Eve.

FREUD Do you have some celebration planned? You're going to watch the fireworks, perhaps?

IDA I'm going home. I promised myself I'd give you until New Year's Eve 1900 to cure me.

FREUD *(taken aback) You* would give *me* until New Year's Eve 1900?

IDA That's what I said, isn't it? Then I would leave for good.

FREUD struggles to maintain his neutral analytic stance.

FREUD Your good or my good, Ida?

IDA I'm past caring.

FREUD When did you decide you were going to leave, for *good*?

IDA Two weeks ago.

FREUD Two weeks! So you gave me two weeks notice. The notice a servant is given.

IDA *(with irony)* Why would I want to treat you like a servant?

FREUD I hope you've thought about this very carefully, Ida.

IDA Of course I have.

She stands.

FREUD You're not cured yet. If you give up now, it will be yourself you're punishing, not me. You could be condemning yourself to a lifetime of neurotic suffering. I've seen how expert you are at inflicting misery on yourself.

IDA You haven't seen *anything*. All *you* see is what you want to see. You haven't seen *me* at all.... Happy New Year!

She exits. FREUD swings his chair around to face the audience. He stares into space, numbed. MARTHA FREUD enters.

MARTHA It's so smoky in here.

FREUD I like it smoky in here.

MARTHA coughs.

MARTHA I don't. I do wish you'd stop.

FREUD Smoking, Martha, is a substitute for masturbation.

MARTHA Please confine comments like that to your work.

Pause.

MARTHA Miss Bauer's left early today, hasn't she?

FREUD Yes. *(Angrily) Schiesse*!

FREUD starts pacing up and down the room.

FREUD Why? Why? Why does she have to leave *now*, when I've almost cured her?

MARTHA She isn't coming back?

FREUD I've put up with her every day for three months now. A living, breathing, argumentative, obnoxious, sensual, surly, defiant, contemptuous eighteen-year-old adolescent. And the last few sessions she's actually been – well, not exactly acquiescing, but certainly not disagreeing with my interpretations.

MARTHA It isn't even as if she were paying for the treatment. Her father is.

FREUD Something must have gone wrong in the analysis. But what? What? I thought I'd got to the root of it. I was almost there. Almost there. I'd almost cured her.

MARTHA And we have such an enormous laundry bill this month, and the school fees...

FREUD ... I know Martha, I know.

Pause. They both look worried.

MARTHA Still, I suppose we can start the celebrations earlier this evening.

FREUD Celebrations?

MARTHA *(smiling)* New Year's Eve celebrations, of course!

FREUD *(grimly)* Of course.

MARTHA You promised the children they could stay up this year – except little Anna. The boys are busy making costumes. They want it to be a surprise.

FREUD I'm not in the mood for any more suprises. Do you think I could be excused – just this once?

MARTHA Certainly not. You could do with some cheering up. You haven't been yourself lately.

FREUD I'm not sure I know what 'myself' is. Perhaps you could enlighten me.

MARTHA Don't talk in riddles. I want us to see this new year in together. You won't let us celebrate the Jewish new year.

FREUD The most interesting thing about this new century is that it contains the dates of our deaths.

MARTHA There you go again.

FREUD *(resigned)* Very well, I'll join you all later.

MARTHA Later?

FREUD Listen Martha, I *have* to find out where I've gone wrong with this girl. I'm feeling enough of a failure as it is, with my book not selling. I need time to reconstruct her case history and recall our analytic sessions.

MARTHA From memory?

FREUD That's all I've got to go on, I'm afraid. I only scribbled down a few after-session notes on a couple of her dreams.

FREUD lies down on the couch.

FREUD Please keep the children out.

MARTHA I shall try. Would you like me to open a window?

FREUD No, thank you.

FREUD closes his eyes.

MARTHA Fresh air might stimulate your memory.

FREUD I'm perfectly comfortable, thank you.

She empties the ashtray.

MARTHA These walls in here have become *so* smoke-stained. I'm sure your patients find them distracting.

FREUD *(becoming impatient) My* patients stare at the ceiling.

MARTHA We really must decorate in here.

She takes out her handkerchief, spits on it, and starts to rub the wall.

MARTHA I wonder how easily the stains will come off.

FREUD *(shouts)* Leave me alone Martha!

SCENE THREE

MEMORY SEQUENCE.

In FREUD's imagination, MARTHA has metamorphosed into the mute KÄTHE BAUER and is flitting around the stage, cleaning everything in sight. IDA is sitting at the ornamental desk, writing a letter.

IDA *(shouts)* Leave me alone, Mother! Don't you *dare* come near my desk. Clean Otto's desk instead. Scrub his homework. Bleach your corsets. Polish the servants. They must be getting pretty grimy, standing around all day with nothing to do. Father says it's a complete waste of money having servants, but a man in his position has to keep up appearances. Why must you do it all yourself, you stupid woman? Just leave my desk alone, will you? It's dusty and filthy, but that's how I want it. Because... because it's my desk. It's MINE. If you *have* to clean something, why don't you clean up your marriage?

IDA puts the letter into an envelope, and places it inside the drawer of the desk. She takes out an exceptionally large key, locks the drawer, and deliberately leaves the key in the lock. She exits. KÄTHE starts dusting the desk. She sees the key, unlocks the drawer, and takes out the letter. She reads it and screams. BAUER comes rushing in. She hands him the letter and exits, distraught. He reads the letter and is visibly shaken.

BAUER *(shouts)* Ida! Ida!

IDA enters, feigning innocence.

IDA Yes, Father?

BAUER Whatever made you write this.... this thing?

IDA What thing?

He hands her the letter. She glances at it and walks over to her desk.

IDA That letter was locked in the drawer of my desk. It's my desk.

She waves the key in his face.

IDA And this is my key. *(Shouts)* My key. IT'S MINE.

BAUER But the letter's addressed to your mother and myself.

IDA I don't care who it's addressed to. It's my private drawer. You stole the key.

BAUER I did not steal the key.

He strokes her hair and her face, tearfully.

BAUER Oh Ida, Ida, why do you want to kill yourself?

IDA I hate my life.

BAUER But why, why? I don't understand. You're pretty and clever. You live in a beautiful apartment. I let you pick and choose your own governesses and attend women's lectures. You know how much I love you.

She pulls away from him angrily. Her voice becomes hoarser and her coughing increases.

IDA You don't love me. You don't give me what I want.

BAUER What do you want then, Ida? Tell me. A trip to the Spa? A kitten? A new hat?

IDA You know what I want! I want you to break with the Zellenkas.

BAUER *(wearily)* Ida, Ida, we've known Hans and Marie for years now. She looked after me when I was ill. I can't just walk away from them.

IDA I looked after you as well.

BAUER And what a superb little nurse you were too! Such a special girl. I really wouldn't know what to do without you. Let's have no more of this suicide talk, please.

IDA *(quiet, pleading)* Then break with the Zellenkas.

BAUER But they're friends of the family. Good friends.

IDA He's a liar.

BAUER Who?

IDA *(irritably)* You know who. Hans.

BAUER Oh, please let's not go over that lake episode again.

IDA He wanted to have sex with me, and you don't believe me.

BAUER Ida, watch your language.

IDA And it wasn't even the first time.

BAUER I confronted him about it, and I was satisfied with his explanation.

IDA You don't care, do you?

BAUER *(soothingly)* You know you have a vivid imagination, Ida. All your governesses have said so. It's a sign of high intelligence.

IDA *(getting increasingly worked up)* It's in your interest to think I made it up, isn't it? If you admitted it was true, you couldn't carry on with her anymore, could you?

BAUER I don't know what you're talking about.

IDA *(screaming, hoarsely, breathlessly)* Oh yes you do. You'd have to stop fucking her, wouldn't you?

He slaps his hand across her mouth to silence her. She starts to hyperventilate, and collapses into his arms in convulsions.

FREUD'S CONSULTING ROOM. IDA is lying unconscious in BAUER's arms. FREUD is in the analyst position.

BAUER Perhaps you could set my mind at rest Doctor. I've never ceased to be grateful to you for the diagnosis and treatment you gave me some years back for a condition resulting from my... er... youthful recklessness. But sometimes I lie awake at night wondering whether this is at the root of Ida's problems.

FREUD Factors of heredity aren't the only cause of hysteria, Herr Bauer. Psycho-sexual factors are also involved, not to mention family and social circumstances.

BAUER That makes sense. Her mother's behaviour can be erratic and extreme. But Ida's relentless illnesses, her tantrums and delusions are destroying everyone's life, including her own.

FREUD Delusions? What kind of delusions?

BAUER She's got it into her head – I've no idea how – that my... er... friendly attachment to a lady called Marie Zellenka is not what you might call... an innocent one. In fact it was her husband Hans who recommended you to me. Do you remember him?

FREUD Zellenka... yes. Similar age to myself. Good-looking chap. Affable.

BAUER I'm fond of his wife, of course. But we're just good friends, nothing more. *(Smiles)* You, of all people, know that with my breathing difficulties, lovemaking is out of the question. It goes without saying, Doctor, that your attempts to alleviate Ida's symptoms and fantasies will be handsomely remunerated.

BAUER lays IDA on the couch and exits. IDA opens her eyes.

IDA I think doctors are a complete waste of time.

FREUD You don't have much respect for the medical profession?

IDA Since I was eight they've been trying to cure me of one thing or another. Chronic dyspnoea, migraines, nervous coughing, appendicitis, amnesia, fits. Sometimes I completely lose my voice.

FREUD You lose your voice.

IDA That's what I just said, isn't it? I've had hydrotherapy, electrotherapy, spa treatment, and every pill under the sun.

FREUD And Doctors of the mind?

IDA You want to control how I think.

FREUD How so?

IDA My father's paying you, and knowing him, he'll want results.

FREUD What sort of results?

IDA *(cynically)* Don't tell me you don't know already! He wants you to convince me he isn't having an affair with Marie Zellenka. Well, he's a liar. They've been carrying on for years.

FREUD Years?

IDA Since we stayed together in the hotel.

BAUER, ZELLENKA and IDA are standing in a hotel lobby.

BAUER An excellent choice of hotel, Hans. Just the place to bring a chap to convalesce.

ZELLENKA Actually, it was Marie who chose it.

BAUER When I was looking out of my bedroom window, I saw a bird with a huge wingspan fly out of the mountain. An eagle do you think?

ZELLENKA Quite possibly, Philipp. There have been sightings.

IDA *(perplexed)* But your bedroom window looks out onto the terrace at the front.

BAUER I've... er... moved to another room at the end of a corridor.

ZELLENKA Is Käthe coming for this walk?

BAUER She's still exhausted after the journey.

IDA We'd better leave soon, or it will be dark.

ZELLENKA Marie's just rounding up the children.

ZELLENKA takes a small box out of his pocket.

ZELLENKA Here, you can play with these while we're waiting.

She opens the box and takes out a small pair of lady's binoculars.

IDA *(excitedly)* They're beautiful. That's tortoise shell, isn't it?

ZELLENKA Yes, with a mother of pearl inlay.

She kisses his cheek.

BAUER You're so kind to my little girl.

IDA puts the binoculars to her eyes. MARIE enters. IDA's face lights up.

IDA Marie!

MARIE I really don't know what to do. I can't get the children to come on the walk. They want to play in the boating pool. Hans, would you mind? You know how I hate wading around in water.

ZELLENKA *(deliberately awkward)* I feel like a walk myself, actually. And anyway, they never do what I tell them.

MARIE Oh Ida, darling, would you *please* give Hans a hand?

IDA I didn't bring my galoshes with me.

MARIE You can borrow mine. They're under the bed.

She hands IDA a key. IDA starts walking away.

MARIE Not that way, Ida! *(Hesitantly)* I've changed rooms. I'm near the end of the corridor.

BAUER and MARIE exit together.

The consulting room. FREUD is in the analyst position. IDA is on the couch. She is coughing fairly continuously throughout the following exchange.

IDA He's so selfish. He stays with her even though he knows what it's doing to me.

FREUD You allow their relationship to dominate your thoughts.

IDA *(angrily)* It's his lies and excuses. Yesterday he said he was going to the South for a few days, because he wasn't feeling well and the climate would do him good. I found out this morning she was on her way there too – to visit a 'sick relative.' It's been like that for years. *(Sadly)* Father always used to take *me* away with him.

FREUD And your brother?

IDA He stayed with Mother. Otto has always been close to Mother.

FREUD And you were close to your father?

IDA Yes. He didn't like anyone else to go into his bedroom when he was sick. Not even Mother.

FREUD So until Marie came along... You were like a wife to him. His confidante.

IDA does not reply.

FREUD It wasn't your mother's role Marie took over, was it? It was yours.

IDA does not reply.

FREUD I think you're in love with your father.

Pause.

IDA In love with my father! (*She laughs scornfully.*) How ridiculous.

FREUD Can't you see that your migraines, fainting fits, coughing fits, asthmatic attacks and amnesia, are disguised attempts – weapons even – to get his sympathy and attention?

IDA No.

FREUD You've tried to manipulate him through begging, arguing and even threatening suicide. You're giving him an ultimatum. "It's her or me".

IDA I had asthma before he even met her. So there!

FREUD But it was your *mother* you were jealous of then.

IDA *(incredulously)* Me? Jealous of my mother? You should meet the woman. All she's interested in is her cleaning and her constipation. She's mad.

In the background, in semi-darkness, BAUER and MARIE are embracing.

FREUD But she was still something you could never be – his wife. And now that Marie has taken over that role, you're out in the cold.

IDA She's only with him because of his money. My father's a man of means, you know.

FREUD A man of means? Now that's an interesting choice of expression. *Ein vermogënder Mann.* It can also mean well-endowed, can't it?

IDA I know Father gives her money. He's much richer than her husband. You want to see the wardrobe and jewellery she has now, compared to when we first knew them.

FREUD But well-endowed also has a sexual meaning, hasn't it?

IDA Everything has a sexual meaning according to you.

FREUD But what are you *really* wishing to communicate by choosing this expression? Let's try looking at its opposite. *Ein unvermogënder Mann.* A man *without* means. You know your father's health is poor. And as he suffers from extreme breathlessness, it's unlikely he could have successful intercourse. Sometimes two opposites can sit quite happily together in the unconscious. On the one hand you're convinced they're having an affair, yet on the other you believe that your father's impotent.

BAUER and MARIE's embrace is becoming increasingly heated. She unbuttons his shirt lets down her hair, and sinks to her knees.

IDA That doesn't have to stop them.

FREUD Attaining satisfaction? Are you suggesting that there are *other* ways a man and woman can achieve sexual satisfaction?

MARIE leads BAUER off-stage. IDA starts to cough. Pause.

FREUD Where did you learn about this, Ida?

MARIE, still with her hair loose and looking dishevelled, enters, takes the mantegazza book off the shelf, and sits on the couch beside IDA. She opens the book. IDA is inquisitive, embarrassed, breathless and giggly.

Slides of erotic Viennese art are projected. Klimt: 'The Kiss', Danae: 'The Embrace'. Schiele: 'Act of Love', 'Reclining Woman', 'Girl Kneeling, resting on both elbows'.

MARIE moves away from IDA and addresses her in a disassociated manner.

MARIE You see Ida... men and women... women and men... can... can... speak to each other in a variety of different ways... different inflections... different rhythms and reverberations...

KÄTHE BAUER walks across the stage.

MARIE *(with bitterness)* Certain women find communication a repugnant activity. Yet their silence is respected... revered even, by society.

IDA starts to cough.

MARIE Sometimes Ida, sometimes a woman has to adapt or curtail the manner of expression that is most familiar and natural to her, in order that the man she loves may feel more... more at ease... and more cherished in her company.

MARIE kisses IDA, returns the book to the shelf, and leaves. IDA starts coughing violently.

FREUD There's a permanent tickle in your throat. You're constantly irritated at the thought of your father and Marie indulging in oral practices. Hysterical symptoms are an expression of secret, suppressed wishes. You fantasise that you're Marie, and that it's happening to you. You can't breathe. You're choking.

IDA exits, choking.

END OF MEMORY SEQUENCE.

SCENE FOUR

MARTHA enters carrying a tray.

FREUD *(to himself)* I did cure the cough. It vanished after that.

MARTHA What cough? You haven't caught Sophie's influenza, have you?

FREUD What have you got there, Martha?

MARTHA A special treat.

FREUD Artichokes?

MARTHA *Italian* artichokes. Now close your eyes and imagine yourself in Rome. I know how you long to visit the place.

FREUD takes an artichoke.

FREUD *(smiling)* So you think the unfathomable neurosis which prohibits me from setting foot in the Eternal City could be suppressing a secret, sensuous desire for artichokes? Doubtful Martha...

FREUD nibbles at it.

FREUD ...nevertheless, they *are* delicious. Thank you my dear.

He kisses her. MARTHA looks pleased.

MARTHA Baroness Ferstel has just arrived. We're all playing charades in the sitting room. She's brought the children some special chocolates from Belgium.

FREUD I'm afraid you'll have to entertain her yourself this evening.

MARTHA But you know she's offered to speak to the Minister of Education about your professorship.

FREUD How many times have I told you, I'm not going to get my professorship through the back door. Especially not through the favours of an ex-patient. I've waited fifteen years already, and I want it to happen in a dignified way, through the proper channels.

MARTHA You know there are no 'proper channels' for Jews. Either you get a person of influence, like the Baroness, to petition on your behalf, or you convert to Catholicism.

FREUD Which you know I would never do.

MARTHA Thank God.

FREUD Perhaps it's some papal phobia that's preventing me from 'marching on Rome.' Like Hannibal, my fellow Semite, I can never get any closer to the damn place than Lake Trasimeno.

MARTHA starts to walk out but stops at the door.

MARTHA *(softly)* Please don't be long. I'm finding it difficult to keep Anna out of here. She shut herself away in the nursery and made a costume, all by herself. Helen of Troy, would you believe! I said she could stay up – just this once. She's dying to show it to you. You know how much you mean to your little girl.

MARTHA looks at him, pleadingly.

FREUD Thank you, Martha. I'd lost my train of thought, and you've put me back on track... I'd just reached the point, in my recollection of Ida's analysis, where I needed to find out why she'd suddenly revived an obsessive, post-oedipal attachment to her father.

MARTHA I don't understand what you're talking about.

FREUD You see, it's perfectly natural for a young girl like Anna to feel so passionately about her father, but Ida, on the other hand, is already a young woman and should have grown out of it.

MARTHA *(under her breath)* Ida Bauer!

FREUD The clue to Ida's unnatural feelings towards her father lay in a dream. The Greeks were right about a lot of things. Do you know what Heraclitus of Ephesus said in 500 BC?

MARTHA No, I don't.

FREUD "We must not act and speak like sleepers, for in our sleep we act and speak."

FREUD lights a cigar and takes up the analyst position.

FREUD Dreams... The guardians of sleep. Dreams... Symbols and disguises the resourceful ego imposes on the sleeper's unbridled unconscious desires and instincts.

MARTHA I'll give the Baroness your apologies, shall I?

FREUD Dreams, dreams. Where two illogical, contrary ambivalent desires can exist side by side, like hate and love, desire and repulsion, longing and rejection, fire and water. Dreams, dreams. It's dreams that provide the key.

MARTHA exits, frustrated.

SCENE FIVE

MEMORY/DREAM SEQUENCE.

Music: Schoenberg. Mirrors. Smoke starts to rise from where FREUD is seated, merging with the smoke of his cigar. IDA enters wearing a nightdress. She puts her clothes at the foot of the couch. She lies down on the couch and falls asleep.

FREUD *(hypnotically)* There's no smoke without fire, Ida. There's no smoke without fire. No smoke without. No smoke. No. There's no smoke without fire, Ida. There's no smoke without fire. No smoke without. No smoke. No. There's no smoke without fire, Ida. There's no smoke without fire. No smoke without. No smoke. No.

KÄTHE enters and rushes around in a state of panic, fanning the smoke. BAUER runs into the room, full of anxiety. He stands over IDA and shakes her – desperate to wake her up. She finally opens her eyes, and in slow motion, rises to her feet, and dresses. KÄTHE starts searching frantically for something.

BAUER You had a dream. The house was on fire. Your father was standing by your bed and woke you up. You dressed quickly. Your mother wanted to stop and save her jewellery box but your father said, "I refuse to let myself and my children be burnt for the sake of your jewellery box."

BAUER impatiently pushes KÄTHE and IDA out of the room. He remains onstage.

BAUER You hurried downstairs. As soon as you were outside you woke up.

BAUER exits.

THE CONSULTING ROOM. IDA runs in excitedly.

IDA Doctor Freud! That dream I had again the other night... I forgot to tell you that when I woke up in the morning, I thought I could smell smoke.

FREUD *(mystified)* You thought you could smell smoke. I wonder why?

IDA I first had the dream two years ago, several nights in succession. Father and I had gone to spend a holiday with the Zellenkas, by the lake at Loibechl.[1] We'd arrived in a thunderstorm. They were staying in a small wooden house, surrounded by trees. Father was worried about fire because the house didn't have a lightning conductor. He could only stay for a few days because of business. I was supposed to stay on with Hans and Marie, but I insisted on leaving with Father.

THE LAKE. ZELLENKA is rowing IDA across the lake. He can't keep his eyes off her. IDA is looking at the scenery through the binoculars he gave her.

ZELLENKA It's so beautiful here.

IDA Isn't it just?

ZELLENKA The indigo lake and salmon sky. The hazy purple alpine peaks. A perfect setting for your loveliness, Ida.

IDA Look at the swans!

ZELLENKA So white, aren't they! The whitest swans I've ever seen. Are you nervous Ida?

IDA *(sharply)* No. Why should I be?

ZELLENKA Let me think. What could you possibly be nervous about? Can you swim?

IDA Not really.

ZELLENKA *(laughing)* So if we sink, I shall have to rescue you. I think you'd better start being nicer to me Ida. A little smile, perhaps?

She looks away. ZELLENKA breathes in.

ZELLENKA The air is as clear as crystal. Such a glorious fragrance of pine. We're getting closer to the shore.

IDA peers at the shore through her binoculars.

---

1. Freud refers to this place in the case study as 'L'. I've substituted the town of Loibechl which is beside a lake in the Alps, a reasonable distance from Vienna.

IDA *(excitedly)* I can see a grey shape – a creature – it's running into the woods – wait a minute, there's two of them!

ZELLENKA Wolves.

IDA *(nervously)* Wolves!

ZELLENKA Yes. There are wolves in this area. Now you really have something to be nervous about.

IDA *(scared)* Let's go back. Please.

He laughs.

ZELLENKA Don't worry, I'll rescue you from the wolves too.

They reach the shore. ZELLENKA helps IDA out of the boat.

ZELLENKA What lush, verdant grass. Shall we sit here for a few moments and be one with nature?

IDA I'd rather not sit down, if you don't mind. I think the grass is probably damp.

ZELLENKA feels the grass.

ZELLENKA No, no, it's quite dry.

IDA All the same, I'd rather not.

ZELLENKA Listen. I was only teasing you about the wolves.

IDA I know.

ZELLENKA They've had to kill them off – to protect holiday-makers like us.

IDA They must have been Wolfhounds.

ZELLENKA Yes. Wolfhounds.

He takes off his coat, and lays it on the grass. IDA remains standing.

ZELLENKA Here, Madam can sit on my coat.

IDA I don't want to.

ZELLENKA Come on, it's nice and dry.

He sits down, then grabs hold of her wrist and starts to pull her down. She resists.

IDA I said I don't want to.

ZELLENKA Then I shall have to stand.

He gets to his feet, and suddenly embraces her passionately.

ZELLENKA Oh Ida, Ida, please, please, please.

IDA What's the matter with you? Stop it!

ZELLENKA I want you so much. So much. You've no idea how much.

She pushes him away.

ZELLENKA *(pained)* My wife refuses to satisfy me, sexually.

She looks at him aghast, then slaps him violently on the right cheek. He gasps. IDA strides angrily away leaving ZELLENKA to nurse his cheek.

IDA I didn't want to return with him in the boat, so I started walking back around the lake, through the woods. But in the end I had no choice. I asked a man how long it would take to walk. He told me two and a half hours. I didn't have the energy.

She climbs back in the boat with ZELLENKA, exhausted.

ZELLENKA Ida, look... I'm sorry. Really sorry. I don't know what came over me. Will you forgive me? ... Look, you won't tell anyone, will you? ... Ida... Ida. Please... say something... speak to me... please.

She deliberately ignores him.

ZELLENKA *(with hostility)* Very well. We can both play that game.

They remain silent as he rows them back across the lake. IDA gets out the boat and hurries away from him.

THE LITTLE WOODEN HOUSE.

IDA By the time I got back to the little wooden house I felt exhausted.

IDA lies down on the couch.

IDA I went to lie down on the sofa in the bedroom and fell asleep.

She closes her eyes. ZELLENKA is standing over her. She opens her eyes.

IDA *(angrily)* What are you doing in here?

ZELLENKA I need to get something from my room. I'm the one who's paying for this place, and I can come and go as I please.

ZELLENKA exits. IDA gets up.

IDA I didn't feel safe. I asked Marie for the key to the room, so I could lock myself in.

MARIE enters, hands IDA a large key, and exits. IDA puts the key on the desk. ZELLENKA enters, picks it up without her noticing and exits. She turns around and sees it's no longer there.

IDA The next day I saw that the key had gone... I had to dress myself in a hurry. I knew I wasn't safe. I insisted on leaving with Father a few days later.

THE CONSULTING ROOM.

IDA lies down on the couch. FREUD is in the analyst position.

FREUD When you wake up in the dream, your father is standing over you – just as Zellenka was when you awoke from your nap on the sofa.

IDA Yes.

FREUD So the dream is expressing the opposite of what actually occurred – your father is saving you from danger, whereas in reality, Zellenka was threatening it.

IDA I suppose so.

FREUD Let's look for some more opposites, shall we? Fire?

IDA Water.

FREUD Were you a bed wetter?

IDA Sometimes.

FREUD Do you remember being woken up in the night...

IDA To prevent it happening?

FREUD Yes.

IDA Father used to wake me.

FREUD Now let's get back to that jewellery box your mother is frantically searching for in the dream. The word for jewellery box is *Schmuckkästchen*, isn't it? Which also has the vulgar meaning of female genitalia.

IDA I knew you'd say that!

FREUD So why do you think your mother is trying to preserve her '*Schmuckkästchen*?'

IDA I know the sort of life my father lived before he married. Once I overheard a relative of his discussing it. He's made my mother sick, I'm sure of it. And I've accompanied my mother to a spa that specialises in that sort of thing.

FREUD And you're afraid of getting the same sickness, aren't you? Like your mother, you want to keep your jewellery box intact.

IDA Hans had given me a jewellery box not long before I had the dream.

FREUD And he wanted to get inside it, didn't he? He hadn't succeeded by the lake in the morning so he let himself into your room that afternoon. In your dream what you're saying to yourself is: "This man is after me. He wants to force his way into my room...

BAUER enters.

BAUER ... my jewellery box is in danger, and if he so much as lays a finger on me it will be my father's fault."

IDA Yes. He's to blame for it all.

BAUER But you still want your father to protect you.

IDA He doesn't care about me.

BAUER He cares about you deeply.

IDA My father sacrificed me.

FREUD Your father and Zellenka appear to have had an unspoken agreement not to look too closely at what the other was doing.

IDA *(bitterly)* My father handed me over to Hans to keep him quiet.

BAUER exits.

FREUD Do you know which desire it is you're repressing in this dream?

IDA No.

FREUD Well I'm going to tell you. What you *really* want is to give Zellenka the sexual satisfaction his wife denies him. At the lake you were severely tempted.

IDA laughs scornfully.

IDA Tempted! I detest Hans Zellenka.

FREUD lights a cigar.

FREUD But why? I've met him myself.

FREUD walks over to the couch, still smoking his cigar.

FREUD He struck me as a handsome, educated sort of person. The type of man a young woman like yourself would feel attracted to.

FREUD becomes ZELLENKA. He takes IDA's hand and leads her away from the couch and into his office.

IDA I was fourteen when you invited me to your office to watch the church festival in the square down below.

ZELLENKA I sent my staff home early, and persuaded Marie to stay at home.

ZELLENKA sucks heavily on the cigar.

IDA I was just turning to look out of the window at the colourful parade going on down below. It was a lovely day. I felt happy and excited. Banners were flying everywhere. The band was approaching. The crowd were cheering. Then suddenly...

ZELLENKA grabs her, thrusts himself against her and kisses her forcefully. After several moments she manages to push him away.

IDA Ugh! Yuk!

IDA looks at ZELLENKA and the cigar and spits in disgust she wipes her mouth and runs away. ZELLENKA catches up with her.

ZELLENKA I sent you flowers every day of the year. And I gave you beautiful gifts. I gave you a lovely, expensive jewellery box.

She stops. He hands her a jewellery box.

IDA A *Schmuckkästchen*! For my jewellery. How beautiful. My father gives your wife beautiful gifts too.

ZELLENKA *(angrily)* And visits her every day when I'm at work.

IDA She used to spend months on end in the sanatorium for nervous disorders. Now she's happy and healthy.

ZELLENKA Except when she's around me.

IDA Every time you get back from travelling, she's sick again.

ZELLENKA So she won't have to sleep with me. *(With a hint of desperation)* It was you I wrote to Ida, when I was away for months on end. It was you alone I told the date of my return.

She carries on walking. He follows her.

IDA When we moved to Vienna I thought I'd got away from you. Then I discovered you and your family had moved there too – a few weeks earlier.

They meet.

ZELLENKA Ida! How lovely to see you.

She carries on walking.

IDA I soon realised that you were following me. To make sure I didn't have a secret rendezvous.

ZELLENKA *(jealously)* With another man.

IDA *(screams)* Just leave me alone, will you!

THE CONSULTING ROOM.

IDA returns to the couch, and FREUD to the analyst position.

FREUD Even though you deny it, I think you really care about Hans Zellenka.

IDA He was an animal.

FREUD Is it his animal nature you're afraid of – or your own?

IDA *(impatiently)* I don't know what you're talking about.

FREUD When he was away travelling, did you miss him?

IDA He wrote to me, and I wrote back.

FREUD Were you ever ill during his absences?

Pause.

IDA My voice would go – sometimes.

FREUD His wife was healthy when he was absent, and you were sick.

IDA I don't understand why.

FREUD When the man you loved was away you couldn't speak to him, so speech lost all meaning.

IDA My cousin told me once that she thought I was crazy about him.

FREUD Yet you still deny you feel any desire for him.

MARIE enters, kneels beside IDA, and applies powder and lipstick to IDA's face.

MARIE Oh Ida, Ida. You're still so young... so young... you don't know what it's like... what it's like to feel... to feel poisoned... poisoned with a silent hatred... a silent hatred of the very... the very sound of a man... his sound... his breathing... his boots squeaking in the hall when he arrives home... the noise he makes when he chews his food at supper... the look in his eye when he knows it's time for bed...

MARIE exits.

IDA I feel nothing for Zellenka.

FREUD Come now Ida, he's a good-looking, virile man. You must surely have felt some sexual desire when he pressed himself up against you.

IDA I felt disgust.

FREUD Disgust! What would give a normal young woman pleasure, has, in your case, been converted into feelings of repugnance.

She starts to become asthmatic.

IDA I can still feel the pressure of him, thrusting himself against my chest.

FREUD Your chest? You've displaced the sensation. What you really felt was his erect member pressing into your genital area. But instead of feeling a healthy arousal, as any normal girl would do, you felt disgust. The physical sensation was displaced to your thorax.

IDA I hate watching lovers embracing in the street.

FREUD Because you're afraid the man might be in a state of sexual arousal.

IDA There was a young German governess who used to work for the Zellenkas. She told me Hans had chased her for weeks. He told her his wife refused to satisfy him sexually. She eventually gave in and afterwards he lost all interest in her. She told her parents what had happened. They refused to take her back.

FREUD She gave into Zellenka, and he ruined her life.

IDA Yes.

FREUD You're afraid the same thing might happen to you.

IDA *(fiercely)* It would never happen to me.

FREUD But when you were by the lake, Zellenka used the same line on you that he'd used on this German governess. "My wife refuses to satisfy me sexually." That's what you objected to, isn't it? He spoke to *you* in the same way he'd spoken to a *servant*. You only rejected him because your pride was hurt.

IDA No.

FREUD You need your father again, don't you? But it isn't to protect you from wetting your bed, as it was in childhood, it's to protect you from your overwhelming feelings of love for Hans Zellenka which keep pressing forward into consciousness.

IDA *(vehemently)* No.

FREUD This is why you're so bitter about your father's affair now. You need him for yourself. After all, you'd known for *years* that he and Marie Zellenka were having an affair. You'd even helped to facilitate their liaison by looking after the Zellenkas' children.

IDA *(more vehemently)* No.

FREUD You are, and have always been, passionately in love with Hans Zellenka.

IDA *(hysterically)* No.

FREUD The very fact you say 'no', means 'yes', Ida. Your unconscious is confirming my premise, even though your conscious mind is denying it. You're madly in love with Hans Zellenka.

IDA *(screams)* *No,* no, no.

BLACKOUT. IDA exits.

END OF DREAM/MEMORY SEQUENCE.

SCENE SIX

The bells slowly start to chime midnight. MARTHA comes in holding a candelabra. FREUD is lying on the couch with his eyes closed.

MARTHA *(fed up)* What are you doing in the dark? Have you fallen asleep?

She shakes him.

FREUD *(confused)* Martha! What time is it?

MARTHA Almost midnight. We're all waiting for you. Hurry up, or we won't see the New Year in together.

MARTHA pushes FREUD out of the room.

INTERVAL.

ACT TWO, SCENE ONE

The early hours of the morning. Bells are ringing in the new year. Laughter is heard, along with snatches of festive music.

CHORUS 1 And so, a new year.

CHORUS 3 A new year.

CHORUS 2 And the century is still so young she has barely learnt to crawl.

CHORUS 3 Still suckling the bitter-sweet milk of her uncertain future.

FREUD walks into the consulting room holding a glass of brandy. He is preoccupied and tipsy. There are some celebratory 'streamers' still hanging off him.

CHORUS 2 Will she be your nurturer or destroyer?

CHORUS 3 Will she lift you up on her shoulders for all to see? Her hero who voyaged into the darkest underworld of the unconscious in search of his dearest love, The Truth?

The laughter becomes jeering and mocking in tone, as the CHORUS take on the role of FREUD's 'internal furies'.

CHORUS 1 Or will she spit you out like the remains of a cheap cigar?

CHORUS 2 Too cancerous to inhale.

CHORUS 3 A moral health hazard.

CHORUS 2 Fit only to be ground into the filthy pavement, and trampled on by street walkers.

Agitated, FREUD takes his book 'AN INTERPRETATION OF DREAMS' from the shelf.

CHORUS 3 All those years of tormented self-analysis to produce 'An Interpretation of Dreams' and you've hardly even sold fifty copies!

CHORUS 2 Vienna is going wild over these new Symbolist Painters.

CHORUS 3 And what is your dream book about but symbols?

CHORUS 1 When Darwin, your hero, published his 'Origin of Species' the first edition was sold out by the evening. But no one wants to know about *your* masterpiece, do they?

FREUD throws the book across the room. The laughter stops abruptly. The CHORUS becomes more empathic.

CHORUS 2 Oh *Mein Herr. Mein Herr.*

CHORUS 1 A candle can light up a cave that has been dark for millions of years. But if no-one wants to enter that cave with you, if they are too afraid of the shadows –

CHORUS 3 Then what has been the point of it all?

CHORUS 2 What, oh what, has been the point of it all?

FREUD *(very controlled)* The defences required to deal with the apocalyptic rage of not being taken seriously... *(less controlled)*... Not being listened to... not being heard. It's, it's maddening... murderous even...

SCENE TWO

MEMORY SEQUENCE

Offstage, IDA immediately follows on from FREUD.

IDA *(screaming, uncontrolled)* ...Mother! *(She chases KÄTHE onstage, shouting)* Listen to me! Listen to me! You've got to listen to me. *(She chases KÄTHE into a corner.)* I have something really horrible to tell you. *(KÄTHE looks up at her, nervously.)* The reason why I left the little wooden house and came home early with father. You've *got* to believe me....

She whispers in her mother's ear and exits. KÄTHE gasps in horror. BAUER enters. KÄTHE whispers in his ear. He looks horrified.

BAUER This is absurd. I can't believe it. Whatever's got into the man? *(Shouts)* Ida! Ida! *(We hear a door slam.)* She's gone out. Damn. I'll have to write to Zellenka immediately and demand an explanation.

He sits down at the desk, takes a pen and starts to compose a letter. KÄTHE looks over his shoulder as he's writing.

As BAUER begins to recite his letter, ZELLENKA enters with a pen and paper, sits down at the ornamental desk, and starts to compose a letter in response. MARIE follows him in and looks over his shoulder as he writes. She's clearly distraught.

BAUER Herr Zellenka. It is my painful duty to bring the following matter to your attention. My daughter claims that when she and I were staying with you at Loibechl recently, as your guests – I repeat – your guests – you apparently showed...

ZELLENKA ... the deepest respect and fondness for Ida. In fact, I have so much regard for her that I promise you I have never, and I repeat, never...

BAUER ... made a sexual advance towards her by the lake.

ZELLENKA Not in a million years would I so much as dream of taking advantage of a young woman...

BAUER ... by forcing yourself upon her in a depraved fashion. This has come as such a shock to her mother and myself. I insist that...

ZELLENKA ... you grant me the opportunity to convince you that I am totally innocent and trustworthy. All I ask is that you let me visit you in person to...

BAUER ... explain your behaviour! Our two families have been on an intimate footing for several years now, but I feel compelled to...

ZELLENKA ... assure you that absolutely nothing has changed to...

BAUER ... affect our longstanding relationship in the future. Yours...

ZELLENKA ... respectfully...

BAUER ... Philipp Bauer.

ZELLENKA Hans Zellenka.

BAUER puts the letter in an envelope, and seals it. He and KÄTHE exit.

ZELLENKA puts the letter in an envelope and seals it. He hands it to MARIE. She exits. Confident, ZELLENKA sets off to meet BAUER.

THE BAUER'S DRAWING ROOM.

BAUER re-enters. The men shake hands briskly. BAUER motions ZELLENKA to sit down.

ZELLENKA You know why I've come Philipp. But I don't think you're quite prepared for what you're about to hear. You might, perhaps, want to pour yourself a stiff drink first.

BAUER You mean you'd like *me* to pour *you* one.

KÄTHE enters with a tray containing a brandy decanter and two glasses. BAUER pours them each a drink. KÄTHE exits with the tray.

ZELLENKA I wish there were an easier way to tell you this... that I could somehow spare your feelings... after all, I'm a father too.

BAUER Get on with it, will you!

ZELLENKA Very well. I know you still look upon Ida as your little girl. But the fact is, Philipp, she isn't quite as innocent as you imagine her to be.

BAUER *(angrily)* Explain yourself.

ZELLENKA I've received information from a most reliable – if reluctant – source, well known to us both, which, sadly, points to the fact that Ida... well...

BAUER Well what!

ZELLENKA To put it bluntly... Ida knows everything there is to know about sexual behaviour.

BAUER All thanks to you, no doubt.

ZELLENKA I swear to you, I've had no part in it. The fact of the matter is that your daughter is unnaturally preoccupied with the subject of sex.

BAUER *(furiously)* What are you talking about? Explain yourself man! She's still only a child.

ZELLENKA Hear me out! Please! As you know, whenever Ida comes to stay with us, she shares a room with Marie, and I sleep in the spare room. Not that I'm complaining. I know how women like to chatter about feminine things. Jewellery, perfumes, petticoats... even the opera...

BAUER *(impatiently)* Yes, yes, yes!

ZELLENKA Marie tells me they often used to confide in each other – as women do. But she became increasingly shocked and upset by Ida's precocious sexual curiosity.

BAUER A desire to know certain basic facts of life is fairly normal in a young person of her age.

ZELLENKA Ida's desire for facts was apparently rapacious.

BAUER How can you prove it?

ZELLENKA My wife tells me she was extremely disturbed one day to find Ida poring over a book by Mantegazza.

BAUER *(shocked)* Mantegazza!

ZELLENKA Yes. His 'Physiology of Love.' As you know, Mantegazza's explicitness can be quite alarming. Certainly not for the consumption of the female sex.

BAUER *(gravely)* Indeed. And Marie caught her reading this you say?

ZELLENKA Yes. She was quite devastated. You know how sensitive Marie is. She was shocked to find a girl as young and well-bred as Ida reading such material. It made her anxious about Ida's reputation and marriage prospects. A girl who's obsessed with this sort of smut loses a man's respect.

BAUER *(pained)* That's enough!

ZELLENKA I think it goes a long way towards explaining Ida's aberration regarding some incident between us at the lake.

BAUER How?

ZELLENKA You know Ida has a vivid imagination. And with all the Mantegazza stuff swimming around in her head...

BAUER You're implying that she made it all up?

ZELLENKA Yes I am.

BAUER And Marie – what does she think?

ZELLENKA Let's just say we think Ida fantasised it all.

BAUER She let her adolescent imagination run away with her?

ZELLENKA Absolutely.

Pause. BAUER reflects for a few moments.

BAUER After all, she didn't mention the incident until *two weeks* after it was supposed to have happened.

ZELLENKA Quite. I'm sure it's just a phase she's going through.

ZELLENKA stands to go.

BAUER She'll grow out of it.

ZELLENKA Of course. And it goes without saying Philipp, that I bear no feelings of resentment towards Ida.

BAUER embraces him.

BAUER I'm sorry I doubted you, Hans.

ZELLENKA Let's just forget it ever happened, shall we?

ZELLENKA exits. MARIE enters, walks over to BAUER and embraces him.

BAUER Why ever didn't you tell me about Ida and all this Mantegazza nonsense?

MARIE I know how you adore her – we all do. I wanted to spare your feelings, my darling.

BAUER What an angel you are!

He pulls her down onto the sofa. They kiss passionately.

FREUD is in the analytic position. IDA enters, and stands watching them.

IDA *(bitterly)* Why did I wait two weeks before telling my parents what had happened by the lake? If I'd told Father straight away perhaps he would have believed me.

She turns angrily on FREUD.

IDA I suppose you don't believe me either, do you Doctor Freud? You're just like the rest of them. You think I made it all up.

FREUD As it happens, I do believe you Ida. I believe your story.

IDA *(surprised and moved)* You believe me? Thank you. Thank you.

FREUD You want to know why you waited two weeks before telling your parents? You wanted to see whether Zellenka would come running after you and try to convince you that he genuinely loved you, that he wasn't playing with you in the same way he'd played with the poor German girl. But instead, the man betrayed you.

MARIE leaves the couch and moves over to IDA. She stares at IDA with hostility.

MARIE You worshipped Marie, and she betrayed you too. The two of you were as close as sisters. Yet she was prepared to sacrifice you to keep her relationship with your father intact.

IDA I had a governess once. I thought we were very close too.

MARIE Then you started to notice how she seemed to lose all interest in you when your father wasn't around. She was in love with him and couldn't care less about you. You got your father to sack her.

FREUD But he won't sack Marie for you, will he?

MARIE laughs in IDA's face and exits. BAUER is now stretched out on the sofa like a corpse.

IDA I had a dream that my father was dead.

FREUD Dead, you say?

IDA *(with relish)* Yes. Dead.

FREUD Your revenge.

BAUER exits. IDA lies down on the couch.

IDA I'm wandering around an unfamiliar town – yet it feels familiar... It could be German.

FREUD German?

IDA Mmm. I think I know why. The afternoon before the dream I'd been showing some relations of ours a picture album that a young engineer had sent me when he went to work in Germany.

FREUD An admirer?

IDA I met him before we moved to Vienna. Later in the afternoon I took one of my cousins to an art exhibition. There was a strange picture there. It disturbed me. I stared at it for quite some time. The picture was in the dream too.

FREUD Describe it.

IDA There was a dense, dark wood. Nymphs were playing in the background. The gallery itself reminded me of one I'd been to in Dresden. Another cousin had taken me there and wanted to show me around. But I asked to be left alone.

FREUD Why?

IDA leaves the couch. She is in the Dresden Gallery, admiring the objets d'art.

IDA Raphael's Sistine Madonna was there. *(Rapturously)* The most glorious piece of work I've ever seen.

THE MADONNA is illuminated.

FREUD The Madonna... The Virgin Madonna... positioned on a pedestal and frequently emulated by girls oppressed by imputations of sexual guilt.

THE MADONNA lifts her veil. It is MARIE ZELLENKA.

IDA I couldn't take my eyes off her for two whole hours. She was so white. So luminous. So beautiful.

She remains staring at The MADONNA, transfixed.

FREUD Before they experience genuine sexual passion for a man...

THE MADONNA (MARIE) ... girls can sometimes feel desire for their own sex – which evaporates once their heterosexual urges are awakened. But if the libido is denied and repressed a current of unconscious erotic feeling can channel itself into intense longing and desire for a woman.

IDA embraces THE MADONNA (MARIE) passionately.

FREUD Particularly in the case of hysterics.

FREUD has a sudden realisation.

FREUD *(excitedly)* It's so obvious! How can I have missed it? You feel an intense, passionate love for Marie Zellenka, don't you?

THE MADONNA (MARIE) But you've hidden it so carefully, so very, very carefully. On a deep, profoundly unconscious level, you want her even more than you want her husband.

FREUD I would even go so far as to say that *she's* the *real* object of your desire.

THE MADONNA (MARIE) And that you resent your father, because it's *him* she loves, and not you.

THE MADONNA vanishes. IDA breaks down in tears.

FREUD *(triumphantly)* Please continue with the dream.

IDA walks over to the desk and picks up a letter.

IDA I return to the house where I'm living. There's a letter from my mother. *(Reads)* "Your father is ill. I didn't bother to let you know before because you left home without telling us. But he's dead now, so you can come home if you like. Mother."

She moves away.

IDA I set off for the station, but I can't find it anywhere. I have to ask a hundred times: "Where's the station? Where's the station? Where's the station?"

FREUD A hundred times?

IDA *(remembering)* Last night. The brandy.

BAUER enters, slightly drunk.

BAUER Ida, fetch the brandy would you?

IDA We had guests for dinner.

BAUER It's in the cabinet. Your mother has the key.

BAUER exits. KÄTHE walks in holding a large key. She ignores IDA and proceeds to communicate silently with invisible dinner guests.

IDA Can I have the key please?... Mother can I have the key?... Mother... I need the key. You know Father can't sleep without brandy...

MARIE and BAUER enter sleepily. Their arms wrapped around each other.

FREUD Except when he's with Marie.

MARIE and BAUER yawn and embrace.

FREUD Sexual satisfaction is the best soporific.

IDA *(shouts)* Mother! The key! I've asked you a hundred times.

Enjoying her power, KÄTHE walks primly between MARIE and BAUER, pushing them apart. MARIE runs out. BAUER looks frozen and traumatised.

IDA One of the guests proposed a toast to Father. That he should remain in good health for many years. A shadow passed over his face. He started to tremble... he looked... he looked....

BAUER Dead.

BAUER and KÄTHE exit, arm in arm. KÄTHE looks triumphant.

FREUD So in your dream, you want to return home now your father is dead...

IDA ... but no-one will tell me where the station is. I look around, and suddenly I'm in a wood, thick with trees. The same woods I saw in the picture.

FREUD You've associated yourself with this admirer you have in Germany. You've become a young man. The woods represent pubic hair. You say there were nymphs in the picture. Nymphae is the name given to the labia minora which lie in the background of the thick forest of pubic hair. You, as a young man, are seeking to penetrate the female genitalia.

IDA I meet a man in the woods and ask him how much longer it will take me to get to the station. He tells me it will take two and a half hours.

FREUD You're in the woods by the lake at Loibechl. You asked a man there how long it would take you to walk around the lake, remember? He told you it would take two and a half hours. You didn't want to return on the boat with Zellenka.

IDA I look up and see the station ahead of me.

She freezes in her tracks and looks terrified.

IDA But I cannot move. I cannot move. I cannot move.

FREUD Sexual anxiety is preventing your life from moving forward, from advancing.

IDA I'm at my parents' home. I knock and knock on the door. Finally the maid answers. She tells me that Mother and the funeral guests are at the cemetery burying Father.

FREUD This dream clearly manifests your deep sadistic wish to punish your father.

IDA takes the encyclopaedia off the shelf.

IDA I walk calmly to my room and begin reading a large book.

She puts the book on the desk, sits down and starts to read it.

FREUD An encyclopaedia.

IDA When I heard my cousin was dangerously ill with appendicitis, I didn't know what it meant, so I looked it up in the encyclopaedia.

FREUD Encyclopaedias are full of graphic medical illustrations – and therefore, forbidden knowledge. They're places where young people like yourself learn terms such as 'nymphae' and 'hymen'. Now that your father is dead, you're no longer afraid he might catch you looking at such material.

IDA After reading about it, I had appendicitis myself.

FREUD You punished yourself for dipping into forbidden pages.

IDA I wasn't able to walk properly, once I'd recovered. I dragged my right foot. The doctors couldn't work out why.

FREUD Did you have this appendicitis before or after the incident at the lake?

IDA Nine months after.

FREUD Nine months! Then the appendicitis pains were an imaginary childbirth! You were dragging your right foot because you'd made a false step.

IDA False step?

FREUD You became pregnant.

IDA *(confused)* Pregnant?

FREUD Yes. In your unconscious you became pregnant! You were already a little mother to Zellenka's children, remember?

IDA Mother?

Dazed, IDA slowly leaves the room.

FREUD You unconsciously fantasised that you *had* lost your virginity by the lake – but you only understood the medical implications when you consulted the encyclopaedia. *(Pleading)* Don't go – I haven't finished!

END OF MEMORY SEQUENCE.

SCENE THREE

MARTHA walks in. She's in her nightdress and her hair is loose.

MARTHA I can't sleep. It's gone three o'clock.

FREUD I had no idea of the time. I'm sorry.

MARTHA Come to bed now.

She strokes his hair.

FREUD My poor Martha. You have to put up with a lot from me, don't you?

He embraces her affectionately.

MARTHA *(gently)* Come to bed.

FREUD And if I do, can I make love to you?

MARTHA *(nervously)* You know we can't afford any more children.

FREUD That doesn't stop me wanting to make love to you.

MARTHA I've had six children in nine years. I only ever wanted three.

She turns away, then notices his brandy glass and ashtray and picks them up.

MARTHA I'll take these to the kitchen.

Feeling rejected, FREUD reaches into his draw and takes out a silver box.

MARTHA Oh, please, please not tonight. You know it keeps you awake.

He tips out a little white powder and proceeds to snort it.

FREUD Put those things down will you! Cocaine helps to suppress my libido. I think yours has been sublimated into a drive for domestic perfection.

MARTHA The maid is off today.

FREUD I wish you'd stop being such a model *hausfrau*. I don't want you to develop 'housewife psychosis' like Käthe Bauer... Although I suppose in her case it's herself she's trying to get clean.

MARTHA Why is she trying to get herself clean?

FREUD Like most men in this city of surplus flesh, her husband lived a loose life before they married.

MARTHA Poor woman.

FREUD Strange, isn't it, I've never indulged in the sexual freedom I advocate.

MARTHA exits, angry and hurt. FREUD snorts some more cocaine.

SCENE FOUR

SEQUENCE OF NARCOTICALLY-INDUCED ABBERATIONS AND HALLUCINATIONS.

High on cocaine, FREUD talks rapidly, gesticulates wildly, and manifests signs of omnipotent behaviour.

Mirroring her movements in the first dream, IDA enters wearing a nightdress. She puts her clothes at the foot of the couch. She lies down on the couch and falls asleep. FREUD lights a cigar and watches her closely as she writhes around in her sleep.

FREUD Why do you have to deny your sexuality? You along with most of the other 'respectable' women of your class? I've seen you there, on that couch, out of the corner of my eye. Your actions betray you. But you're a vicious one, Ida. You have claws, you scratch, and you bite, you tear and you slap. I want to let you out of your birdcage, Ida Bauer – let you fly free – out of your birdcage of repression and denial.

IDA suddenly opens her eyes. She sniffs.

IDA When I woke up in the morning, after the dream, I could smell smoke.

IDA gets up and dresses in slow motion.

FREUD *(exasperated)* Smoke. She could smell smoke. Why? Why? Why did the dream she'd had by the lake reoccur during analysis? Why, after recounting the dream, did it take her several days to recall smelling smoke? The memory must have had to overcome an incredibly strong repression. It represents a real threat to her... *(IDA exits.)* Mmm... I wonder. Could the smell of smoke have something to do with me, perhaps?

IDA *(offstage)* Why you?

FREUD Well, I'm a smoker...

IDA *(offstage)* So? Father and Hans are smokers.

FREUD When I'm trying to convince you that there's a hidden agenda to your behaviour I repeat the phrase: "There's no smoke without fire".

IDA *(offstage, mimicking him)* There's no smoke without fire. There's no smoke without fire.

FREUD paces up and down.

FREUD She must sense she's in danger again. From her own desires. What desire could she be concealing from herself and from me? *(Pause. A thought occurs to him. He smiles.)* I think she wanted me to kiss her. And she knew if I kissed her, because of my cigar habit, it would have been a smoky kiss. Just as Zellenka's kiss was a smoky kiss. *(IDA comes in and kisses FREUD passionately.)* The dream was clearly a warning. It brought back her deep fear of having sex with Zellenka. So although, unconsciously, she desperately desired the kiss, she couldn't help but react with fear and disgust. In her unconscious, I became Zellenka. *Now* I understand why she walked out on me.

IDA slaps FREUD around the face and exits.

FREUD It was equivalent to the slap around the face she administered to Zellenka. *(Excitedly)* Transference! That's what it is. Transference! I had no idea how powerful it was – or what an extremely useful analytic tool it could be. I must publish the case history – even though it's only a fragment... *(He goes over to his desk, opens a notebook, takes up a pen, and then pauses.)* ...and writing about a young woman's sexuality will cause a stir... Those involved should remain anonymous, of course... The Zellenkas shall become... Herr K and Frau K. And what name shall I give to Ida? *(Pause.)* Dora. Yes, I think I shall call her Dora.

FREUD remains at his desk, in darkness.

SCENE FIVE

The BAUERS' home. BAUER enters and looks impatiently at his watch.

BAUER *(calls)* Ida my dear, it's time for your visit to Dr Freud.

IDA enters.

IDA Time, time, Dr Freud says time doesn't exist in the unconscious.

BAUER I don't give a damn what he thinks about time in the unconscious. It's real enough to him in the here and now. I have to pay for your hour whether you're there or not. Well that's the Jews for you. No wonder they're taking over Vienna.

IDA I thought we were Jews too.

BAUER *(angrily)* Well, are you going?

IDA No, I'm not.

IDA exits.

THE CONSULTING ROOM.

FREUD gets up from behind his desk to greet BAUER. They shake hands.

BAUER It would appear that your attempts to cure Ida have been unsuccessful. I seem unable to persuade her to continue her analysis.

FREUD A pity.

BAUER Do you know some other way of curing her hysterical delusions?

FREUD Delusions?

BAUER Why, that I'm having a... a liaison with Marie Zellenka, for example.

FREUD *(firmly)* Herr Bauer, your daughter harbours many delusions, but after treating her for eleven weeks I'm absolutely convinced that isn't one of them.

BAUER *(shocked)* In that case, I suggest we terminate our arrangement.

BLACKOUT.

SCENE SIX

The ZELLENKAS' home. MARIE is sitting on the couch in a state of mourning. ZELLENKA enters.

ZELLENKA We have a visitor.

IDA follows him in. Surprised, MARIE rises to her feet.

MARIE Ida!

IDA I heard your sad news and came to offer my condolences. Klara was such a lovely little girl.

MARIE It was kind of you to come.

IDA You must miss her dreadfully.

MARIE We do, we do. She was always fragile, as you know, but we certainly weren't prepared for... for... for this.

ZELLENKA Can we tempt you to stay for afternoon tea?

IDA No. Thank you very much. But while I'm here, there are one or two things I'd like to sort out. It won't take long.

IDA turns to ZELLENKA.

IDA You. You *did* force yourself upon me at the lake, didn't you? And then you tried to make my parents believe I was obsessed with sex, and that I'd invented the whole thing.

ZELLENKA Ida, is this the right time to bring this up? As far as we're concerned, the past is dead and buried.

MARIE Dead and buried!

MARIE starts to weep.

IDA I don't care. I want the truth. You know you tried to seduce me, then you lied to cover it up, didn't you? Well, didn't you?

ZELLENKA *(quietly)* Yes Ida, I am afraid that I did.

He exits, slowly. IDA turns to MARIE.

IDA And you. You're having an affair with my father, aren't you?

Pause. MARIE does not reply.

IDA And it's been going on for several years. Well, it's true, isn't it?

MARIE nods.

MARIE Yes Ida, it's true.

IDA Good... Now tell me something Marie, why did you betray me?

MARIE Betray you?... Betray you?

IDA Why did you tell him about the books?

MARIE Books?

IDA You know which books.

MARIE breaks down.

MARIE I spent time in a sanatorium, before I met your father...

IDA *(impatiently)* Don't blame it on your nervous diseases.

MARIE *(through her tears)* I'd stopped sleeping... I'd stopped eating... I'd stopped living... But worst of all, I'd lost all feeling for my poor little children. My poor little children. They meant nothing to me at all. Nothing. Nothing. Nothing.

IDA I meant nothing to you, too.

MARIE Do you have any idea what it feels like, Ida? To feel nothing?

IDA does not reply.

MARIE I wanted you on my side... Yes... But I was fond of you too, Ida. Very fond. I was prepared to be your friend, confidante – even the mother you craved... *(angrily)* But I wasn't prepared to allow my husband's clumsy, puerile fumblings, or your spiteful accusations to destroy the joy and stability I *thought* I had, at last, regained.

MARIE exits. IDA remains on stage, weeping.

SCENE SEVEN

The city of Vienna. Apart from general street noise, we hear the sound of carriage wheels and horses' hooves in the distance.

ZELLENKA enters dressed for the street, carrying a briefcase. He stops dead in his tracks when he sees IDA. There's an expression of acute pain on his face. IDA is trembling.

IDA I said I never wanted to see you again... What are you staring at me like that for? You're a coward, a fool. I trusted you; I could have loved you even...

He takes a step towards her. The sound of horses' hooves and carriage wheels gets louder and louder.

IDA *(shouting)* Why are you standing in the middle of the street? Get out the way! Look out! Look out!

He continues to stare at her, transfixed. There's an almighty crash. IDA screams. ZELLENKA falls to the ground.

BLACKOUT.

SCENE EIGHT

THE CONSULTING ROOM. MARTHA is ushering IDA in.

MARTHA What a charming hat, Miss Bauer.

IDA smiles at MARTHA and looks around the consulting room. It clearly evokes memories for her.

MARTHA He should be back shortly. I'm sure he'll spare you a few minutes. It's been some time since we last saw you.

IDA Fifteen months.

MARTHA And your father? How is he now?

IDA Still in poor health. Thank you.

MARTHA Do excuse me. I have to keep an eye on the children. They are supposed to be doing their homework.

MARTHA leaves. IDA wanders around the consulting room. She sees a box of cigars and takes one out. It's larger than the cigars FREUD has been smoking up until now.

IDA So, now we can afford bigger and better cigars, *Professor* Freud!

She lights the cigar and starts coughing, then takes up the analyst position and addresses an invisible FREUD on the couch.

IDA *(tongue in cheek)* Now then, let's see... I wonder what desire it is you're repressing in this dream, Sigmund?... You feel anxious... *and* jubilant? Don't forget, two opposites can sit quite happily together in the unconscious... Ooh. You're in a wood, are you? A *dense* wood?... 'Dense wood' has a sexual meaning, surely... you see a house... there's a girl inside... *(in mock horror)* The house is on fire! There's no smoke without fire, is there?... The door is locked?... Ahh! You have the key. A great big shiny key... It won't fit into the lock, you say?... You *have* to get inside?...

You shake the house... You plunge the key into the lock again and again... What's your unconscious trying to tell you?... *(gasps)* Suddenly you hear a noise and look up. She opens the door. *(Laughs)* It was unlocked all along...

FREUD enters. He sees IDA and steps back in amazement.

FREUD Ida! What are you doing here?

IDA I've helped myself to one of your cigars.

FREUD So I see.

IDA It's all right. Don't look so shocked. I've smoked before. Hans Zellenka used to roll cigarettes for me. In fact he'd rolled me one just before the lake debacle... Oops! Ash all over the carpet.

She treads it in.

FREUD It won't be the first time.

IDA Do you know what day it is today?

FREUD Tuesday I believe. End of March. Why?

IDA Wrong. It's April.

FREUD The first of April?

IDA laughs loudly.

IDA Yes. The first of April

FREUD *(smiling)* Your timing, Ida, is as immaculate as ever.

IDA Congratulations on your Professorship. I read about it in the newspaper two weeks ago.

FREUD *(embarrassed)* Oh it was all a matter of bribery.

IDA Bribery?

FREUD Baroness Ferstel gave the Minister of Education a painting for his new gallery. Why are you here?

IDA For two weeks now I've had this dreadful neuralgia down the right side of my face.

FREUD Well, what do you expect? You did leave before the end of your treatment. We were almost there. You denied me the satisfaction of a cure. More to the point, you denied yourself one.

IDA The Zellenkas' daughter died recently. I decided to pay them a visit. Marie admitted she was having an affair with my father, and Hans confessed he'd lied about what happened at the lake.

FREUD Their daughter had just *died*? You have quite a sadistic streak, Ida.

IDA And you don't?... I saw Zellenka again, in the city, not long afterwards. When he saw me he stopped dead in the middle of the street. A carriage ran over him...

FREUD A carriage!

IDA I ran away.

FREUD Hmm. How long have you had this neuralgia?

IDA Two weeks.

FREUD And on the right side, you say?

IDA You heard me.

FREUD *(animated)* You hit Zellenka on the right cheek too, didn't you?

IDA You know I did.

FREUD And then, because of you, he was knocked down by a carriage.

IDA He was knocked down by a carriage because he was stupid.

FREUD You quite naturally felt guilty, but suppressed it, of course.

IDA He didn't die.

FREUD No matter. He must have been badly injured. Then you read about my Professorship in the newspaper and succumbed to feelings of acute guilt on account of causing so much pain to the man you loved.

IDA That's *your* view of it.

FREUD You see, in your unconscious Ida, Zellenka and myself are one and the same man.

IDA sighs.

IDA You always have to have the last word, don't you?

They remain onstage.

SCENE NINE

Weeping and sighing is heard. The CHORUS is invisible.

CHORUS 1 After her final visit, you added a post-script to 'Dora, Fragment of a Case of Analysis.'

CHORUS 2 Your bewildering case study of heterosexual longing –

CHORUS 3 Incestuous love –

CHORUS 2 And sapphic desire.

CHORUS 3 But she was no longer a threat to you, was she?

CHORUS 2 Your darkness had already lifted.

CHORUS 1 The summer before you had finally penetrated the sacred citadel of suppressed savagery –

CHORUS 2 And secret longing –

CHORUS 3 You 'entered' Rome.

Pause.

CHORUS 2 Her darkness remained, for years.

CHORUS 3 For years her multiple, fragmented sexuality was devoured by your greedy students of psychoanalysis.

CHORUS 2 She was eclipsed.

CHORUS 3 In darkness.

CHORUS 1 For years she remained in darkness.

The weeping and sighing stops. Mirrors are illuminated. The CHORUS is visible.

CHORUS 3 Then the voices came.

CHORUS 1 Silently at first.

CHORUS 2 Bewildering, multiple, fragmented voices.

CHORUS 1 Voices like stars illuminating her night.

CHORUS 2 Women's voices – but not all.

CHORUS 3 Not all the voices were women's.

CHORUS 1 Their glare was on you.

In a choreographed sequence, the CHORUS weaves in and out of each other, and around FREUD. Their stance and delivery are distinctly modern. They whisper at first, but later their voices reach a crescendo of accusation.

CHORUS 2 What does *he* know about a woman's sexuality?

CHORUS 1 *Culture* determines destiny, not anatomy.

CHORUS 3 He got it wrong about gender identity.

CHORUS 1 And sexuality.

CHORUS 3 What about *his* unconscious?

CHORUS 2 What about his *counter*transference?

CHORUS 3 What did *he* repress?

CHORUS 1 Frau K. should have been part of Dora's transference.

CHORUS 2 After all, he claimed Dora was in love with her too.

CHORUS 3 Too threatening for him, wasn't it?

CHORUS 1 Being the recipient of homosexual desire.

CHORUS 3 For him, fragmentary knowledge implied impotence.

CHORUS 1 He was afraid of identifying himself with Dora's father.

CHORUS 2 An impotent invalid.

CHORUS 1 Instead he chose the virile Herr K.

CHORUS 3 Those fellatio fantasies he attributed to Dora must have been his own desires.

CHORUS 1 An impotent male would resort to cunnilingus, surely?

CHORUS 3 It's not the penis women envy. It's power.

CHORUS 2 Hysterics crave mothers, not penises.

CHORUS 1 He rejected Dora's mother.

CHORUS 2 It was her mother she was really exacting revenge on.

CHORUS 1 Not him.

CHORUS 3 Not Herr K.

CHORUS 1 And he wrote her mother off as foolish and uncultivated.

CHORUS 3 He never gave her mother a voice.

CHORUS 2 He never gave *Mothers* a voice.

CHORUS 3 "I do not like to be the mother in transference," he was later to say.

CHORUS 1 "It always surprises and shocks me a little. I feel very masculine."

CHORUS 3 You're being a bit tough on the old boy. Twenty or so years later he acknowledged the importance of the pre-oedipal mother.

CHORUS 1 For girls.

CHORUS 3 Dora represents his feminine side.

CHORUS 2 The side he fears.

CHORUS 1 The side he rejects.

CHORUS 2 His hysterical side.

CHORUS 1 Hysteria is the disease of women in a patriarchal society.

CHORUS 3 Dora was most definitely a victim.

CHORUS 2 No she wasn't. She was a heroine.

CHORUS 3 She was a victim.

CHORUS 2 She was a heroine.

CHORUS 1 She was an adolescent!

FREUD *(shouting louder)* She walked out on me!

FREUD addresses the audience.

FREUD If only she hadn't walked out on me. You see, she continued to suffer from hysterical symptoms all her life. *Ménière's* syndrome, migraine, anxiety attacks. She became a heavy smoker. Marriage did nothing for her. She was convinced her husband, a failed composer, was unfaithful – just as her father had been. A colleague of mine who examined her in 1922 claimed her marriage only served to cover up her distaste for men. *(Tearfully)* If she'd stayed I could have cured her. I *know* I could have cured her.

IDA addresses the audience.

IDA It's true, I was plagued with illness all my life, and my marriage was anything but happy. But our son became an internationally renowned musician, and I myself eventually managed to excel in something apart from hysteria. The game of bridge became a fashionable craze in Vienna between the wars. And I was a Bridge Master. I taught all the ladies in all the best salons in Vienna how to play. My skill came quite naturally, of course. I was brilliant at concealing my hand and knew about all the intricacies and subterfuge involved when playing in a foursome. I'd had excellent teachers, after all. And my companion in bridge was none other than Frau Marie Zellenka.

FREUD laughs and turns to IDA. Music. They start dancing together – mirroring the opening dance sequence.

CHORUS 3 And so they continue their endless dance –

CHORUS 2 Of contraction,

CHORUS 1 Volition,

CHORUS 2 Submission,

CHORUS 3 Control.

CHORUS 1 The dance of life.

CHORUS 3 The dance of death.

CHORUS 1 Freud's death. Dora's death.

CHORUS 2 She died of colonic cancer in New York,

CHORUS 1 A refugee,

CHORUS 2 The year the war ended.

CHORUS 3 He died in London, of throat cancer,

CHORUS 2 The year the war began,

CHORUS 1 A refugee, too.

CHORUS 3 Little did he realise that such a pleasurable, tenacious little vice would cause him years of endless suffering, some thirty or so operations, and eat away half his face.

CHORUS 2 All those cigars. All that smoke.

CHORUS 1 Smoke never left him alone.

CHORUS 3 His books consigned to the flames of the Berlin bonfires. His sisters incinerated in the ovens of Auschwitz.

CHORUS 2 But still they dance on.

CHORUS 3 Icons of a faded century.

CHORUS 1 They dance on.

CHORUS 3 Until the music finally ends.

CHORUS 2 And they remain crystallised in time, as Fragments of an Analysis of the Twentieth Century.

Lights down.

The end.

THE COMPANY

Sphinx Theatre Company (founded as the Women's Theatre Group in 1973 and relaunched as Sphinx in 1990) is the longest established women's theatre company in the UK. The company was an Arts Council Regularly Funded client from 1975 to 2006, and subsequently project-funded.

A pioneering force of the Women's Liberation Movement, the WTG was founded as a separatist, radical fringe theatre group for the first 'Women's Festival' at the Almost Free Theatre in 1973. The WTG toured education, community venues and studio theatres across the UK with company-devised shows, and in 1978, began to commission women playwrights.

In 1990, Sue Parrish was appointed Artistic Director, and the company was relaunched as Sphinx Theatre Company. Sphinx had a renewed mission to advance women as theatre artists, from 'the barricades to the mainstream' and to demand a cultural revolution in which women could take centre stage. For the Company, the era of consciousness raising was over.

In addition to annual touring shows, Sphinx organised ten years of conferences featuring the most influential feminist directors, playwrights and performers. From 1991–2002, these took the form of the landmark 'Glass Ceiling' conferences; the first was held at the Institute of the Contemporary Arts (ICA), in 1991 with subsequent annual events held mainly in the National Theatre Cottesloe Theatre from 1992-2002. The 'Vamps, Vixens and Feminists' conferences followed from 2009-2012, and the 'Women Centre Stage' conferences from 2015-16. Many major women artists, journalists and politicians became regular speakers, including Hélène Cixous, Taslima Nasrin, Germaine Greer, Sarah Kane, Fiona Shaw, Dame Janet Suzman, Juliet Stevenson, Kathryn Hunter and Bidisha.

In 2020, the writers' project Sphinx 30 commissioned 30 diverse women playwrights in a unique collaboration with 15 regional theatres and was showcased brilliantly at the Royal Central School of Speech and Drama in 2021 – 2022. A lifelong engagement with the work of Bertolt Brecht inspired by his gallery of iconic female protagonists produced *A Berlin Kabaret*, winner of Best Cabaret at the 2014 Brighton Fringe Festival and Argus Angel for Artistic Excellence.

In collaboration with academic and playwright Jennifer Tuckett, Sphinx produced the Women in Theatre Report (2020). In 2023, this report was developed to consider the impact of the COVID-19 pandemic on the position of women in the theatre industry.

Tegan Verheul, Clarisse Zamba and Anni Epstein,
in *She Wolf* written by Morgan Lloyd Malcolm
Photo © Pau Ros 2021

TIMELINE

1973 The Women's Theatre Group is founded as a separatist feminist theatre group for the first Women's Festival at The 'Almost Free Theatre'.

1978 The Women's Theatre Group begins to commission women playwrights.

1980 The Conference of Women Theatre Directors and Administrators is founded to address the lack of women in top arts positions.

1981 ***New Anatomies*** by Timberlake Wertenbaker

1982 The Women's Playhouse Trust is established, with Dame Peggy Ashcroft as President, Pam Gems, Jane Lapotaire, Glenda Jackson, Diana Quick, Fiona Shaw and Juliet Stevenson as Associates, and Jules Wright, Rosemary Squire, Nicole Penn-Symons and Sue Parrish as Directors.

1983 Several conferences are held at the ICA to discuss the status of women in British Theatre, including those run by the Women's Playhouse Trust.

Sue Parrish curates and publishes 'THE STATUS OF WOMEN IN THE BRITISH THEATRE, 1982-83' for the Conference of Women Theatre Directors and Administrators (CWTDA). This survey finds that only 12% of artistic directors are female and only 11% of produced playwrights are female. From Sep. 1982-Sep. 1983, 42 of 622 plays performed in Repertory Theatres were written by women. Once you exclude 22 productions of Agatha Christie's works, only 6 of these plays were performed on the theatre's main stages (only 0.0096% of the plays in Rep. Theatres that year), while the remaining 14 were performed in smaller studio spaces.

1990 Sue Parrish is appointed as Artistic Director and The Women's Theatre Group is relaunched as SPHINX THEATRE COMPANY.

Mortal by Maro Green and Caroline Griffin

Her Aching Heart by Bryony Lavery

Christmas Without Herods by Lisa Evans

1991 ***The Roaring Girl's Hamlet*** in a new setting by Claire Luckham

GLASS CEILING – 'WEARING THEIR CLOTHES', *SADLER'S WELLS.*

GLASS CEILING CONFERENCE I – 'FROM SHAKESPEARE TO APHRA BEHN & THE POST FEMINIST MYTH', *THE ICA*.

1992 ***Every Bit Of It*** by Jackie Kay

GLASS CEILING II: 'AN ART FORM NOT A PLATFORM', *THE ICA.*

1993 ***Playhouse Creatures*** by April De Angelis

1994 ***Chandralekha*** by Amrit Wilson

Black Sail, White Sail by Hélène Cixous

GLASS CEILING III: 'THE PERSONAL AND THE POLITICAL & INSPIRATIONS AND TRANSFORMATIONS', *THE NATIONAL THEATRE*.

GLASS CEILING IV: 'BLOOD AND LETTERS', *THE NATIONAL THEATRE.* Taslima Nasrin is a keynote speaker at this event. The Bangladeshi writer gained global attention in the 1990s, due to her feminist essays and novels, which criticise what she characterises as all "misogynistic" religions. Nasrin has been living in exile since 1994, with multiple *fatwas* calling for her death. The event is monitored by Special Branch, and police snipers are stationed on the neighbouring roofs to ensure her safety.

1995 ***Hanjo*** by Seami and Yukio Mishima, adapted by Diane Esguerra

GLASS CEILING V: 'FROM VICTIM TO DIVA', *THE NATIONAL THEATRE.*

1996 ***Voyage In The Dark*** by Jean Rhys, adapted by Joan Wiles

GLASS CEILING VI: 'SLIP-SHOD SIBYLS WITH GERMAINE GREER', *THE NATIONAL THEATRE*. FEATURING A READING OF SARAH KANE'S *BLASTED*.

1997 ***Goliath*** by Bryony Lavery, adapted from the book by Beatrix Campbell

GLASS CEILING VII: 'SHIFTING FOCUS', *THE ALMEIDA*.

1998 ***The Snow Palace*** by Pam Gems

The Snow Palace British Council tour to Poland

GLASS CEILING VIII: 'GENDER ON THE MODERN STAGE', *THE NATIONAL THEATRE*.

1999 ***Vita And Virginia*** by Eileen Atkins

1999/2000/2001/2004 ***Sweet Dreams*** by Diane Esguerra

2000 ***A Wedding Story*** by Bryony Lavery

2001 ***Cherished Disappointments In Love*** by Jouko and Juha Turkka, adapted by Bryony Lavery

2003 ***As You Like It*** directed by Sue Parrish

2004 ***The Little Mermaid*** by Pam Gems

2005 Sphinx celebrates over 30 years of theatre with *Flogging the Jewels: A Celebratory Exhibition* at the National Theatre.

GLASS CEILING IX: 'COLLABORATION', *SOHO THEATRE*.

2006 ***Yellow*** by Rachel Barnett and Geraldine Pilgrim

Sweet Dreams by Diane Esguerra is performed at the Charleston Festival.

Blame by Beatrix Campbell and Judith Jones is produced in collaboration with York Theatre Royal.

The Brave New Roles Play Competition, sponsored by Oberon Books, seeks submissions featuring strong roles for women.

Sphinx publishes the WOMEN IN THEATRE SURVEY, which finds that only 19% of companies had female Artistic Directors, and (across 140 productions in 112 UK venues), only 9% of playwrights were female.

2007 ***Blame*** by Beatrix Campbell and Judith Jones is revived at London's Arcola Theatre.

2009 VAMPS, VIXENS AND FEMINISTS CONFERENCE I: 'THE ELEPHANT IN THE ROOM', THE OLIVIER THEATRE, *THE NATIONAL THEATRE*.

Sphinx publishes THE ELEPHANT IN THE ROOM report.

2010 VAMPS, VIXENS AND FEMINISTS CONFERENCE II: 'FIGHTING THE BACKLASH', *THE YOUNG VIC*.

Sphinx publishes FIGHTING THE BACKLASH. This report shows that women make up 35% of actors, 17% of playwrights, 23% of directors – despite being 52% of the population.

2011 VAMPS, VIXENS AND FEMINISTS CONFERENCE III: 'THE FEMINIST ROADSHOW', WOW SOUTHBANK CENTRE. Featuring a performance of 'All Girl Band', from *My Name is Alice,* by students of Mountview Academy of Dramatic Arts.

2012 VAMPS, VIXENS AND FEMINISTS... IN THE NORTH! CONFERENCE IV, *LEEDS PLAYHOUSE.*

2013/2014 ***A Berlin Kabaret*** by Peter Cox, Sue Parrish and Joseph Atkins

2015 WOMEN CENTRE STAGE FESTIVAL I: 'HEROINES', *THE NATIONAL THEATRE*.

THE SPHINX TEST is published, providing a theatre-specific strategy for exploring and expanding women's stage roles.

2016 WOMEN CENTRE STAGE FESTIVAL II: 'POWERPLAY', *HAMPSTEAD THEATRE.*

2018 ***Women Centre Stage: Eight Short Plays By and About Women*** is published by Sphinx Theatre and Nick Hern Books.

2019 WOMEN CENTRE STAGE SYMPOSIUM III: 'ARE WE AT THE TIPPING POINT?', *HAMPSTEAD THEATRE*. Sphinx subsequently publishes the symposium's findings as research papers.

2020 WOMEN CENTRE STAGE FORUM IV: 'WHAT SHARE OF THE CAKE', *TRAFALGAR STUDIOS*.

WHAT SHARE OF THE CAKE report shows that 31% of The Arts Council's National Portfolio Organisations (NPOs) have female Artistic Directors, controlling only 21% of NPO funding.

2021 SPHINX 30 project begins, developing 30 women playwrights over five years. The playwrights were April De Angelis, Tutku Barbaros, Gemma Bedeau, Satinder Chohan, Sarah Connors, Suzette Coon, Matilda Feyisayo Ibini, Beth Flintoff, Sarah Grochala, Ming Ho, Anita Kelly, Joanne Lau, Maureen Lennon, Morgan Lloyd Malcolm, Ginni Manning, Sarah McDonald Hughes, Yolanda Mercy, Guleraana Mir, Janice Okoh, Julia Pascal, Winsome Pinnock, Punam Ramchurn, Alli Smith, Kathrine Smith, Rommi Smith, Hannah Treadaway, Chloe Todd Fordham, Jane Upton, Bea Webster and Polly Wiseman.

Sphinx publishes the WOMEN IN THEATRE REPORT, in collaboration with academic and playwright Jennifer Tuckett, which finds that only 21% of Artistic Directors are female. It also finds that only 0.64% of NPO funding went to women's theatre companies from 2015-2018. The report recognises "a new era" of theatrical work which looks "towards a redrawing of the cultural landscape".

2022 *The Stage Report* finds that (across 500 productions at 132 UK venues), only 26% of playwrights were female.

2023 The WOMEN IN THEATRE REPORT is updated in light of the impact of the COVID-19 pandemic.

2025 SPHINX 30 Project holds its final meeting at Kings College London, led by Timberlake Wertenbaker and April De Angelis, on the topic "What is the responsibility of the female voice on stage in these dark times?"

Tania Khan and Aleeza Humranwala,
in *Empire of The Mind* by Satinder Chohan
Photo © Pau Ros 2021

Diana Feng and Fabrizio Matteini,
in *The Queen's Body* by Julia Pascal
Photo © Pau Ros 2021

ACKNOWLEDGEMENTS

Arts Council England, Elaine Aston, April De Angelis, Peter Cox, Brigid Larmour, Paulette Randall MBE, Susan McGoun, Julia Pascal, Kathryn Pogson, Nicole Penn-Symons, Toni Racklin, Maggie Saxon, Jane Seymour, Dame Rosemary Squire DBE, Dame Janet Suzman DBE and Timberlake Wertenbaker.

The collaborating theatres of Sphinx 30: The Bush Theatre, Derby Theatre, Graeae Theatre Company, Hull Truck Theatre, Kali Theatre Company, Leeds Playhouse, Everyman, Liverpool Everyman and Playhouse Theatres, New Earth Theatre Company, Nottingham Playhouse, Octagon Theatre Bolton, Red Ladder Theatre Company, Salisbury Playhouse, Stephen Joseph Theatre Scarborough, Theatr Clwyd and Watford Palace Theatre.

Grateful thanks to Josette Bushell-Mingo, Principal, and the Royal Central School of Speech and Drama for their brilliant collaboration and production of the Sphinx 30 Showcases.

Special thanks to Cheryl Robson, Amie Brian, Tiffany Woodsmith and Susannah Kraft.

More from Aurora Metro

PLAYS FOR TODAY BY WOMEN
eds. Cheryl Robson and Rebecca Gillieron
SBN 978-1-906582-11-1 £15.99

VOTES FOR WOMEN AND OTHER PLAYS
edited and introduced by Susan Croft
ISBN 978-1-906582-01-2 £12.99

CLASSIC PLAYS BY WOMEN
ed. Susan Croft
ISBN 978-1-9065820-0-5 £16.99

SIX PLAYS BY BLACK AND ASIAN WOMEN WRITERS
ed. Kadija George
ISBN 978-0-9515877-2-0 £14.99

PLAYS BY MEDITERRANEAN WOMEN
ed. Marion Baraitser
ISBN 978-0-9515877-3-7 £9.95

50 WOMEN IN THEATRE
introduced by Susan Croft
ISBN 978-1-913641-05-4 £24.99

FEMINIST THEATRE THEN & NOW
introduced by Elaine Aston and ed. Cheryl Robson
ISBN 978-1-913641-38-2 £16.99